Handbook of Inclusive Knowledge Management

Handbook of Inclusive Knowledge Management: Ensuring Inclusivity, Diversity, and Equity in Knowledge Processing Activities examines the role that diversity, equity and inclusivity (DEI) plays in the field and discipline of knowledge management (KM). With the premise that DEI is the inclusion and equal treatment of all types of people, things and viewpoints, the book aims to increase awareness of DEI among KM practitioners and researchers. It is a starting point for adopting knowledge processing activities that ensure all knowledge voices are represented in knowledge creation and capture. The book explains how this valuable knowledge can be shared and disseminated so that there is equitable access as well as knowledge. The focus of this handbook is on inclusivity in KM, its current state, specific challenges and an exploration of the best path forward.

Currently, inclusivity does not appear to be on many KM road maps, and this book provides insights into the state-of-the-art of inclusivity in KM. In alignment with the book's central theme, it presents a diverse range of perspectives that includes KM researchers, KM educators and KM practitioners. Addressing different stages of knowledge processing, as well as the KM bookends of KM culture, KM competencies and KM governance, the book features in-depth case studies to illustrate how inclusivity can be integrated into KM. The handbook concludes with concrete recommendations on how to integrate inclusivity into KM in organizations. Reviewing both the theory and practice of inclusive KM, the book helps readers gain actionable insights into an inclusive KM approach that includes standards, guidelines and checklists.

Kimiz Dalkir is an Associate Professor and the Director of the School of Information Studies, McGill University, Montreal.

Handbook of Inclusive Knowledge Management

Ensuring Inclusivity, Diversity, and Equity in Knowledge Processing Activities

Edited by
Kimiz Dalkir

CRC Press
Taylor & Francis Group
Boca Raton London New York

CRC Press is an imprint of the
Taylor & Francis Group, an **informa** business

AN AUERBACH BOOK

First edition published 2025
2385 NW Executive Center Drive, Suite 320, Boca Raton FL 33431

and by CRC Press
4 Park Square, Milton Park, Abingdon, Oxon, OX14 4RN

CRC Press is an imprint of Taylor & Francis Group, LLC

© *2025 Taylor & Francis Group, LLC*

ISBN: 978-1-032-52132-9 (hbk)
ISBN: 978-1-032-52131-2 (pbk)
ISBN: 978-1-003-40796-6 (ebk)

DOI: 10.1201/9781003407966

Typeset in Minion
by SPi Technologies India Pvt Ltd (Straive)

Contents

Preface

This handbook represents a characterization of the degree the discipline of knowledge management (KM). As a good practice, the term "inclusivity" will be used to represent concept of DEI and we will begin with a definition.

> the fact of including all types of people, things or ideas and treating them all fairly and equally. (Cambridge Dictionary[1])

Another way of looking at inclusion is to identify where there is exclusion: where certain groups of people or ideas are excluded. Examples include the digital divide where some socioeconomic groups do not have the same level of access to resources such as technology. However, the situation is not always so cut and dried as unfair or inequitable situations are often more subtle, harder to detect but just as damaging. Examples include deciding which voices should be heard or which "correct" ideas should be valued. Inclusivity is of course a broad issue and a global or societal challenge. The focus of this handbook is on inclusivity in KM: what is the current state, what are some of the specific challenges, and what is the best path forward?

Inclusivity should play an active role in all stages of the KM cycle. All knowledge processing activities should be inclusive, beginning with the creation or capture of knowledge, which refers to identifying valuable knowledge within an organization. At this initial stage, it is important to ask the following: Are we using inclusive criteria? Are we flagging knowledge as valuable that is representative of all the knowledge workers in the organization? Are our knowledge elicitation processes actively ensuring that diverse content is being collected?

Once valuable knowledge has been identified and organized (typically classified and rendered tangible and "findable" through search), the second stage of knowledge processing involves sharing and disseminating this valuable knowledge throughout the organization. How can we ensure that everyone can have access to this content? What about employees with disabilities? What about non-native English speakers?

The final stage involves the preservation of valuable knowledge so that people can apply it, use it now but also so that future (often unknown users) will also be able to find, access and understand how to apply this knowledge. Again, are we using inclusive criteria to decide what knowledge to preserve? How can we ensure that we are thinking of the broadest possible range of users with different knowledge needs?

Inclusivity does not appear to be on many KM road maps yet. The following chapters will provide insights into the state-of-the-art of inclusivity in KM. True to our central theme, a diverse range of perspectives will be provided, including KM researchers, KM educators and KM practitioners. Different chapters address different stages of knowledge processing, as well as the KM "bookends" of KM culture, KM competencies and KM governance. There are a number of in-depth case studies to illustrate how inclusivity can be integrated into KM. The handbook then concludes with chapters with concrete recommendations on how to integrate inclusivity into KM in your organization. Readers will thus benefit from a review of both the theory and practice of inclusive KM and gain actionable insights into a more inclusive KM approach that includes standards, guidelines and checklists.

In the first chapter, Susanne Durst and Samuel Foli set the stage in a call for action for more inclusive KM. She was one of the first to recognize the need for more inclusivity in what she terms more responsible KM (rKM). Durst describes rKM as an approach that transcends organizational/national/etc. boundaries, is collaborative and inclusive, and involves different and diverse partners on an equal footing. She uses the example of a higher education institution to outline the key questions to address to help overcome the disparities that exist in knowledge access, sharing, dissemination and preservation activities. The key questions form a framework or checklist that can be used by KM researchers, educators and practitioners to ensure inclusivity requirements are being addressed.

The second chapter is an ethnographic study on knowledge processing activities during strategy formulation sessions at a university by Martie Mearns. This is a comprehensive and in-depth methodology that is very well suited to better understanding the complexities in ensuring inclusivity in general, and in this case study, ensuring inclusive KM strategy development. There is also an interesting finding that remote or virtual knowledge acquisition and sharing was found to be *less* inclusive. Other research found that remote meetings had the potential to be more inclusive in terms of everyone participating more equally. However, the importance of face-to-face knowledge sharing activities is well established in the field of KM, and this may also be the case for inclusive knowledge processing activities.

In Chapter 3, Patricia de Sá Freire and Yuqing Yao highlight the importance of valuing inclusivity in knowledge governance. Inclusivity is needed in the initial steps of identifying and mapping where critical knowledge exists within an organization. The authors went beyond a single organization and looked at an interorganizational case study involving academia, industry and government. They describe how they ensured a diversity of knowledge contributors were involved in the mapping. They describe their methodology which can help ensure inclusive knowledge governance through transdisciplinary co-creation. The use of knowledge visualization also serves as a common "language" for a broader range of diverse knowledge workers.

Chapter 4 looks at inclusive KM in the healthcare sector. Deborah Swain discusses barriers to collaboration and sharing in a more inclusive way as well as some enablers. For example, the author also discusses policies that can support measures to improve inclusivity such as the U.S. National Institute of Health requirement that all funded projects are required to share their data. She proposes a framework that goes beyond the traditional KM models to create a collaboration model for KM professionals, healthcare stakeholders and patients. This framework integrates both tacit and explicit knowledge in an open access formula to break the siloes separating data librarians, knowledge managers and healthcare researchers. More effective collaboration between all healthcare stakeholders as well as more patient voices being heard will help reduce biases in healthcare and increase inclusivity in KM moving forward.

There are two case studies on inclusive KM education in Chapter 5. Kendra S. Albright, Andreas Brandner and Annet K. Nabattanzi-Muyimba look at social inclusion and exclusion as it relates to knowledge inclusion and exclusion throughout knowledge processing activities. The authors discuss how to ensure inclusiveness is a critical element in KM education by discussing the inclusiveness strategies used by two institutions: the MSc in KM program at the University of Kent in Kent, Ohio, and the KM certification courses at the Knowledge Management Academy in Vienna, Austria. The importance of inclusive course content and pedagogy together with ensuring diversity in course instructors such as guest lecturers from underrepresented populations are highlighted. The authors provide comprehensive guidelines on how to ensure maximum accessibility and equity while minimizing any biases, whether they be conscious or unconscious.

Angel Y. Ford and Daniel Gelaw Alemneh examine epistemic injustice, which is discrimination that specifically targets a person's knowledge in Chapter 6. While the authors review the forms in which this bias can exist, their focus is on identifying how they can be effectively addressed. The example of scholarly publishing is used which is essentially publications from academics and researchers, typically in peer-reviewed academic journals. A number of recommendations are made as to how we can each, as individuals, reduce discrimination. An example is being aware of any biases when we conduct a peer review: do we judge more harshly if the study uses a different methodology than ours? Another is to look at the composition of editorial boards of academic journals. At the collective level, they note that there is still room for institutions despite advances in Open Access. An example would be for universities to populate their institutional repositories and facilitate access to their contents.

The next chapter also looks at scholarly publishing but adopted a different approach. Irene Kitimbo and Cynthia Kumah did a content analysis for the top five journals in KM. These were: *The Journal of KM, KM Research and Practice, Organizational Learning, Journal of Intellectual Capital* and *VINE: Journal of Information and Knowledge Management Systems*. They looked at evidence of different types of diversity in these journals such as authors' country of residence, the term diversity in journal article titles and editorial board diversity. Among their recommendations are for key KM journals to adopt DEI statements and to actively promote citation diversity. The authors also recommend increasing diversity in the editorial boards as did the previous chapter authors and they specifically target the higher ranked KM journals.

Chapter 8 is predominantly from a practitioner's perspective, Yang Lin, on the current state-of-the-art of inclusivity in artificial intelligence, including the new Large Language Models (LLMs) and generative AI applications such as ChatGPT. There was surprisingly little found in terms of inclusive KM practices despite consulting with key KM stakeholders. While this is not great news, it does confirm that inclusive KM is still in its infancy. The better news is that effective guidelines to help mitigate biases AI systems appear to be highly transferable to knowledge processing activities. These biases are reviewed, mitigation strategies are presented for each, and a series of guidelines are proposed to improve diversity, equity and inclusivity in KM practice. These include frequent audits and assessments that use fairness metrics and ideally integrative DEI components into the KM ISO 30401-2018 standard (which is discussed in more detail in the next chapter).

The final chapter by Susan McIntyre also presents a practitioner's perspective and presents an illustrative case study from the Government of Canada's networked anti-terrorism initiative. This is an excellent how-to guide to adding inclusivity to all stages of the KM cycle when processing organizational knowledge. There is a link to the KM ISO standard as well as to an outcomes-based measurement tool that can be very valuable in tracking progress and goal attainment. The chapter concludes with an Inclusive KM checklist that can help the KM community to take stock of what their current DEI situation is and then plot a concrete course to attaining their KM inclusivity goals.

It is clear that we need to not only increase awareness but start adopting proven practices for all knowledge processing activities to ensure that all knowledge voices are represented in knowledge creation and capture, that this valuable knowledge is then shared and disseminated in such a way that there is equitable access and that we ensure that knowledge preservation for continued use and reuse is representative. This handbook serves as a good starting point for KM researchers, KM educators and KM practitioners to look at their own inclusivity practices and create their own roadmap to more inclusive KM. As we began with a definition, we will conclude with one: a possible definition of what inclusive KM should be, presented in the form of a checklist:

Inclusive knowledge management should be[2]:
1. the *ongoing creation* of knowledge by members of the organization who are from different power-levels (from front-line workers to top management), pertaining to their organization's tasks,
2. the *integration* of knowledge from diverse individual interactions and different organizational contexts and cultures (or micro-culture),
3. the *contribution* of tacit knowledge from members regardless of their culture, socio-economic background, education level, ethnicity, gender and sexual orientation, indigenous status, belonging to a visible minority group or physical and mental abilities,
4. the *codification* of knowledge through technology that is accessible to all stakeholders and that they can access,
5. the *transfer* of knowledge from subject matter experts to staff members and from other stakeholders and communities of practice through accessible channels that can be accessed,

6. the *dissemination* of knowledge to stakeholders and other organizations to establish evolving best practices, thus fostering trust and innovation successfully in the field of practice,

7. and *governed* by an ethical and transparent KM strategy, organizational policy and applicable legislation throughout the organization, the interorganizational KM ecosystem and society.

NOTES

1 https://dictionary.cambridge.org/dictionary/english/inclusivity.
2 Developed in collaboration with Mélanie Vachon.

Acknowledgments

I would like to thank Bénédicte Anjou and Mélanie Vachon for their collaboration and contributions to this book.

1

Responsible and Inclusive Knowledge Management Made Concrete

Susanne Durst and Samuel Foli
Reykjavik University, Reykjavik, Iceland

1.1 INTRODUCTION

Recent events and developments, such as the pandemic, the war in Ukraine, but also the introduction of ChatGPT in November 2022, have led to significant consequences at various levels. For example, recent publications report that the digital divide, educational disadvantage, poverty, child labor and violence against minorities or certain professional groups have increased again or even further (Bhatia, 2023; Signé, 2023; United Nations Human Rights, 2023; International Labour Organization, 2023; World Bank, 2022). This is very worrying because it makes activities involving many different social groups, which are necessary to address the societal challenges, even more difficult. Additionally, these events and developments also significantly affect knowledge, the perception of knowledge and access to knowledge, in short, knowledge management (KM).

In fact, in this highly changed environment KM is facing a new challenge. The importance of developing one's own knowledge in order to be able to follow and weigh the different developments accordingly is not only questioned against the backdrop of the possibilities offered by ChatGPT and similar artificial intelligence (AI)-based chatbots, but also against the backdrop of rapid technological developments and its environmental impact (Kumar and Davenport, 2023) as well as other challenges, e.g., increased cyberattacks (Schulze and Kerttunen, 2023) or spread of fake news (Beauvais, 2022) which make it increasingly difficult for any

DOI: 10.1201/9781003407966-1

individual to keep track of things at all. This situation is exacerbated if the person is facing one or more of the challenges mentioned before (Olanrewaju et al., 2021; Pahl, 2023).

In 2021, Susanne Durst has proposed responsible knowledge management (rKM) as a possible solution to address these challenges. Durst describes rKM as an approach that transcends organizational/national/ etc. boundaries, is collaborative and inclusive, and involves different and diverse partners on an equal footing. Moreover, rKM focuses on KM practices such as creating, sharing and preserving knowledge for the common good, understood as anything that benefits the entire society or that contributes to better society.

In this chapter, the authors aim to show how rKM could be used specifically in an educational context to help (1) demonstrate the benefits of rKM in education and (2) emphasize how important it is that knowledge is not only accessible to all, but also jointly developed, shared and constantly discussed (improved and also discarded). In the discussion, knowledge is viewed as something that can be both positive and negative, depending on the perspective chosen. An example of positive knowledge in education is knowledge developed by students, regardless of their background, that aims to contribute to addressing societal challenges. Negative knowledge, on the other hand, can manifest itself in the fact that different forms/types of knowledge are not desired and only knowledge that comes from a certain group of students or the lecturer is viewed as "correct."

Additionally, and to do justice to the original idea of the rKM, the discussions are conducted from a world perspective. From an educational perspective, this would mean that relevant and solution-oriented knowledge for the learning challenge is drawn from all parts of the world and not just from a Western or an Eastern perspective or from the "louder" countries or "higher ranked" universities. Eventually, a collaborative and inclusive rKM from an educational point of view would mean that every student uses his/her voice and that it is also heard to make an active contribution to creating, sharing and preserving knowledge for the common good. The authors of this chapter hope that the insights conveyed in this chapter will be considered valuable for different target groups. The proposed approach can provide new insights for both academics and practitioners, as they not only get to know a different way of thinking about KM, but also first ideas to implement this way of thinking in a concrete way. The chapter is structured as follows. In the following section, the relevant concepts and terms are briefly outlined to frame the chapter. This is followed by sections that describe how rKM could be applied in education. The chapter ends with a conclusion.

1.2 KNOWLEDGE MANAGEMENT

The importance of knowledge as a key strategic factor for business operations is well known (Spender, 1996; Teece, 2001). This is true for all types of organizations, for profit and non-for-profit ones (Durst et al., 2020). Consequently, organizations should find continual ways to manage this factor appropriately. Knowledge management can be considered as the processes and structures developed and maintained in organizations to support various knowledge processes such as knowledge identification, knowledge creation, transfer and retention (Alavi and Leidner, 2001). It is embedded in and aligned with the organization's overall strategy (Lönnqvist, 2017). Given the importance of educational institutions, such as universities, for the creation and transfer of knowledge (Edvardsson and Durst, 2017), it is not difficult to attribute a fundamental role to KM as well.

To improve KM activities in organizations, more recent research suggests that the possible downsides of knowledge should be viewed as well (Massingham, 2010; Durst and Aisenberg Ferenhof, 2016). This means that depending on the situation knowledge can be a positive risk, i.e., knowledge as an asset, something valuable while in other situations, this knowledge would be a negative risk, i.e., something dangerous, etc. For example, knowledge about vulnerabilities and threats is invaluable for protecting digital systems in cybersecurity. Organizations can use this knowledge as a positive risk, allowing them to strengthen their defenses. However, if this knowledge falls into the hands of cybercriminals, this knowledge becomes a negative risk, because they can exploit vulnerabilities to launch cyberattacks and compromise sensitive data. Supporters behind the knowledge-at-risk perspective argue that a comprehensive approach to KM should approach knowledge from both sides. A knowledge-at-risk perspective can also be transferred to the educational context. Educational institutions such as universities are also increasingly exposed to cyberattack. Furthermore, there is also a risk at universities that different opinions and different knowledge are not desired; are even suppressed. In addition, there is also a risk in educational institutions that the increased use/integration of AI-based tools and solutions will downplay, suppress and even forget old knowledge as a result of non-application. The preservation of knowledge could take a back seat. However, the increasing availability of AI-based tools for information query and generation or knowledge retrieval, which makes information and documented knowledge accessible to broader groups, can be seen as a positive risk.

1.2.1 From Knowledge Management to Responsible Knowledge Management

KM certainly has its merits, but as it was developed primarily for private companies that are clearly focused on creating and maintaining competitive advantage, this approach falls short when it comes to challenges that occur at a higher, overarching level. In other words, challenges that were emphasized in the introduction to this chapter. Knowledge in these challenges should not only be diverse and up to date, but also freely available, shared, used, and retained for the benefit of a variety of different people.

In this context, Durst (2021) has proposed a move toward rKM to support the challenges of humanity through an alternative approach. An approach that takes a bird's-eye view, Durst speaks of a world perspective, and thus goes beyond individual, organizational, industry, national and intergovernmental levels usually found in existing KM research.

The proposed rKM is based on collaboration and inclusiveness and has people in the core, i.e., technology is subordinate to people (society) and not vice versa. As for the different KM processes, rKM aims at increasing the quality of knowledge creation by not only making sure that old and still relevant knowledge is not discarded but also including knowledge that has been developed in different parts of the world/different actors. At the same time the need for strategic unlearning is stressed in case knowledge has become obsolete. RKM thus emphasizes the importance of understanding knowledge and its (longer-term) significance for humanity, regardless of certain hypes. The focus is on the collective, which is made up of people with equal rights and responsibilities who jointly develop solutions to social challenges using the skills and competences available. By emphasizing the collective, the individual is part of the whole but never the decisive part.

Durst in her essay stresses that rKM is at an early stage of development and requires further reflection and thought. This call is attempted to be met in the following. An attempt is made to present a possible application of rKM in education to contribute to the resolution of societal challenges. The focus here is on educational institutions such as universities that offer both teaching and research.

1.2.2 The Application of Responsible Knowledge Management in Educational Institutions

Recent advances in technology, including AI, are changing education policy, not only at a national and regional level, but also at a global level. These changes will have a far-reaching impact and will affect various areas of education, from teaching methods to assessment techniques (Ratten and Jones, 2023). Even if the educational approach, educational practices and educational policy can vary from country to country, region to region and even university to university, its core objective remains constant: to empower individuals to acquire knowledge and skills for productive and responsible participation in society (World Bank, 2021). In view of this fundamental objective, it can be assumed that there is a certain need for change in the field of education in order to do justice to changing social developments and changes. This harmonization provides a basis for the application of rKM. In Durst's (2021) proposal of rKM, there is a deliberate and collective endeavor to confront the challenges that humanity faces through an inclusive and collaborative approach, departing from traditional KM research. Moreover, rKM emphasizes three KM practices to be used for the overarching goal of serving the common good. Higher education institutions are essential for driving societal changes as they not only have the capacity to develop skills and competences and foster knowledge, but they also possess the potential to mobilize educational resources and provide learning opportunities for diverse groups of learners (UNESCO Institute for Lifelong Learning, 2022). Knowledge creation and sharing in this context should therefore be the result of an environment that favors critical thinking, creativity and innovation (Baena-Morales et al., 2023; Ferrari et al., 2009). These processes are further facilitated when teachers and students actively engage in research, exploration and experimentation through various initiatives, including collaborative projects, hands-on experiences and interdisciplinary studies (Gamage et al., 2022; Chhabra et al., 2021).

With the introduction of rKM into these KM processes and related ones, the activities and their impact on education can be raised to a higher level, as the collaborative and inclusive approach is at the center from the beginning and is not just another option among many. Consequently, rKM has the potential to reshape higher education by making cooperation, equality and the shared responsibility of all stakeholders (students, teachers and university leadership in particular) an essential element of all activities. An education that is focused on rKM can therefore play a central role not only in overcoming pressing societal challenges, but also in shaping a better society. In view of the existential threat posed by climate change, for example, educational institutions have the opportunity to use rKM to formulate improved (more contemporary) pedagogical approaches and research agendas. Through this lens, they can prioritize collaborative responsible actions as a core principle, instilling it in the DNA of their teaching and research pursuits and institutional practices. In the classroom, rKM can drive students and teachers to focus on environmental ethics, promote responsible resource management and foster a deeper understanding of the interconnectedness of ecosystems and the resulting consequences. In the case of research, rKM can encourage groups of diverse researchers to explore innovative collaborative green business models and strategies, sustainable agricultural practices and climate modeling techniques which draw on real-time data from different parts of the world.

Knowledge dissemination takes on paramount importance in today's world characterized by the rampant spread of fake news and misinformation (Dame Adjin-Tettey, 2022; Council of Europe, 2023). In an era characterized by information overload and the rapid spread of falsehoods, it is even more crucial for educational institutions to give the highest priority to ethical knowledge transfer. This entails not only the delivery of accurate and dependable information and knowledge but also the cultivation of critical thinking and digital literacy skills among students and teachers, so that they are able to better distinguish credible sources from misinformation (Council of Europe, 2023). Moreover, educational institutions, which are pivotal in the dissemination of knowledge through research (Edvardsson and Durst, 2017), bear a significant responsibility in ensuring that principles of research ethics are strictly adhered to. This adherence is crucial to prevent the falsification of data or results and their dissemination, as such misconduct can have severe and detrimental effects on society as a whole. Furthermore, ensuring that knowledge is disseminated ethically is not solely a matter of accuracy; it also involves making this knowledge accessible to a broad audience, particularly in underprivileged areas. Recent reports by intergovernmental organizations like

UNESCO[1], UNICEF[2], UN[3] underscore the alarming expansion of the digital divide, which is a cause for concern. RKM, in this context, strives to guarantee that knowledge and educational opportunities are within reach of everyone, irrespective of their geographical location, socioeconomic status or background. This may encompass initiatives such as providing free or affordable educational resources and advocating for digital inclusion. In addition, an rKM-based higher education policy advocates that everyone makes and should make an active contribution to knowledge creation and dissemination; and that his/her voice is heard. In this way, rKM aims to mobilize the various rKM processes in each individual and the results should be brought together with those of others in order to facilitate the core idea of rKM.

The preservation of knowledge also plays an indispensable role in overcoming current and future societal challenges. Educational institutions, often regarded as repositories of knowledge (Veer Ramjeawon and Rowley, 2018), can greatly contribute to better society through rKM. A rKM-focused approach ensures that the relevant knowledge held by educational institutions is not only preserved and made accessible, but that this knowledge is also continually reviewed for relevance. This is done by actors acting responsibly and together, who are aware that knowledge can also have a half-life date; however, this must be carefully examined to prevent old knowledge from being lost. Furthermore, actors accept different types of knowledge and recognize that combining these types can enable new alternative solutions.

Therefore, the importance of quality preservation of knowledge cannot be overstated. When relevant knowledge is effectively preserved, it stands the test of time and remains relevant for generations to come. This prevents the unnecessary and expensive re-creation of lost or forgotten knowledge, averting a scenario where the world reinvents the wheel and thus wasting scarce resources that could be better used elsewhere (Durst and Aisenberg Ferenhof, 2016). In this interconnected world, teachers worldwide are particularly encouraged to embrace and spread the spirit of open collaboration. By working together and exchanging their existing knowledge, they can make an active contribution to a better world together and across borders. The understanding of the relevance for this approach should come from the individual (intrinsic motivation) and ideally be supported and encouraged by the environment, i.e., in this specific case by the university leadership but also by the students. The individual must recognize that he/she has a responsibility toward society and especially a better society for

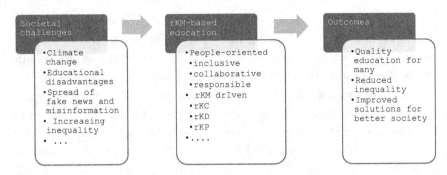

FIGURE 1.1
Framework for responsible knowledge management in education.

(Note: rKC = responsible knowledge creation; rKD = responsible knowledge dissemination; rKP = responsible knowledge preservation).

everyone. At the same time, this person is aware that social change requires many people who are willing to act together and is therefore actively looking for them. It is assumed that rKM literacy helps with this.

Bringing together the discussion above, Figure 1.1 presents a framework outlining societal challenges such as climate change and educational disadvantages, as shown on the left side of the diagram. The framework emphasizes that the incorporation of rKM in education is expected to yield positive outcomes, as illustrated on the right side of the diagram. As depicted in the framework, rKM-driven education is based on principles that can not only improve current education policy but also actively address social challenges.

1.3 CONCLUSIONS

The objective of this chapter was to present rKM from an educational perspective as a means of contributing to the resolution of societal challenges. As delineated within the chapter, rKM principles seem to offer a robust framework for tackling a diverse range of complex societal issues. The discourse here has highlighted the link between rKM and education and its potential central role in shaping and implementing a landscape characterized by responsibility, equity, inclusion and collaboration. As this chapter has shown, integrating the basic principles of rKM into the education system could contribute to solving urgent societal challenges.

More precisely, this integration could support in achieving the United Nation's Sustainable Development Goals (SDGs) such as no. 4 quality education, no. 5 gender equality, no. 10 reduced inequalities and no. 17 partnerships for the goals.

RKM has the power to transcend geographical and socioeconomic boundaries, facilitating global access to the wealth of knowledge housed and continuously developed and updated within educational institutions. If this is utilized for the benefit of many, it can promote not only cooperation at different levels, but also integrative and collaborative approaches to tackling societal problems at the global level—approaches based on collective actorhood and responsibility.

Educational institutions, with their central importance for social change, are encouraged to take responsibility in order to fulfill their role. Adopting the rKM principles could help.

In order to initiate further discourse and the next concrete steps, some specific research questions and areas for future investigations are presented below:

General
- How can the assumptions underlying the rKM approach be effectively integrated into educational institutions in order to contribute to urgent societal challenges?
- What role do the individual members of society play in this? How do they recognize not only that action must be taken, but that they must act together?
- What is needed to develop and maintain collective actorhood and responsibility in education?
- What are the key factors that influence the successful dissemination and use of knowledge in a responsible and ethical manner, and how can educational institutions, intergovernmental organizations and the individual person promote these factors?
- How can cultural and indigenous knowledge be preserved, shared and integrated into modern education systems to promote cultural diversity and intercultural understanding in the face of globalization?
- Recognizing that critical thinking and inclusion of all people regardless of background is not universally desired or will shift the power position of individuals/groups, there is a need for more research into how any tensions can be addressed for the benefit of many and collaborative activities.

Impact Measurement and Evaluation:

- What measures are appropriate to demonstrate a successful integration of rKM in education?
- What measures are appropriate to assess the contribution of rKM-led education initiatives to global challenges/the ESGs?

Emerging Technologies:

- What role can emerging technologies play in advancing rKM-based education and addressing global challenges?
  - For example, how can blockchain technology be used to demonstrate greater inclusiveness and more togetherness in education?
- What are the ethical considerations and potential pitfalls associated with the dissemination of knowledge, especially in the era of digital misinformation, and how can rKM mitigate these challenges?

NOTES

1 UNESCO (2023) Bridging the digital divide and ensuring online protection https://www.unesco.org/en/right-education/digitalization (Accessed on 22 September 2023).
2 UNICEF (2021) What we know about the gender digital divide for girls: A literature review https://www.unicef.org/eap/media/8311/file/What%20we%20know%20about%20the%20gender%20digital%20divide%20for%20girls:%20A%20literature%20review.pdf (Accessed on 22 September 2023).
3 United Nations (2023) Digital Divide https://news.un.org/en/tags/digital-divide (Accessed on 22 September 2023).

REFERENCES

Alavi, M., & Leidner, D. E. (2001). Knowledge management and knowledge management systems: Conceptual foundations and research issues. *MIS Quarterly*, *25*(1), 107–136.

Beauvais, C. (2022). Fake news: Why do we believe it? *Joint Bone Spine*, *89*(4), 105371.

Baena-Morales, S., Merma-Molina, G., & Ferriz-Valero, A. (2023). Integrating education for sustainable development in physical education: Fostering critical and systemic thinking. *International Journal of Sustainability in Higher Education*, *24*(8), 1915–1931.

Bhatia, V. (2023). Bridging the digital divide in the European Union. https://www.weforum.org/agenda/2023/08/how-to-bridge-the-digital-divide-in-the-eu/. Retrieved 4 September 2023.

Chhabra, M., Dana, L. P., Malik, S., & Chaudhary, N. S. (2021). Entrepreneurship education and training in Indian higher education institutions: A suggested framework. *Education+ Training*, *63*(7/8), 1154–1174.

Council of Europe (2023). Dealing with propaganda, misinformation, and fake news. https://www.coe.int/en/web/campaign-free-to-speak-safe-to-learn/dealing-with-propaganda-misinformation-and-fake-news. Retrieved from 22 September 2023.

Dame Adjin-Tettey, T. (2022). Combating fake news, disinformation, and misinformation: Experimental evidence for media literacy education. *Cogent Arts & Humanities, 9*(1), 2037229.

Durst, S. (2021). A plea for responsible and inclusive knowledge management at the world level. *VINE Journal of Information and Knowledge Management Systems*, Vol. ahead-of-print No. ahead-of-print. https://doi.org/10.1108/VJIKMS-09-2021-0204

Durst, S., & Aisenberg Ferenhof, H. (2016). Knowledge risk management in turbulent times. In K. North and G. Varvakis (eds.), *Competitive Strategies for small and medium enterprises: Increasing crisis resilience, agility, and innovation in turbulent times* (pp. 195–209).

Durst, S., Lindvall, B., & Bruns, G. (2020). Knowledge risk management in the public sector: Insights into a Swedish municipality. *Journal of Knowledge Management, 24*(4), 717–735. https://doi.org/10.1108/JKM-12-2017-0558

Edvardsson, I. R., & Durst, S. (2017). Universities and knowledge-based development: A literature review. *International Journal of Knowledge-Based Development, 8*(2), 105–134.

Ferrari, A., Cachia, R., & Punie, Y. (2009). Innovation and creativity in education and training in the EU member states: Fostering creative learning and supporting innovative teaching. *JRC Technical Note, 52374*, 64.

Gamage, K. A., Ekanayake, S. Y., & Dehideniya, S. C. (2022). Embedding sustainability in learning and teaching: Lessons learned and moving forward—approaches in STEM higher education programs. *Education Sciences, 12*(3), 225.

International Labour Organization (2023). To bring social justice to all we must end child labour. https://www.ilo.org/global/about-the-ilo/how-the-ilo-works/ilo-director-general/statements-and-speeches/WCMS_884696/lang--en/index.htm. Retrieved 4 September 2023.

Kumar, A., & Davenport, T. (2023). How to Make Generative AI Greener. *Harvard Business Review*, 20 July 2023. https://hbr.org/2023/07/how-to-make-generative-ai-greener

Lönnqvist, A. (2017). Embedded knowledge management: towards improved managerial relevance. *Knowledge Management Research & Practice, 15*(2), 184–191. https://doi.org/10.1057/s41275-017-0053-y

Massingham, P. (2010). Knowledge risk management: a framework. *Journal of Knowledge Management, 14*(3), 464–485. https://doi.org/10.1108/13673271011050166

Olanrewaju, G. S., Adebayo, S. B., Omotosho, A. Y., & Olajide, C. F. (2021). Left behind? The effects of digital gaps on e-learning in rural secondary schools and remote communities across Nigeria during the COVID-19 pandemic. *International Journal of Educational Research Open, 2*, 100092. https://doi.org/10.1016/j.ijedro.2021.100092

Pahl, S. (2023). An emerging divide: Who is benefiting from AI? https://iap.unido.org/articles/emerging-divide-who-benefiting-ai. Retrieved 4 September 2023.

Ratten, V., & Jones, P. (2023). Generative artificial intelligence (ChatGPT): Implications for management educators. *The International Journal of Management Education, 21*(3), 100857.

Schulze, M., & Kerttunen, M. (2023). Cyber operations in Russia's war against Ukraine: uses, limitations, and lessons learned so far. *SWP Comment 2023/C 23*, 17.04.2023, https://doi.org/10.18449/2023C23

Signé, L. (2023). Fixing the global digital divide and digital access gap. https://www.brookings.edu/articles/fixing-the-global-digital-divide-and-digital-access-gap/. Retrieved 4 September 2023.

Spender, J.-C. (1996). Making knowledge the basis of a dynamic theory of the firm. *Strategic Management Journal, 17*, 45–62.

Teece, D. J. (2001). Strategies for managing knowledge assets: The role of firm structure and industrial context. In I. Nonaka & D. J. Teece (Eds.), *Managing Industrial Knowledge: Creation, Transfer and Utilization* (pp. 125–144). London: Sage.

United Nations Human Rights (2023). HC: The digital divide is leaving young people behind. https://www.ohchr.org/en/stories/2023/03/hc-digital-divide-leaving-young-people-behind. Retrieved 4 September 2023.

UNESCO Institute for Lifelong Learning (2022). Policy brief: the contribution of higher education institutions to lifelong learning. UIL/2022/ME/H/9. https://unesdoc.unesco.org/ark:/48223/pf0000381924. Retrieved 3 December 2023.

Veer Ramjeawon, P., & Rowley, J. (2018). Knowledge management in higher education institutions in Mauritius. *International Journal of Educational Management, 32*(7), 1319–1332.

World Bank (2021). Tertiary education overview. https://www.worldbank.org/en/topic/tertiaryeducation. Retrieved 11 September 2023.

World Bank (2022). Violence against women and girls – what the data tell us. https://genderdata.worldbank.org/data-stories/overview-of. Retrieved 4 September 2023.

2

Facilitation of Knowledge Sharing and Capturing Practices in Organisational Strategy Development

Martie Mearns
University of Pretoria, Pretoria, South Africa

2.1 INTRODUCTION

In preparation for college strategy development, the Deanery generally embarks on retreats to elicit contributions from the chairs of schools, heads of academic departments, a few experienced tenured professors, and the middle and top management administrators in the college's support roles. Their collective knowledge and experience are usually sufficient to align the college's unique present accomplishments and potential future contribution to the higher education institution's specific strategic vision, direction, and mandate. Yet, the current junior faculty are silent recipients of the strategic direction, expected to co-deliver the strategic destination of the future institution. But, when an academic department of knowledge management at one such institution is tasked to facilitate the strategic breakaway from a knowledge management perspective, a whole new set of voices actively contributes to the strategic direction of the college. This chapter proposes to provide an ethnographic discussion of three strategic breakaway sessions for a university college through a restructuring process as the initial facilitation session, a think tank some years later conducted remotely during global lockdowns, and again in-person at the end of the Dean's term looking towards the succession of leadership and future strategy.

DOI: 10.1201/9781003407966-2

The planning process and stages of the strategic breakaway sessions are discussed to indicate the inclusivity of involving voices that are generally not involved in strategic planning sessions. The age and experience of this diversified group required the application of a variety of techniques to elicit conversation to socialise knowledge. Trust was probably the most difficult to create within the discussion space due to the top-down oversight function of the deanery which can be described as a hierarchical organisational culture as opposed to adhocracy or clan cultures typical of academic departments. Another assortment of techniques was applied to externalise and capture the discussion and sharing of knowledge in the room. A combination of verbal, paper-based, whiteboarding, and electronic techniques used by the facilitation team ensured better inclusivity of input from as many voices willing to participate. The unconventional nature of the techniques elicited a mixed response but challenged the traditional approach to strategic sessions.

2.1.1 Background

A rapidly changing and highly competitive world necessitates pressure on organisations to modify their strategies to respond to environmental threats and opportunities (Mezias, Grinyer & Guth, 2001). Strategy formulation is an inseparable activity paired with strategy implementation and remains an ongoing, continuous activity central to everything an organisation does (Dyson, Bryant, Morecroft and O'Brien, 2007). Dyson et al. (2007) view strategy-making as the crafting of deliberate actions, intentionally steering and shaping an organisation's future in a specific desired direction.

The desired direction is seen as a key driver of strategy development often articulated through mission or vision statements, strategic objectives or goals that are measured by targets and other performance metrics (Dyson et al., 2007). Strategic development implies direction-driven organisational change represented by Dyson et al. (2007) as a virtuous cycle that stimulates behavioural change through an articulated direction (Figure 2.1). The behavioural response then results in organisational change that takes the organisation towards the desired direction.

Often in organisations, the desired direction is different from the realised direction caused by incentives for senior managers or targets pursued for easy options rather than for the sake of the original vision or even unrealistic or misguided original visions and missions (Dyson et al.,

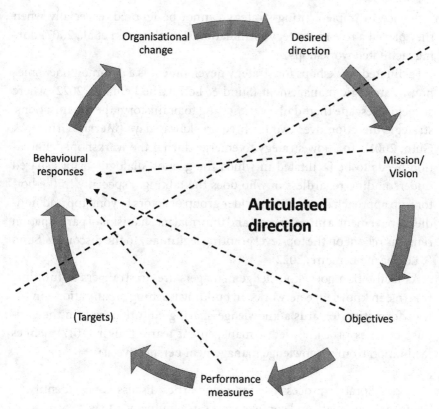

FIGURE 2.1
Direction-driven Organisational Change. (Adapted from Dyson et al., 2007).

2007). One of the main themes identified by Burgelman et al. (2018) in strategy process research is the actors involved in the strategy formulation. While executives and top management teams play a significant role in strategy formulation, it is now well known that including other employees in strategy formulation can have a positive influence on strategy implementation consistent with the emergence of the concept of open strategy (Burgelman et al., 2018; Sund & Le Loarne Lemaire, 2022). In deciding who the strategist should be, a view beyond the traditional top-down process is needed that includes potential strategists from a wider group of actors with individual experiences of agency that are innately connected to their experiences that they can bring to their role in constructing strategy (Jarzabkowski, Balogun & Seidl, 2007). For that reason, middle and lower-level managers as well as operational-level employees have the social, interpretative, linguistic, and personal knowledge bases through which they shape strategy, but more importantly their actions and influence in implementing strategy cannot be ignored, especially when they played a role in strategy formulation (Jarzabkowski et al., 2007) during facilitated workshops.

Facilitated workshops for strategy development is a common phenomenon in strategic management (Sund & Le Loarne Lemaire, 2022) where strategists escape their daily work setting to brainstorm the organisations' strategic direction over two to three breakaway days (Mezias, Grinyer & Guth, 2001). To allow strategy to emerge during the workshop, deliberation needs to be facilitated in which the groups' dialogue brings shared understanding regardless of who does the talking. Especially in the bottom-up approach of allowing a wider group of actors beyond top and middle management, a mix of formal and informal mechanisms of participation remains reliant on the top-level granting legitimacy to the discourse (Sund & Le Loarne Lemaire, 2022).

As facilitation goes, knowledge managers are no strangers to fulfilling this role in knowledge networks, in building learning organisations, in the transformation towards a knowledge-sharing culture or within the various activities of a knowledge management team. Dalkir (2017) defines facilitation from a knowledge management perspective as:

> A collaborative process used to help parties discuss issues, identify, and achieve goals, and complete tasks in a mutually satisfactory manner. This process uses an impartial third party, the facilitator, who focuses on the processes and procedures of dispute resolution and decision-making. The facilitator is impartial to the issues being discussed, rarely contributes substantive ideas, and has no decision-making authority.

In preparation for a college's strategy development at a Higher Education Institution (HEI), the Executive Dean of College approached an academic department of knowledge management to facilitate strategy formulation deliberations during three two-day retreats. The facilitation of these strategic breakaways, spanning eight years between 2014 and 2022, allowed a whole new set of voices to actively contribute to the strategic direction of the college. This chapter provides an ethnographic study of three strategic breakaway sessions for this HEI college through a restructuring process as the initial facilitation session, a think tank a number of years later conducted remotely during global lockdowns, and again in-person at the end of the Dean's term looking towards the succession of leadership and future strategy.

2.2 METHODOLOGY

Typical to ethnographic research the study does not begin with a research question but rather a research interest (Pickard, 2013:138), namely the application of knowledge management facilitation techniques in strategy formulation workshops. The fieldwork happened over a prolonged period from 2014 to 2022. The author acted as the main facilitator during each of the three workshops, analysed and wrote up the narratives and data collected at each of the workshops and had the added benefit of witnessing strategic changes forthcoming from these workshops as a member of the faculty in the College. An essential element in ethnographic research is that the researcher is the primary instrument, combining the researcher as a participant observer and qualitative data collection techniques in a collaborative process of interpreting data and using that interpretation to present a description of the context and to tell a story (Pickard, 2013:139). The researcher acted as the main facilitator of a facilitation team of five for the first workshop, the main facilitator of a co-facilitation team for the second workshop and the sole facilitator of the third and final workshop (Figure 2.2).

This role of researcher and facilitator allowed for the data collection of the ethnographic research from a participative engagement perspective,

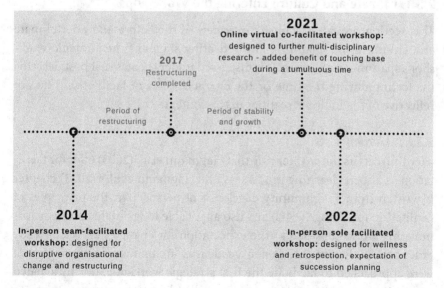

FIGURE 2.2
Timeline of Workshop Facilitation.

immersed in the context and observing from the inside during the planning, facilitation, discourse analysis of the deliberations, and the report writing phases of the workshops. As Pickard (2013:141–143) points out multiple perspectives, multiple realities, and multiple views of the context were gathered through diverse data collection and resulted in descriptive storytelling.

2.3 CHARACTERISTICS OF FACILITATION DURING STRATEGY FORMULATION

During the facilitation of a strategy workshop, the facilitator needs to be mindful and acknowledge the diversity and uniqueness of the individuals who are required to share a collaborative space. This next section offers some insight into the climate and change in culture observed during the facilitation of the series of workshops. A mindfulness of the context that could explain a possible resistance to sharing is also required. This is then followed by a discussion of the knowledge management approaches applied during the facilitation of each of the workshops.

2.3.1 Climate and Culture Entering the Workshops

This section provides a holistic overview of the before and after climate and culture of the planning and reflecting stages of the strategic workshops spanning eight years. It is discussed under themes that best describe the feeling during the time or the characteristics of facilitation that are reflective of the multiple realities of the context.

2.3.1.1 Herding Cats

'Herding cats' is the chapter title that Hagmann et al. (2023) offer for facilitation as a social learning process. While Hagmann et al.'s (2023) chapter is written from a community development perspective, the principles of facilitation for change (F4C) are also applicable to facilitated strategy formulating workshops due to the expectation for change that was already described in Figure 2.1. When academics in knowledge management were approached to facilitate the first strategic workshop, the anticipated disruptive organisational change, overall reluctance, and resistance to change were expressed by all departments and faculty. A recent merger of multiple HEIs still negatively affected several employees, and department leadership maintained a reluctance and outright refusal to undergo a further restructuring process.

The first of several planning meetings for this first workshop with executive leadership soon revealed a clear agenda that restructuring is inevitable and that the workshop is perhaps an exercise in 'propaganda'. When this question was posed to the executive leadership clear offence was taken and a somewhat patronising response given that the word 'propaganda' is a very loaded term and not to be confused with strategy direction from the executive management. The mandate for facilitation, however, was to get clear direction from all levels of faculty to ensure and clarify that the most dynamic strategy for the organisation is ensured. This required the inclusion of strategists beyond only the chairs of schools, heads of academic departments, a few experienced tenured professors, or some middle and top management administrators in the college's support roles. While their collective knowledge and experience may be sufficient to align the college's unique present accomplishments and potential future contribution to the HEI's specific strategic vision, more voices were needed to ensure a smooth transition that the disruptive change of a restructuring process would result in. Dynamic junior faculty were identified from each department and invited to actively contribute to the new strategic direction of the college as they would be instrumental in implementing the change that would come with the restructuring of departments.

Reflecting on this melting pot of attendees to this first workshop, all nine (9) practitioner profiles (Table 2.1) as identified by Sund and Le Loarne Lemaire (2022) could be identified in the 80 strategists that were invited to attend the first strategic workshop.

Having these different characters in the same room along with seasoned and tenured professors required the key factor and important mediator in knowledge sharing, namely trust, to counter the feeling of 'herding cats' in the facilitation process.

2.3.1.2 Trust

Dalkir (2017: 93) states *'without a common base of shared identify (e.g., profession) and trust, knowledge sharing will not succeed'*. And again Dalkir (2017: 149) says the following about trust:

> Networks operate informally with few rules. They depend on trust.
> The first dimension of trust is competence: 'I can trust you if you're
> good at what you do'. Second, trust needs a community. Networks
> naturally spawn internal groups of like-minded individuals.

TABLE 2.1

Practitioner Profile (Sund & Le Loarne Lemaire, 2022:48)

Strategist	Practitioner Profile	Profile Description
a) Profiles of practitioners who are in the spotlight and use the workshop setting as a stage for proposals		
Strategist A	The over-achiever	The over-achiever stands out for a nothing-to-lose mentality and comparably rugged and tempestuous behaviour. When in a discourse, the over-achiever does not shy away from brusque and controversial behaviour.
Strategist B	The diplomat	The diplomat is seen as someone wanting to move forwards, but not at any cost, knowing when to step down.
Strategist D	The sniper	The sniper applies a focussed and driven approach and seeks to steer discourses towards stated organisational goals to get ideas through.
Strategist E	The judge	The judge provides informed input based on prior experience.
Strategist G	The newbie	The newbie provides detailed accounts of experiences and reasoning and shows a curious approach to what is going on in the organisation without dependence on or hindrance by relationships and history.
Strategist H	The realist	The realist shows using a personal approach, a good story can make the difference.
b) Profiles of practitioners who are in the shadow, but are not silent bystanders		
Strategist C	The advisor	The advisor serves top management and the group at large in workshop settings as the go-to-resource for fact-based advice and input.
Strategist F	The go-between	The go-between while without the support of the masses this voice tries to find a middle ground.
Strategist I	The pertinence pursuer	The pertinence pursuer sticks to the facts and is to the point when an intervention is made and makes others listen.

Because trust is so central to knowledge management facilitation, it is the most important aspect to have emerged in a facilitation process, to nurture throughout the facilitation and its loss or absence is immediately felt and once lost, seldom regained. Hagmann et al. (2023:143) offers the first step in facilitation as the opening up or warming up where people familiarise with each other, create an inclusive and open atmosphere, develop personal bonds, make a safe space in which people are comfortable to speak, reduce hierarchies, and match expectations. The trust developed in the room during the first workshop was influenced by what was formulated in the strategy document that followed and the extent to which it remained true to the discourse during the workshop. Rouleau (2005) is of the opinion that selling a new strategy to the organisation requires to gain the trust of the strategists contributing to the discourse and those in the organisation who were not present as strategists in the workshop need good reasons to adopt the change presented by the strategy. If the trust of the strategists was lost, their role in giving good reason to adopt the change by those who were not in the strategy workshop is diminished, even destroyed.

2.3.1.3 Virtuous Cycle
The meaning of a virtuous cycle is a recurring cycle of events, the result of each one being to increase the beneficial effect of the next (Figure 2.1). Direction-driven strategic development is intended to operate in such cycles (Dyson et al., 2007:8). The smaller the gap between the realised direction and the desired direction, the more successful the task of strategic development. Therefore, subsequent cycles of articulated direction should ensure better sense-making and ultimately the long-term success of an organisation.

Volatility and distrust almost derailed the first workshop because the expectations that were created in the opening-up stage of that workshop did not match what revealed itself during the first day of the workshop. Some strategists present in the first workshop also asked the 'propaganda' question behind closed doors and in whispered conversations along passages. Although disillusioned for a brief moment during the first workshop the restructuring process took three years to finalise. While mid-term reviews of the strategy were done as part of the virtuous circle, facilitation with a knowledge management focus was again requested only in 2021 for a college-wide strategic session towards developing a research strategy and postgraduate research offering which was facilitated amidst the global lockdowns of the COVID-19 pandemic.

2.3.1.4 Unlocking Organisational Ecologies

A second main theme identified by Burgelman et al. (2018) in strategy process research is the organisation as a set of ecologies of strategic initiatives subject to the selection forces of guided evolution. This means that organisations have internal ecologies that develop different types of strategic initiatives. These strategic initiatives emerge and evolve within smaller ecologies or business units but contribute collectively to the larger organisations' measured targets and performance metrics.

The facilitation for the second workshop took place via online virtual conferencing during which time a value proposition for a five-year strategy for postgraduate research topics and research programmes was developed. A value proposition was crafted as a statement that clearly identifies the benefits of the College's postgraduate research focus and programme offering to its stakeholders. Six ecologies emerged from this discussion with clear strategic direction and intent. Deep analysis of the value proposition allowed people to reflect, evaluate, and challenge their thinking and potential to buy into this value proposition and the change it would bring to their research focus and postgraduate teaching offerings. Hagmann et al. (2023:143) state that the deeper you go into the analysis, the fewer solutions there are and therefore consensus lies in depth. Before global lockdowns, the virtual platform would never have been considered as a workshop space and the initial apprehension to facilitate the workshop virtually allowed depth in the discussions beyond expectation.

2.3.1.5 Expectation Management

Expectation was perhaps the most difficult aspect to manage through the entire first two workshops, including the planning, the duration of the workshop, and the report writing of the deliberations. The executive of this college was tremendously dynamic and demanded very high standards and return on investment, not only from the workshop outcome itself but also from the implementation of the strategy.

After the first day of the first workshop, a debriefing meeting resulted in a completely different plan for the second day based on what transpired during the first day, falling short of the expectations of the executive. The facilitation yet again changed midway through the second day of the first workshop to salvage the loss of trust as a result of misaligned expectations. The facilitation of the second workshop took place in a co-facilitated partnership with a consultant with whom the main facilitator had not worked before. The interpretation of the expectations of the executive took longer than usual to fully comprehend by both facilitators and the virtual environment did not make this process easier. Several trial-and-error programmes and processes were suggested for the facilitation which were not aligned with the executive's expectations. As a result, the facilitator needs to be willing and capable of on-the-fly facilitation to adapt to what works and what does not work for the current players in the current situation (Van Laere, Lindblom & De Wijse-van Heeswijk, 2021:348). Van Laere et al. (2021:347) recognise on-the-fly facilitation as instantaneous but draws simultaneously on awareness of the past, present, and future, which requires multiple skills and courage from the facilitator. Lessons learned from the first workshop gave the main facilitator in the second workshop an advantage which the consultant did not have in interpreting the executive's expectations.

2.3.1.6 Record, Reflect, Report

The methodology for the facilitation of these workshops maintained a knowledge management focus and is based on the concept of the SECI model by Nonaka and Takeuchi as developed in 1995 (Nonaka, 2022). The SECI model was proposed in the theory of organisational knowledge creation and approaches strategy development with humans as the central role instead of the analytical strategy methods of the plan, do, check, act (PDCA) cycle planning (Nonaka, 2022).

The SECI model described the ongoing upward spiralled process of knowledge creation within an organisation where employees' tacit knowledge (the knowledge people have in their heads, experiences, values, beliefs, and emotions) is converted into explicit knowledge that can be codified or written down, stored, and managed.

The four steps of the SECI model start with socialisation as a tacit-to-tacit knowledge exchange engaged in dialogue. In a presentation-based environment like the one dictated by the third strategy workshop the sharing through socialisation was somewhat one-sided. However, socialisation was achieved to some extent through deliberately involving strategist participation by encouraging continuous posting of thoughts on the deliberation as written responses, suggestions, concerns, or questions. This process of writing thoughts down represented the second step of the knowledge creation cycle, namely externalisation by codifying tacit knowledge to explicit knowledge. The third step, combination, implies the collation of different concepts and ideas together to form a holistic, coherent system, theory, or narrative. This third step usually starts at the respective workshops but continuous in the form of reflections by the facilitator and is captured by assigned scribes of narratives offered during the deliberations. Combination continues during the analysis of the data collected during the workshops that are coded and clustered into specific categories or themes in the report. In some cases, post-workshop contributions were requested to be included in the report which allows for the realisation of the fourth step of the SECI model namely, internalisation, to put the strategy narrative into practice through action.

Workshop facilitation focusses on creating opportunities and platforms for the socialisation of the tacit-to-tacit knowledge exchange. Techniques to capture these exchanges in explicit form also need to be created during the workshops. In some cases, the codification is done by the participating strategists themselves and in other cases assigned scribes were used. In Dalkir's (2017) integrated KM cycle the techniques for socialisation and externalisation can be seen as the techniques used in the knowledge capture and knowledge creation phases.

2.3.2 Facilitation Techniques Used in Workshop 1

This two-day workshop was facilitated by the author along with five assistants. During the planning phase, their roles were to brainstorm which techniques would be best suited to socialise and externalise strategists' contributions. During the workshop they assisted in various roles including co-facilitation, administration, video recordings, and scribing. After the workshop they assisted in documentation, transcription, analysis, and report writing. The layout of the workshop accommodated 80 strategists around 10 large round tables, placed café style in a very large conference room. There was ample space to move around, and tables were spaced in such a way that movement between them was very easy. Initially those attending were left to find their own seats with colleagues they were familiar with. This allowed the building of trust as people are more likely to share knowledge in a space where there is trust and goodwill, and for successful collaboration it is important to capitalise in teams where there are pre-existing or heritage relationships (Gratton & Erickson 2007). Team members who already know and trust one another will become nodes for newly formed teams to evolve further trust from (Gratton & Erickson, 2007). As often observed, attendees would bring their mobile devices and computers to the workshop venues to keep the day-to-day business going and keep email messages under control. Ground rules were established and agreed to ensure undivided attention, full presence, and complete participation from everyone (Johnson et al., 2010:1599). The following techniques regularly applied in knowledge management were used during the workshop to elicit conversations and capture discussions.

2.3.2.1 A Weblog

A weblog is usually an informal website that contains a log or diary of information, and serves as a platform for individuals to communicate, and share ideas, opinions, and knowledge (Lefika & Mearns 2015:28). It captures information in such a way that it is codified and ready for organisational use. While it is usually written in the form of a story or a diary entry, it presents a historical account of a topic, usually in reverse chronological order.

During the workshop one of the facilitation assistants captured the discussions and deliberations of the workshop by scribing quotes, taking and posting photographs or any other media in real-time, and sharing it like a film reel on multiple screens in the room. A platform called *keeep* was used for this purpose. *keeep* was a Software as a Service (SaaS) platform designed in 2011[1] to leverage collective corporate intelligence by capturing, creating, and sharing text, images, videos, ideas, and any professional work across an organisation. Not only did this collect quotes, narratives, and key discussion from all strategists, it recorded the history of the workshop and more importantly a glance at the screen in the venue would serve to trigger additional conversation as a 'silent' but visual prompt as discussions continued around several tables. Two quotes that were collected from sticky notes written by one of the strategists while the executive dean was still delivering an introductory address at the workshop were:

'We definitely focus on profit…What about people and planet?'

'It is not necessary to restructure the Faculty to enable
Innovation & collaboration. Maintain a flat structure.'

2.3.2.2 Collaborative Whiteboarding

As visible in the second quote in Figure 2.4, the introduction to the two-day workshop already reflected a resistance to the suggested restructuring process that was recognised during the planning stages of the strategic workshop. Szulanski (2000:10) speaks of stickiness in knowledge transfer, referring to the difficulty in transferring knowledge, that it is not an act of transfer but rather a process. To facilitate the transfer of knowledge as a process early in the workshop, strategists were encouraged to make use of physical collaborative whiteboarding by writing whatever comes to mind at any moment during the workshop on sticky notes and place it on a central whiteboard. These quotes were captured and displayed on the *keeep* platform but were also thematically categorised after the workshop and formed part of the narrative of the holistic post-workshop report. The fact that strategists could anonymously and confidentially contribute difficult to discuss and contentious issues without victimisation or recourse meant that the formation of the transfer seed in the initiation stage of the process of transfer, as discussed by Szulanski (2000:13), was planted. While Szulanski (2000) focusses on knowledge transfer, the potential linkage between the process of knowledge transfer and the direction-driven organisational change (Figure 2.1) for strategic development deserves further investigation. The trust that developed in the room was evident from one of the top seven observations that the executive dean shared as the morning progressed, captured on the *keeep*. Observation number 6 was:

> Healthy organisations are marked by tensions of opposites, for example, in the faculty we find tension between those stretching towards the bigger picture and the reality of getting the job done. We need both voices to be heard in finding the truth. Thank you for speaking up.

Collaborative whiteboarding was also used per academic or administrative service department on large flipchart papers armed with random magazine pictures, coloured pens, scissors, and glue (Figure 2.3). At the time a number of conservative pre-retirement professors initially frowned upon this activity, reached for their computers to answer emails to avoid stepping out of their comfort zone. They re-engaged after a gentle reminder of the ground rules they agreed to and proceeded to create diagrammatic representations of visions and missions (Figure 2.4) with what can only be described in the end as youthful enthusiasm.

Having by this time achieved full participation through co-creation and collective strategising (Sund & Le Loarne Lemaire, 2022:53) and established substantial trust in the room it was time to generate different energy using a knowledge café.

FIGURE 2.3
Challenged Comfort Zone.

2.3.2.3 Knowledge Café

Knowledge cafés are characterised by a guest speaker who speaks for 5–30 min contextualising a topic, followed by posting one to three open-ended questions (Lefika & Mearns 2015). The questions serve as the basis for conversation that initially takes place in small groups in a café style setting, with four to five iterations. Each iteration requires delegates to move around the room finding new groups to interact with. The facilitator discerns when saturation of the question discussion is reached and calls the entire room to a final feedback session, standing in one large circle. Each person then briefly shares one key insight they gained from the inter-action. To avoid the repetition of insights already mentioned a delegate merely says 'skip'. This also applies to shy individuals not willing to speak

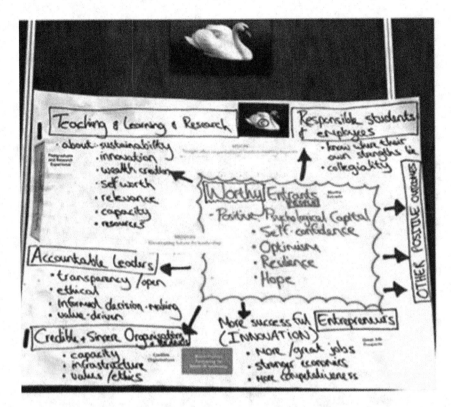

FIGURE 2.4
Collaborative Vision and Mission.

publicly. Only the last circles' insights are captured. The stand-up meeting also ensures that the feedback from each individual is to the point, without repetition or any individual monopolising the conversation. The knowledge café concluded the first day of the workshop.

2.3.2.4 Retrospect

On the morning of the second day, a retrospect was held to review the events of the first day. Some analysis done through the night was presented to start making sense of the initial insights collected (Figure 2.5).

The dean delivered a lengthy discussion of his plans of restructuring and the intense trust that was created through the processes of the first day, coupled with the now confirmed suspicion that the workshop was an exercise in 'propaganda' revealed anonymous contributions such as:

> We discussed the Dean's ideas around the proposed restructuring, and we are not happy about it. The naming of the school bothers us;

Question 1 *Which strengths can I contribute in supporting the notion of sustainability?*	Question 2 *What hurdles should we overcome to embrace sustainability at the HEI level, Faculty level, Departmental level, and at an individual level?*	Question 3 *To which elements of sustainability can I contribute?*	Question 4 *How do we sustain momentum towards end 2015?*	Question 5 *Formulate the way towards 2020*	Question 6 *How do we contribute towards the stature and excellence of higher learning?*
Create a work-life balance	Departmental level: To dream again	Contributing to people	Actively seek interdisciplinary collaboration within U21	Harnessing the use technology to enhance learning	Become a true subject expert with industry links
Research in Sustainability (students & through international partnerships)	Lack of skills & capacity constraints	Profit: Develop SLPs to support "profit" element	Maintain current position as first choice for retail & marketing education	Define where we want to be in 2020	Attract, appoint and retain excellent staff

FIGURE 2.5
Excerpt of the Initial Analysis of Colour-coded Sticky Notes towards Sensemaking.

we have a fear of getting lost in the system; the grouping together of departments might exclude opportunities for innovation and collaboration; there is a need for more interdisciplinary collaboration across the board; we want to keep the flat structure and rather create more opportunities for networking and collaboration across the entire college.

This interim feedback threatened to derail the entire strategic session and a palpable change in atmosphere was observed with strategists starting to completely disengage from the process. In a bold move, the facilitators consulted with the Dean, explained what a fishbowl is and suggested to close the workshop with a candid fishbowl conversation.

2.3.2.5 Fishbowl Conversation Technique

A fishbowl conversation is used to keep a focussed conversation when a large group of people needs to engage on the same topic. Generally, five chairs are placed in a circle in the centre of a larger circle or a double circle. The inner circle of five chairs has four people seated (with one open chair) and have a conversation which the outer circle(s) observe. At any time, a person from the outer circle(s) can join the conversation after seating themselves in the open chair, requiring one of the other four inner circle conversationists to vacate their chair, always leaving a chair open in the centre that can be occupied by anyone in the room.

The Dean realised the volatility of the moment and agreed to proceed with the fishbowl, with the exception that he would occupy the only chair in the centre, inviting open questions with no repercussions from all 80 strategists. He was made well aware of the importance of truthful, yet diplomatic answers honouring that any questions be allowed without fear or favour. Questions that were asked openly reflected raw honesty:

- Strategist 1: *'I am concerned about hearing what we are hearing, and questions are really unanswered. We are concerned that you actually want direction about exactly what you wanted to know. Is this what you wanted to hear?'*
- Strategist 2: *'Issues were raised on the observations and we have a feeling of disappointment. This feeling is shared and people might be disappointed for different reasons. Despite the fact that we don't want a hierarchical structure we might need a multi-layer organisation. From where you sit you are a custodian of decisions that still need to*

be sold to the rest of the organisation. You came to the meeting with
certain expectations. How do we know if all of us came with the same
expectations?'
- *Strategist 3: 'We are not where you are and you need to give us time
  to catch up with you. Your slides reflect months of thinking and in
  an hour and a half, we need to take the journey and enter into your
  world. We need to have time to catch up with you.'*

As much as the conversation appeared to have derailed, the progression
started to resemble Szulanski's (2000:13) process of knowledge transfer
where the key stages are initiation, implementation, ramp-up, and integration. The key milestones are formation of the transfer seed, decision
to transfer, first day of use, and finally achievement of satisfactory performance. Day 1 initiated the formulation of the transfer seed and the retrospect on the morning of day 2 resulted in a total resistance to change. The
fishbowl conversation accelerated the decision to transfer, as it started to
take shape in the responses from some individuals.

- *Strategist 4: 'Scared [of change], should not be misinterpreted as not
  being on board - our headspace is different. Now that this energy is
  going, do not drop us. I do not want to be unsure again in the future.'*
- *Dean: "I am also scared; my weakness is not always knowing how
  to operationalise things. Thank you for being honest. Thank you for
  pointing it out. We are scared to acknowledge our fears, but it is part of
  trust-building to admit what we are battling with. We learn by enriching experience and acknowledging each other."*
- *Strategist 5: 'In summary, [Dean], we are behind you. We would like to
  have you as our leader, the reality is that the college is running really
  well which differs from the past. It is about the distillation process and
  finding our feet. We need the distillation process and we need to move
  forward and know that our future is not secure unless we are willing to
  walk the road.'*

The conversation then proceeded to suggest ideas of how to start the move
forward and what to do to know where to move to. The conversation closed
with several strategists offering advice and gentle warnings:

- *Strategist 6: 'I hope you will hear us. I am not sure that you always
  hear us. We need to be careful of the quiet rumbles in the corner'.*

- *Strategist 7: 'Once, as a leadership team, the strategy has been sorted out, the staff on the ground should not be forgotten, so that they too can embrace your direction. The strategy will bring us to greater relevance and the dynamics and excitement in the college shows that the staff is ready to hear your voice more and less anxiety will ensue.'*
- *Strategist 8: 'To maintain the speed I propose that you will consult in this way again. Afford the people sufficient freedom, there has been no suppression and we could speak, helping us to see the future better. And to state to you that I am not going to do something and that we will be able to say that.'*

The Dean concluded with the following statement and closed the Workshop:

- *Dean: 'The moment where you realise you know nothing...now that I have insight I realise I know nothing.'*

The techniques applied in this first workshop were varied and purposefully designed to take people out of their comfort zone yet create trust. On both these scores they were successful. Had it not been for the facilitation teams' insight into knowledge management techniques and organisational culture paired with their skills in facilitation and their agility to make quick changes, this workshop could easily have failed midway. The deliberations did deliver a report of the findings and a strategy was developed and implemented that resulted in a major restructuring of the college. The next request for facilitation came seven years later in 2021 amidst global lockdowns during the COVID-19 pandemic.

2.3.3 Facilitation Techniques Used in Workshop 2

In this co-facilitated online workshop, many of the strategists who were present in the first workshop were again invited to this think tank and those heritage relationships that Gratton and Erickson (2007) mentioned assisted team members who already knew each other and who knew the facilitators ensuring that trust was already developed and could also act as nodes for trust with new members. By the time the online workshop took place attendees had been familiar with the online environment for more than a year due to online remote work and teaching during COVID-19 lockdowns.

The online nature of virtual conference rooms and breakaway rooms allowed for discussion and besides a few initial technical issues ran smoothly over the single day of discussions. Three discussions took place, the first in multidisciplinary breakaway discussions with six questions guiding the conversation. The second round of discussions was conducted in a schools-based conversation and used four questions as a guide. Discussions were documented by delegates who volunteered or were group-appointed scribes and recorded their discussions on Google Docs on a shared Google Drive. The third round of discussions resulted from a plenary session using a transcript generated by the recording of the plenary sessions and documenting the chat of the session. Ad hoc email discussions with scribes were conducted after the workshop to clarify cryptic points from the workshop documentation where necessary. All these sources served as the text-based data collected for the analysis and report writing.

Due to the breakaway nature of multiple virtual rooms and having only two facilitators, it was not possible to enter rooms and where rooms were entered by facilitators it was disruptive and stopped the conversation instead of being supportive. The ease of immediate documentation of the discussion and the fact that everybody could see the document being edited in real-time is probably the most valuable feature of this type of facilitation. It is however very impersonal and difficult to manage. To ensure good data connectivity some delegates opted to travel to the campus and maintain social distancing guidelines and protocols. These in-person encounters were celebrated by those individuals on campus in light of the lengthy duration of strict lockdowns that were enforced at the time.

This online workshop was very taxing. Limited bandwidth and weak connectivity resulted in most individuals deactivating cameras and therefore it was impossible to read energy levels, participation, facial expressions, or other body language. The strategist profiles as indicated in Table 2.1 were also lost to the facilitation process and the role they play in strategy discussion was only visible in their breakaway groups, if they actively participated, and could not be drawn upon from a facilitation perspective.

The plenary session was also rather one-sided, but the chat function allowed for the contribution of multiple perspectives. Contributing to the chat was however optional and, in some cases, some contributions were rather cryptic and required clarification. Multiple thoughts posted in close succession tended to be distracting during the discussion and required cross-referencing to the transcript of the audio recording afterwards.

The author experienced the online workshop to be less effective from a knowledge management approach facilitation perspective. The same level of trust was not established compared to the in-person workshops and unless more quiet voices placed their thoughts in writing, they remained silent during this workshop.

Nevertheless, from this workshop two Directors of Schools requested facilitation in a similar vein for their schools specifically, and regular updates of the progress of one of the schools are still being sent to the author. In 2022, immediately after the complete lifting of enforced lockdowns a third workshop facilitation was requested that took place at a retreat location and marked the end of the Dean of College's term.

2.3.4 Facilitation Techniques Used in Workshop 3

While the planning for this workshop and how it was advertised to the attendees was focussed to prioritise wellbeing and to get reconnected post-global and national lockdowns of 2020–2021, there was an expectation from the delegates that there would be some form of succession planning and direction for the future leadership to follow. The Dean, Deputy Deans, various Directors of Schools, and Heads of Departments provided feedback and celebrated what had been the collective best performance since the college and schools' inception. Continuous contributions using sticky notes were again encouraged.

2.3.4.1 Structured Collaborative Whiteboarding
In structured collaborative whiteboarding contributions were encouraged according to pre-determined themes:

- Cultivation or aspects that require time to nurture.
- Pruning refers to aspects that come from lessons learned that need to be tidied up or cut back now that we know what works, does not work or needs to change.
- Harvesting would imply quick wins or low-hanging fruits that can be capitalised on.
- Refinement requires a process analysis to modify the aspects that need to improve or be moulded to produce the required output.
- Uses imply that some aspects could potentially have many purposes – what can we do to work smarter, not harder?
- Threats identified and ideas on how to approach threats or initiatives to protect against such threats with or without support from other units.

- Nourishment and support refer to specifically what the colleges' administrative office could do to aid schools', departments', or individuals' outputs and efforts.

The conversations and presentations that prompted these contributions took place during the first day. Partial analyses were again done during the night of the first day and resulted in a spreadsheet that was offered as a retrospect as part of a plenary discussion. However, pressured for time during the breakaway, planned retrospect was not sufficiently completed to put the narrative into practice to create further tacit knowledge on generating solutions for the contributions collected. A collaborated shared document was used instead during a brief post-workshop period.

2.3.4.2 Software as a Service
Software as a Service or SaaS platform allows for storage, sharing, and accessing files and documents over the internet in which multiple users can collaborate. The spreadsheet was therefore shared post breakaway with directors of schools to populate representing the collective knowledge and wisdom from the college who might have implemented good practice or ground-breaking initiatives or have experience in response to the issues that have been indicated during day 1 of the workshop that needed specific attention.

The spreadsheet summarises the collective insight from the delegates on the shared strengths, weaknesses, opportunities, and threats of each school or department. Delegates were also invited to write down pertinent questions that were to be addressed on Day 2 of the breakaway. The honesty and trust of these processes are what Nonaka, Toyama, and Konno (2000) refer to as *Ba*, a difficult-to-translate Japanese term that refers to the shared context for knowledge creation. The integrity and authenticity with which delegates' questions are treated determine the willingness of employees to openly participate in subsequent knowledge-creating spirals. Although some of the questions posed at the 2022 breakaway were answered during Day 2 of the breakaway, disillusionment was expressed by delegates in informal debriefing conversations that some questions were treated nonchalantly or totally dismissed. Considering that the questions were posed anonymously it was not possible to identify the unsatisfactory answers received to the list of questions that were shared in the post-workshop report. It was recommended that the questions that were pointed out in the report be properly answered and circulated to the delegates.

Considering that *Ba* is seen as a shared platform for knowledge creation, it refers to physical and/or mental spaces foundational to tacit knowledge sharing. It not only involves emotions, feelings, experiences, and mental images of individuals active in a knowledge-sharing context, but also involves the formation of a collective relationship that is open to the sharing of practices, values, processes, and culture. By paying attention to *Ba*, the focus in the knowledge-creation context is on the individual as a person who holds the knowledge rather than just on the knowledge itself. This proved to be equally important in strategy development workshops. Without this kind of trust environment present in *Ba*, employees do not feel safe in common spaces and are unwilling to engage in dialogue to share and create knowledge or to develop strategy. Relationships are formed in *Ba* not only because employees share knowledge, but also because they share values, beliefs, and emotions. It is this connectedness and dialogue that allows the development of new knowledge 'with others' rather than 'to others' (Attard, et al., 2022). The concept of *Ba* in the SECI model would probably be the ideal place where knowledge managers should develop conscious awareness around the issues of diversity, equity and inclusion because this is the place where relationships are formed and the willingness to engage is born.

The SECI model is an extensively researched, respected, and trusted model in the knowledge-creation process of converting tacit knowledge into explicit knowledge in organisations. The conscious application of this model assists in creating trusting environments where knowledge sharing can be facilitated to create knowledge assets. However, the knowledge-creating process is not managed in the traditional sense of managing the flow of information. It is rather an active and dynamic process that creates knowledge by providing specific conditions. A university as a knowledge-creating organisation can benefit from the application of the SECI model in strategy development too.

2.4 THE VALUE OF KNOWLEDGE MANAGEMENT FACILITATION IN INCLUSIVE STRATEGY DEVELOPMENT

'Knowledge management is not just a practice of moving knowledge about, it is an act of equity, it is building an inclusive culture' (Trees, 2022). Good knowledge management is regarded as an approach to democratising access to knowledge and expertise. Inclusive facilitation through knowledge management approaches, as was done in these three workshops, facilitates inclusivity in strategy development. Not only does such inclusivity give a voice to the traditional voiceless 'victims' of strategy development, but it also gives them agency to own and navigate major changes that result from new strategic direction.

Knowledge management approaches during the facilitation of the workshops created psychologically safe spaces (SECI's *Ba*) to exchange ideas and experiences between diverse colleagues in terms of age, rank, and position. Durst (2021:216) reiterates that the probability of success towards responsible knowledge management increases when one seeks and appreciates the skills and competencies of everyone regardless of the person's role, function, education, age, or ethnic background. Traditionally younger, lower-ranked faculty would not have been in a shared collaboration space with older higher-ranking faculty, let alone fulfil the role of strategists to decide the desired direction for the College. Inclusion and diversity are key components of knowledge management success and the same seems to apply to strategy development.

Inclusivity in knowledge management, and for that matter strategy development, the facilitator needs to remain mindful that the capability to share one's insights, knowledge, and experiences does not only depend on one's age, rank, role, or background but can also be related to personality types such as introverts, and situational or environmental context such as organisational culture (Kakkar & Tangirala, 2018). The inclusive, diverse group of strategists should be selected for the workshop regardless of visible differences (age, ethnicity) or known differences (rank, position). Once they physically enter the collaboration space it becomes a dynamic and intuitive process to gain trust, tease out the silent voices, and gently tone down the overly loud voices. Knowledge management has a long history of doing exactly that.

2.5 CONCLUSION

To create knowledge dynamically and continuously, an organisation needs a vision that synchronises the entire organisation. It is top management's role to articulate the knowledge vision and communicate it throughout (and outside) the company. The knowledge vision defines what kind of knowledge the company should create in what domain. The knowledge vision gives a direction to the knowledge-creating process, and the knowledge created by it, by asking such fundamental questions as 'What are we?', 'What should we create?', 'How can we do it?', 'Why are we doing this?', and 'Where are we going?'.

(Nonaka, Toyama & Konno, 2000:23)

Not only is this the language of knowledge sharing and knowledge management, but it is also most certainly the language of strategy development. Having several iterations through the virtuous cycle an organisation would know who they are, what they should create, how and why they are doing it, and where they are going. All this is stimulated through behavioural change towards an articulated direction, aiming for a desired direction hoping that the realised direction is as close as possible, or hopefully, spot-on. The techniques typical to knowledge sharing and knowledge management proved to be very useful in navigating the strategic direction for an HEI college not only in terms of overcoming the stickiness to change but also in teasing out the generally quieter voices and managing the overly loud voices in a room.

NOTE

1 https://pitchbook.com/profiles/company/96277-78#overview keeep was founded in 2011 and in 2021 went out of business.

REFERENCES

Attard, C., Elliot, M., Grech, P. and McCormack, B. (2022). Adopting the concept of 'Ba' and the 'SECI' model in developing person-centered practices in child and adolescent mental health services. *Frontiers in Rehabilitation Science*. 2, 744146. https://www.frontiersin.org/articles/10.3389/fresc.2021.744146/full

Burgelman, RA, Floyd, SW, Laamanen, T, Mantere, S, Vaara, E, Whittington, R. (2018). Strategy processes and practices: Dialogues and intersections. *Strategic Management Journal*. 39,531–558. https://doi.org/10.1002/smj.2741

Dalkir, K. (2017). *Knowledge management in theory and practice*. 3rd ed. Cambridge, MA: MIT Press.

Durst, S. (2021). A plea for responsible and inclusive knowledge management at the world level. *VINE Journal of Information and Knowledge Management Systems*. 54(1), 211–219.

Dyson, R.G., Bryant, J., Morecroft, J. and O'Brien, F. (2007). The Strategic Development Process. In: O'Brien, F. and Dyson, R.G., (Eds.) *Supporting strategy: Frameworks, methods and models*, (1st Ed) pp. 3–24. Chichester, UK: John Wiley & Sons Ltd.

Gratton, L. & Erickson, T.J. (2007). Eight ways to build collaborative teams. *Harvard Business Review*. November 2007. Available: https://hbr.org/2007/11/eight-ways-to-build-collaborative-teams

Hagmann, J., Chuma, E., Ramaru, J., Peter, H., Murwira, K., Ficarelli, P., Ngwenya, H., Krebs, K. (2023). Herding cats: Facilitation in social learning processes. In: Colfer, C.J.P. and Prabhu, R. [eds.], *Responding to environmental issues through adaptive aollaborative management: From forest communities to global actors*. London, UK: Routledge. https://doi.org/10.4324/9781003325932-11

Jarzabkowski, P., Balogun, J., & Seidl, D. (2007). Strategizing: he challenges of a practice perspective. *Human Relations*, 60(1), 5–27.

Johnson, G., Prashantham, S., Floyd, S. W., & Bourque, N. (2010). The Ritualization of strategy workshops. *Organization Studies*, 31(12), 1589–1618.

Kakkar, H. & Tangirala, S. (2018). If your employees aren't speaking up, blame company culture. *Harvard Business Review*. November 2018. Available: https://hbr.org/2018/11/if-your-employees-arent-speaking-up-blame-company-culture

Lefika, P.T. & Mearns, M.A. (2015). Adding knowledge cafés to the repertoire of knowledge sharing techniques. *International Journal of Information Management*, 35(1), 26–32. https://doi.org/10.1016/j.ijinfomgt.2014.09.005

Mezias, J., Grinyer, P., & Guth, W. D. (2001). Changing collective cognition: a process model for strategic change. *Long Range Planning*, 34(1), 71–95.

Nonaka, I. (2022). *Management based on human empathy: For building a future of better living in a dynamic world*. Available: https://www.hitachi.com/rev/column/ei/vol15/index.html

Nonaka, I., Toyama, R. and Konno, N. (2000). SECI, *Ba* and leadership: a unified model of dynamic knowledge creation. *Long Range Planning*. 33(1), 5–35.

Pickard, A.J. (2013). *Research methods in information*. 2nd ed. London, UK: Facet.

Rouleau, L. (2005). Micro-practices of strategic sensemaking and sensegiving: how middle managers interpret and sell change every day. *Journal of Management Studies*, 42(7), 1413–1441.

Sund, C. & Le Loarne Lemaire, S. (2022). The Practitioner's identity and participation in strategy workshops. an ethnographic study. *Management international*, 26(1), 42–58. https://doi.org/10.7202/1088436ar

Szulanski, G. (2000). The Process of knowledge transfer: a diachronic analysis of stickiness, *Organizational Behavior and Human Decision Processes*, 82(1), 9–27. https://doi.org/10.1006/obhd.2000.2884

Trees, L. (2022). How KM can support diversity, equity, and inclusion. *APQC Blog*. Available: https://www.apqc.org/blog/how-km-can-support-diversity-equity-and-inclusion

Van Laere, J., Lindblom, J., & de Wijse-van Heeswijk, M. (2021). Complexifying facilitation by immersing in lived experiences of on-the-fly facilitation. *Simulation & Gaming*, 52(3), 346–363. https://doi.org/10.1177/10468781211006751

3

Integrated Map of Critical Knowledge: A Tool for Knowledge Governance in Interorganizational Networks

Patricia de Sá Freire and Yuqing Yao
Federal University of Santa Catarina, Florianopolis, Brazil

3.1 INTRODUCTION

The digital age has transformed the way organizations operate and interact (Castells, 2011). In the midst of this scenario, knowledge management (KM) has emerged as a fundamental pillar to ensure competitive advantage and sustained innovation (Davenport & Prusak, 1998a; Nonaka & Takeuchi, 1995). It functions not only as an operational mechanism but also as a vital driver for networked organizational learning (Contractor, Wasserman, & Faust, 2006).

Essentially, KM, through its mechanisms, catalyzes the learning process within organizations, leveraging both individual and collective knowledge with a perspective of continuous enhancement of organizational performance (Rizzatti & Freire, 2020). In this context, the interconnection of organizations in complex networks, whether formal or informal, not only requires effective knowledge management for the exchange and co-creation of knowledge but also a system that encourages permeable learning at all organizational levels (Powell & Grodal, 2005).

Organizational Learning (OL) and KM are notably interconnected, with KM providing the necessary infrastructure for learning to be captured, encoded, and distributed throughout the organization and beyond (Rizzatti & Freire, 2020). In interorganizational networks, characterized

DOI: 10.1201/9781003407966-3

by their heterogeneity and interdependence (Provan, Fish, & Sydow, 2007), the need for efficient KM that fosters learning and innovation through the sharing and co-creation of knowledge becomes imperative (Tsoukas & Vladimirou, 2001).

It is in this context that integrated maps of data, information, and knowledge are introduced as a pragmatic solution to simplify the representation and facilitate access and dissemination of knowledge within organizational networks (Eppler, 2004, 2006). These maps go beyond being mere visual representations; they act as a strategic tool that enables the understanding of all stakeholders, consequently guiding organizations to navigate securely in complex and ever-evolving environments (Börner, Chen, & Boyack, 2003). This is where KM shapes itself as an essential mechanism for organizational networks involving multiple stakeholders, not only for the equitable storage and distribution of knowledge but also for facilitating the continuous learning of all network participants.

Knowledge governance, referring to the set of policies, processes, and tools that ensure the effective management and utilization of knowledge at different levels of the organization and among distinct organizations (Renzl, 2008), becomes crucial for aligning efforts and optimizing outcomes, especially in networks where various entities pursue different objectives and practice diverse cultures (Miles, Snow, Meyer, & Coleman, 1978). Governance, by embracing robust KM practices, including those aimed at facilitating learning at multiple levels, creates a conducive environment for systematically absorbing, distributing, and using knowledge to enhance existing practices and drive innovation (Rizzatti & Freire, 2020).

In summary, by emphasizing the importance of dialogic communication among stakeholders, recognizing that knowledge is not static but indispensable for OL, shaped by continuous interactions and exchanges (Brown & Duguid, 2001; Rizzatti & Freire, 2020), this chapter, generated from intricate research on the stages of a method for creating integrated maps of critical knowledge, aims not only to introduce the fundamentals of knowledge governance in interorganizational networks but also to contribute to the detailed understanding and practical application of a method for creating integrated maps of critical knowledge. Thus, it advances the academic and practical discourse on the subject and moves toward empowering organizations to thrive, collaborate, and innovate in an increasingly interconnected and dynamic world (Senge, 2006).

3.2 THEORETICAL FOUNDATIONS

3.2.1 Knowledge Governance in Interorganizational Networks

Since Davenport and Prusak (1998b), who affirmed that knowledge is a valuable resource for organizations, organizational studies have sought ways to manage and govern this asset. In the interorganizational context, Probst, Raub, and Romhardt (2001a) identify that KM is crucial for sustainability and innovation. In Brazil, Terra (2001) emphasizes the importance of KM in collaborative environments and its implications for competitiveness.

Going further, Anna Grandori (2001), Nicholas Foss (2007), and in Brazil, Freire et al. (2017), in their research, warn that knowledge governance is fundamental to KM because it establishes the rules, processes, and mechanisms necessary to ensure that knowledge is managed effectively and efficiently. Knowledge governance enables organizations to identify, capture, store, share, and strategically use knowledge aligned with the organization's objectives and goals. Furthermore, knowledge governance also helps minimize the risks associated with KM, such as the loss of critical knowledge, lack of collaboration, and improper use of knowledge (Bresolin, Souto, & Freire, 2023). Therefore, knowledge governance is essential for KM and the success of organizations in today's competitive environment

According to Grandori (2008), the importance of intra and interorganizational network mechanisms for the effectiveness and intensity of innovative knowledge is highlighted. She mentions that organizations become highly effective when they decentralize and are governed by communities and project teams that facilitate the sharing of property rights, rather than centralized islands of tacit knowledge. Furthermore, she mentions that Bart Nooteboom from the Rotterdam School of Management at Erasmus University emphasizes the importance of governing the knowledge created in interorganizational relationships. Therefore, knowledge governance in interorganizational networks is grounded in decentralization, collaboration, and knowledge sharing among the organizations involved.

Continuing, Kempner-Moreira, Freire, and Souza (2022) reinforce the significance of both intra and interorganizational network mechanisms for effectiveness and the generation of innovative knowledge. The authors suggest that organizations become more effective when they decentralize, adopting shared and multilevel governance. This movement promotes the sharing of property rights and discourages the formation of centralized "islands" of tacit knowledge. This perspective aligns with the seminal article by Bart Nooteboom and his co-authors Berger and Noorderhaven (1997), emphasizing the importance of governing knowledge originating from the state of trust in interorganizational relationships.

However, despite the recognized value of knowledge governance, substantial challenges emerge, especially in the complex contexts typical of interorganizational networks. These networks, with multiple stakeholders and their respective agendas and visions, demand highly refined KM. Collaboration, coordination, and communication among these parties are crucial and simultaneously challenging (Martins and Freire, 2021).

We must also bear in mind that the increased speed of information flows and the abundance of data in the digital age require more sophisticated tools to filter, analyze, and integrate this data into actionable knowledge reliably and qualitatively by multiple stakeholders (Mayer-Schönberger & Cukier, 2013).

To overcome these challenges, the creation of Integrated Maps for Knowledge Governance in Interorganizational Networks is posited as a promising solution.

3.2.2 Maps of Critical Knowledge

Among seminal publications in KM, various models of knowledge maps are used in organizational contexts.

Cognitive Maps, which are hierarchical diagrams representing an individual's or a group's knowledge of a specific domain, illustrate how different concepts are interconnected and how knowledge is organized (Eden, 1992). **Concept Maps**, developed by Novak, represent relationships between concepts through propositions. They are particularly useful for illustrating and structuring knowledge in educational and training fields (Novak and Canas, 2008). **Argumentation Maps** visualize the logical structure of arguments, facilitating the understanding and evaluation of claims, reasons, evidence, and counterarguments (Gelder, 2001). **Topic Maps** are diagrams representing topics and their relationships within a specific knowledge area. They are common in educational settings for outlining the structure of a course or discipline (Jonassen, Beissner, & Yacci, 1993). **Social Knowledge Maps** are visual representations illustrating how knowledge is distributed and shared within a community or social network. This type of map helps organizations identify experts, communities of practice, and information flows (Cross & Parker, 2004). Additionally, ontologies are structured representations defining concepts and their relationships within a domain. They are common in semantic web and artificial intelligence contexts, assisting machines and humans in understanding and sharing knowledge (Gruber, 1993).

All of these maps are constructed through a knowledge mapping process, resulting in the discovery of the location, value, and use cases of organizational knowledge (Ermine et al., 2006). In the end, they serve as valuable tools for organizing, representing, and sharing knowledge in an accessible and understandable manner. The choice of the most appropriate model largely depends on the organization's goals, the target audience, and the nature of the knowledge to be mapped (Marques, Freire, Dos Santos & Mattar, 2017).

However, for knowledge governance in interorganizational networks, where multiple data, information, and knowledge related to each stakeholder are recorded, a model of Integrated Map of Critical Knowledge for the interorganizational network is required.

We know that it is currently a consensus, both in academic literature and in organizations, that knowledge is a valuable resource, especially in such environments where interoperability and collaboration are essential. In other words, knowledge governance in interorganizational environments, with its multitude of stakeholders, represents a scenario of complexity and dynamism. Each stakeholder carries a diverse set of data, information, and knowledge that are essential for the network as a whole.

A new design like an **Integrated Map of Critical Knowledge** emerges as a necessary solution for this scenario. According to the French researchers Jean-Louis Ermine, Imed Boughzala, and Thierno Tounkara (2006), a critical knowledge map is a tool used to identify the most critical knowledge domains within an organization. It is used to assess the risks and opportunities associated with different knowledge domains, such as the risks of knowledge loss or the interest in developing a domain to gain advantages for the company. By identifying the most critical knowledge domains, organizations can prioritize their knowledge transfer actions and focus on transferring the most valuable knowledge to the right people. In their research, the authors mention that the Critical Knowledge Map can be used as a gateway to the knowledge capital, indicating experts, publications, or attached documents, suggesting that its use can be beneficial for sharing knowledge between organizations; in other words, it can serve to integrate knowledge from multiple stakeholders for the common good.

The central purpose of this type of map, the Integrated Map of Critical Knowledge, is to visualize and integrate critical knowledge from various stakeholders, making it accessible and usable for everyone within the network (Probst, Raub & Romhardt, 2001b)

- Diversity Capture: Each stakeholder in an interorganizational network has a unique perspective and set of knowledge. The map aims to consolidate this diversity, reflecting the richness of the network (Nonaka & Takeuchi, 1995).
- Unified Structure: In environments where knowledge is dispersed, a unified structure, as proposed by Snowdon (2002), is essential to make sense of the complexity.
- Promoting Interoperability: Organizations need to work together to achieve common goals. The integrated map promotes this interoperability, showing where knowledge interconnects and where gaps may exist (Alavi & Leidner, 2001).
- Strategic Action: For an interorganizational network to operate effectively, it must act strategically. A map that highlights critical knowledge helps guide this action, providing insights into where to invest efforts and resources (Levitt & March, 1988).

Given the importance of knowledge governance in interorganizational environments, the existence of an Integrated Map of Critical Knowledge is imperative. It not only centralizes and structures knowledge but also allows for a holistic view, crucial for navigating the complexities of networks. As a result, it empowers organizations to collaborate more effectively, innovate, and thrive in an interconnected and dynamic environment.

In the contemporary corporate landscape, a deep understanding of organizational knowledge is essential for guiding strategies, empowering teams, and sustaining competitive advantages. As clarified by Nonaka and Takeuchi (1995), understanding the nature of both tacit and explicit knowledge and their interrelation is crucial. Tacit knowledge, being intuitive and internalized, is often more challenging to codify and transfer, while explicit knowledge is more easily articulated and documented (Polanyi, 1966).

The map of critical knowledge serves as a bridge between these two categories. It not only identifies areas of tacit knowledge that are vital for the organization's operation and innovation but also provides guidelines on how this knowledge can be translated or transformed into explicit forms for easy dissemination (Choo, 2002). The clear and concise visualization of critical knowledge areas allows organizations to prioritize resources and efforts for their protection, development, and distribution (Bolisani & Bratianu, 2017).

In addition to identifying crucial knowledge areas, the map also helps in identifying knowledge gaps, which are vital for planning OL and training initiatives (Dalkir, 2011). For example, if a critical area of knowledge is predominantly tacit and held by a small group within the organization, this may indicate the need for mentoring programs or communities of practice to ensure its broader dissemination (Wenger, McDermott & Snyder, 2002).

It is imperative, however, that critical knowledge maps be treated as dynamic tools and not as static representations of an organization's knowledge. The business environment, technology, and market demands are constantly evolving. Therefore, these maps need to be reviewed and updated periodically to reflect the ever-changing reality of the business environment (Jennex, 2007).

Finally, it is important to note that the effectiveness of a critical knowledge map is directly proportional to the involvement of stakeholders in the process of its creation and maintenance. The active involvement of various stakeholders—from frontline employees to top management—ensures that the map is comprehensive, accurate, and aligned with the organization's real needs (Zack, 1999). This complexity arises from their creation.

3.2.3 Inclusion through an Integrated Map of Critical Knowledge in Interorganizational Networks

Having considered the discussions addressed in the two previous sections, this section will expand the discussion on how an integrated map of critical knowledge may promote inclusion in interorganizational networks. This section will build upon the concepts and theories already introduced, aiming to deepen the understanding of the interplay between knowledge governance, inclusion, and innovation in complex interorganizational environments.

As seen, in today's dynamic and interconnected environment, interorganizational networks are not just groupings of distinct entities but vibrant ecosystems where inclusion and collaboration are fundamental for sustainability and innovation (Huxham & Vangen, 2005). Inclusion here is understood not only in the sense of integrating different organizations but also in incorporating a variety of knowledge, skills, and perspectives. This diversity is crucial for stimulating innovation and organizational resilience (Burt, 2004).

Interoperability is a prerequisite for effective collaboration in interorganizational networks. An integrated map of critical knowledge helps identify and connect different knowledge areas, facilitating strategic cooperation. By making explicit the connections between different types of knowledge, organizations can identify synergy opportunities and collaborate more efficiently to achieve common goals (Kogut & Zander, 1992).

The inclusion promoted by an integrated knowledge map is not only an end in itself but also a lever for innovation. By incorporating a variety of perspectives and knowledge, interorganizational networks can foster an environment conducive to generating innovative ideas and creative solutions. The diversity of insights and experiences can lead to innovative approaches to solving complex problems and exploring new opportunities (Bessant & Tidd, 2011).

The implementation of an integrated map of critical knowledge is not without challenges. Issues of confidentiality, data governance, and the complexity of managing contributions from a variety of stakeholders are just some of the obstacles that must be carefully managed. Additionally, power dynamics and cultural differences among participating organizations can affect how knowledge is shared and used. To overcome these challenges, it is essential to adopt an inclusive and participatory approach from the outset, ensuring that all stakeholders have a voice in the mapping process and that their interests and concerns are duly considered (Powell, Koput & Smith-Doerr, 1996).

In this context, the necessary integration of a critical knowledge map in interorganizational networks is justified, representing a strategic and inclusive approach to managing knowledge in dynamic and diverse environments. This approach offers a promising path for organizations seeking to thrive in an increasingly interconnected and competitive world.

3.3 METHOD CREATION

The development of the method was based on both solid theoretical knowledge and established practices in the field of KM. A careful literature review was conducted, considering works by seminal authors responsible for the theoretical foundations of KM (Polanyi, 1966; Levitt & March, 1988; Wiig, 1993; Nonaka & Takeuchi, 1995; Nooteboom, Berger, & Noorderhaven, 1997; Probst, Raub, & Romhardt, 2001a and 2001b; Dalkir, 2011), as well as taking into account new studies that have been validating these theories with empirical research applied to organizational practices, resulting in the selection of accepted concepts and the identification of opportunities for innovation in current research.

The adoption of a transdisciplinary co-production methodology (Alvares & Freire, 2022), involving the ENGIN laboratory, enabled the creation of an environment that encouraged the development of a method that is both applicable and grounded in solid scientific foundations, connecting theory and practice. This synergy between academia and organizations, whether public or private, provided a conducive environment to test, evaluate, and refine the method, ensuring its relevance and applicability in various contexts.

Collaboration with entities such as the Ministries MCTI, MPA, MAPA, MJSP, the Civil Police of Santa Catarina, the Federal Highway Police, the Department of Finance of Mato Grosso do Sul, Softplan, and Neogrid Sistemas presented a diverse range of scenarios and challenges, allowing the method to be validated and adjusted as needed. Each application provided valuable insights that informed the refinement of the method, considering different challenges and organizational dynamics.

In the academic context, the application of the method as an educational tool in the researcher's courses within a leading Postgraduate Program in Brazil expanded its validation spectrum, serving not only as a practical learning mechanism but also producing case studies that provided more data for the analysis and evaluation of the method.

In the end, the method underwent a complete cycle of development, from theoretical conception to practical validation, encompassing various scenarios and challenges, reinforcing its robustness and validity. The adopted methodological approach and the constant iteration between theory and practice enhance the applicability and effectiveness of the method in real organizational environments, contributing to the evolution of the KM field.

3.4 METHOD FOR CREATING INTEGRATED ORGANIZATIONAL CRITICAL KNOWLEDGE MAPS: STEPS AND PRACTICES

To make use of the method, we first identify the central categories: data, information, and knowledge. In the context of data, these manifest as raw elements, such as usage metrics for software or applications, which, by themselves, do not allow for a concrete analysis of the situation.

Information, on the other hand, arises when these data are analyzed and interrelated, providing a clearer and more applicable view of the situation. Technology companies, for example, can convert raw data into information by analyzing user behavior patterns, helping to understand how users interact with their platforms and services.

Knowledge, which can be classified as essential or critical, is vital for informing decisions and strategies. Essential knowledge refers to fundamental knowledge for the company's daily operations, such as the technical knowledge required to keep software running efficiently. On the other hand, critical knowledge is the kind that has the potential to provide the company with a significant advantage in the market. In a context of strategic redefinition, certain knowledge may shift from one category to another. In technology-based companies, for example, a unique machine learning algorithm that enhances the user experience can be considered critical knowledge.

Having outlined the categories to be worked with, we proceed to describe the method through its six stages and the respective methodological procedures for its implementation.

3.4.1 Recognition of Critical Data, Information, and Knowledge

Definition of the Stage: In this phase of knowledge governance, organizations aim to discern and identify which knowledge is critical for decision-making, innovation, and strategy. This stage is crucial to ensure that efforts and resources are channeled effectively (Choo, 2006).

Procedures with Suggested Practices and Tools:
1. Establishing relevance criteria
    - Practice: Knowledge audiences, where collaborative sessions between various departments and stakeholders are organized to

discuss and define what is "essential" and what is "critical" based on the organization's mission and vision (Nonaka & Takeuchi, 1995).

- **Tool**: Use of project management software such as Trello or Asana to record and prioritize information.

2. Promoting deep dialogue
   - **Practice**: Dialogic workshops, deep discussion spaces among members of the organization to identify essential and critical knowledge (Isaacs, 1993).
   - **Tool**: Video conferencing platforms such as Zoom or Teams to facilitate virtual collaboration.

3. Extracting tacit knowledge
   - **Practice**: Semi-structured interviews, a method that employs open-ended and guided questions to gain insights from stake-holders, focusing primarily on tacit knowledge (Polanyi, 1966).
   - **Tool**: Audio recorders or automated transcription to document interviews.

4. Holistic organization assessment
   - **Practice**: SWOT Analysis, a strategic approach that helps understand the organization's strengths, weaknesses, opportunities, and threats (Helms & Nixon, 2010).
   - **Tool**: Specific SWOT templates or mind mapping software such as MindMeister.

5. Data consolidation and analysis
   - **Practice**: Knowledge mapping, using techniques to create visual representations of tacit and explicit knowledge (Polanyi, 1966).
   - **Tool**: Business intelligence software such as Tableau or Power BI for data visualization.

3.4.2 Identification of Essential Databases

Definition of the stage: The stage of "Identification of Essential Databases" involves the selection and categorization of the main sources of data, information, and knowledge identified in the previous stage, whether they are internal or external to the organization. These databases are considered vital to ensure the quality of decision-making, optimize operations, and promote innovations. Correctly identifying these databases is crucial for the organization to avoid redundancies and inconsistencies and make the most of the available information.

Procedures with suggested practices and tools:
1. Evaluation of current data infrastructure
   - **Practice**: IT audits, to understand the existing storage solutions and databases in the organization (Pearlson & Saunders, 2016).
   - **Tool**: IT audit software, such as Nmap or Nessus.
2. Identification of information needs
   - **Practice**: Internal surveys and questionnaires, to capture the information needs of various departments and stakeholders (Kaplan & Norton, 2004).
   - **Tool**: Online survey platforms, such as SurveyMonkey or Google Forms.
3. Data categorization
   - **Practice**: Hierarchical classification, using criteria of importance and applicability to determine which databases are essential (Davenport & Harris, 2007).
   - **Tool**: Data management software, such as Microsoft SQL Server or Oracle Database.
4. Data integrity and reliability verification
   - **Practice**: Data validation, to ensure that the information contained in the databases is accurate and reliable (Redman, 1998).
   - **Tool**: Data validation and cleaning tools, such as DataWrangler or OpenRefine.
5. Definition of access protocols
   - **Practice**: Permission modeling, determining who has access to which data and under what circumstances (Mell & Grance, 2011).
   - **Tool**: Permission management systems, integrated with databases or content management systems.
6. Assessment of future needs
   - **Practice**: Trend projections, analyzing future trends to anticipate new data requirements (Courtney, 2001).
   - **Tool**: Trend analysis and forecasting software, such as IBM SPSS or R.

3.4.3 Monitoring Formal and Multilevel Flows of Critical Data, Information, and Knowledge

Definition of the stage: Monitoring these flows refers to the continuous monitoring and analysis of how critical data, information, and knowledge circulate within an organization. This process allows for the identification of how information moves between different hierarchical levels, departments, and stakeholders, ensuring that the flows are efficient and knowledge is disseminated appropriately.

Procedures with suggested practices and tools:

1. Mapping current flows
   - **Practice**: Organizational social network analysis, to visualize interactions and information flows among organization members (Cross & Parker, 2004).
   - **Tool**: Social network analysis software, such as UCINet or Gephi.
2. Identification of bottlenecks and inefficiencies
   - **Practice**: Process modeling, to detail and understand workflow flows and detect inefficiencies (Dumas et al., 2018).
   - **Tool**: Process modeling software, such as Bizagi or ARIS Express.
3. Analysis of communication channels
   - **Practice**: Internal communication assessment, observing which channels are most effective and which need improvement (Quirke, 2008).
   - **Tool**: Communication analysis tools, such as Slack Analytics or Microsoft Teams Insights.
4. Real-Time monitoring
   - **Practice**: Dashboarding, to visualize real-time information flows and identify possible deviations or issues (Few, 2006).
   - **Tool**: Dashboard platforms, such as Tableau or Power BI.
5. Assessment of hierarchical flow levels
   - **Practice**: Hierarchical analysis, to understand how information flows between different levels of the organization (Saaty, 1980).
   - **Tool**: Hierarchical analysis software, such as Expert Choice or SuperDecisions.
6. Review and adjustment of flows
   - **Practice**: Dialogic workshops, where members from different levels of the organization come together to discuss and refine information flows (Isaacs, 1999).
   - **Tool**: Workshop facilitation techniques, supported by collaborative tools like Miro or MURAL.

3.4.4 Analysis of the Quality of Essential Data and Information

Definition of the stage: The analysis of data and information quality refers to the assessment of the accuracy, consistency, relevance, and timeliness of critical data and information. This stage ensures that the data used in the organization's operations and decisions are reliable and accurately represent reality.

Procedures with suggested practices and tools:
1. Evaluation of data accuracy
   - **Practice**: Verification and validation, to ensure that data is accurate and correctly represents real events or transactions (Wang & Strong, 1996).
   - **Tool**: Data quality tools, such as Informatica Data Quality or Talend.
2. Identification of inconsistent data
   - **Practice**: Anomaly detection, to identify records that deviate from expected patterns or are inconsistent with other data (Hawkins, 1980).
   - **Tool**: Data analysis software, such as KNIME or RapidMiner.
3. Assessment of data relevance
   - **Practice**: Relevance analysis, reviewing data to ensure that it is relevant to the organization's needs (English, 2005).
   - **Tool**: Database management systems (DBMS), such as Oracle or SQL Server, with analysis functionalities.
4. Verification of data timeliness
   - **Practice**: Temporal audits, to determine whether data is current or has become outdated over time (Orr, 1998).
   - **Tool**: Data audit tools, such as IBM InfoSphere Information Analyzer.
5. Analysis of data completeness
   - **Practice**: Gap verification, to identify if essential data is missing from any data set or system (Redman, 1996).
   - **Tool**: ETL (Extract, Transform, Load) tools that allow completeness verification, such as DataStage or Microsoft SSIS.
6. Assessment of data integrity
   - **Practice**: Referential integrity verification, to ensure that relationships between tables and data sets remain consistent (Date, 2003).
   - **Tool**: Database design and analysis tools, such as ERwin or Navicat.

3.4.5 Representation of the Critical Knowledge Map

Definition of the stage: "The 'Representation of the Critical Knowledge Map' involves the visualization and presentation of knowledge that is considered essential for the organization. This representation facilitates the understanding, transmission, and management of this vital knowledge, enabling stakeholders to quickly identify and act on key areas."

Procedures with suggested practices and tools:

1. Selection of visualization formats
   - **Practice**: Evaluation of best practices for data and knowledge visualization to ensure clarity and effectiveness (Few, 2009).
   - **Tool**: Data visualization software such as Tableau or Power BI.
2. Creation of icons and legends
   - **Practice**: Development of visual symbols and legends to represent different types or categories of knowledge (Bertin, 1983).
   - **Tool**: Graphic design tools like Adobe Illustrator or CorelDRAW.
3. Interaction and navigability
   - **Practice**: Incorporation of interactive features to allow users to explore the knowledge map dynamically (Shneiderman, 1996).
   - **Tool**: Interactive design platforms like Figma or Sketch.
4. Integration with other data sources
   - **Practice**: Establishing connections with databases or information systems to keep the map up to date (Wurman, 2001).
   - **Tool**: Data integration systems like Apache Nifi or Microsoft Azure Data Factory.
5. Feedback and iteration
   - **Practice**: Collecting and incorporating feedback from stakeholders to refine the map representation (Norman, 2013).
   - **Tool**: Collaboration and feedback platforms like Slack or Microsoft Teams
6. Distribution and sharing
   - **Practice**: Sharing and distribution strategies to ensure that the map is accessible to all relevant stakeholders (Duhigg, 2016).
   - **Tool**: Document management and sharing systems, such as SharePoint or Google Workspace.

3.4.6 Verification of Consistency, Applicability, and Validity of the Representation of the Critical Knowledge Map

Definition of the stage: This stage aims to evaluate and ensure that the graphical representation of critical knowledge is not only consistent in its presentation but also applicable in the organization's daily operations and valid in terms of its purpose and stakeholder needs.

Procedures with suggested practices and tools:

1. Review of representation for consistency
   - **Practice**: Comparison and alignment of the representation with established standards and best practices for visualization (Tufte, 2001).
   - **Tool**: Design review software such as InVision or Marvel.
2. Assessment of applicability with key users
   - **Practice**: Conducting feedback sessions with key stakeholders to assess the usability and applicability of the map in the operational environment (Nielsen, 1993).
   - **Tool**: Usability testing tools, such as UserTesting or Lookback.
3. Validity testing
   - **Practice**: Application of statistical and qualitative methods to determine the validity of the map's representation in relation to established objectives (Cronbach, 1951).
   - **Tool**: Statistical software such as SPSS or R.
4. Analysis of integrated data consistency
   - **Practice**: Evaluation of the integrity and quality of the data that feeds the critical knowledge map (Pipino, Lee & Yang, 2002).
   - **Tool**: Data quality tools, such as Informatica Data Quality or Talend.
5. Peer and expert review
   - **Practice**: Submission of the map to experts and peers in the field of KM to assess its suitability and effectiveness (Boud, Cohen & Sampson, 2001).
   - **Tool**: Collaborative review platforms, such as GitHub or Bitbucket.
6. Feedback-Based iterations and updates
   - **Practice**: Implementation of changes and improvements to the map based on received feedback, ensuring its continuous update (Argyris & Schön, 1978).
   - **Tool**: Project and task management tools, such as Trello or JIRA.

3.5 CONCLUSION

The proposed method in this chapter systematically addresses knowledge governance in interorganizational contexts. Nonaka and Takeuchi (1995) emphasize the importance of mapping and understanding both tacit and explicit knowledge, serving as a starting point for this method.

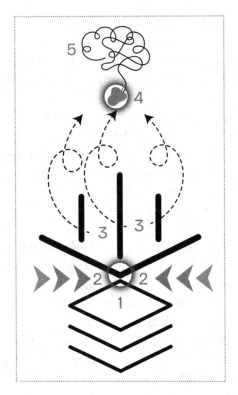

FIGURE 3.1
Integrated Knowledge Mapping Method in Interorganizational Networks.

The visual representation (Figure 3.1) is intended to illustrate the method's process, from inception to validation. The idea is that it can be easily understood by those familiar with the methodology as well as by those who already have in-depth knowledge of it. The image combines the key concepts and discussed stages, providing a concise and informative graphical representation of the proposed method.

The detailed method reflects a logical and integrated path in KM for interorganizational networks. The visual representation of the method for knowledge governance in interorganizational networks has several interrelated elements. These include: a solid foundation with reliable databases and information, arrows representing the flow of information and the transition between tacit and explicit knowledge, magnifying glasses depicting quality analysis, a brain representing critical areas of knowledge, and finally, "check" marks pointing to earlier areas, symbolizing adaptation and learning.

As identified in Figure 3.1 representing the method, the first step, "Identification of Essential Databases," establishes a solid foundation, focusing on the accuracy, consistency, relevance, and timeliness of data to ensure its reliability and representativeness, as highlighted by Wang & Strong (1996).

The method sequence moves on to "Monitoring Formal and Multilevel Flows of Data, Information, and Critical Knowledge." This phase emphasizes the proper circulation of information, in line with Choo's (2006) view of the information cycle and the transition between tacit and explicit knowledge. Next, "Analysis of the Quality of Essential Data and Information" seeks to assess the sustainability of data quality over time, based on Redman's contributions (1996).

Advancing to the "Creation of the Critical Knowledge Map" and its subsequent "Representation," the focus is on visualizing and understanding knowledge. Polanyi's (1966) thinking on tacit knowledge is instrumental in these stages, demonstrating that even when unarticulated, knowledge can be represented in an understandable way. The final step, "Verification of Consistency, Applicability, and Validity of the Representation of the Critical Knowledge Map," is influenced by Argyris and Schön (1978) and highlights the importance of OL and continuous adaptation.

This method distinguishes itself by integrating established concepts from the literature with practices tailored to interorganizational contexts. In addition to providing a framework for mapping and visualizing knowledge, it ensures practical applicability and relevance in various operational scenarios.

Progress in the realm of scientific and organizational knowledge is evident through the fusion of established theories and approaches aimed at complex interorganizational environments. Thus, it fills an existing gap by proposing an integrated and robust approach to knowledge governance.

When considering knowledge governance in interorganizational networks, it becomes essential to adopt a systematic and validated framework. The method presented serves as a consolidated path for implementing multilevel knowledge governance, enhancing benefits, and mitigating risks in complex network environments.

In summary, an integrated map of critical knowledge is not just a management tool; it is a platform for inclusion. By visualizing and integrating critical knowledge from various stakeholders, it not only clarifies the landscape of existing knowledge but also reveals gaps and areas of potential collaboration. This encourages the active participation of different actors, promoting an environment where inclusion is a constant practice (Tsoukas & Vladimirou, 2001).

There is consensus that the diversity of knowledge is an invaluable asset in interorganizational networks. Each participating individual and each entity brings their own experience, tacit and explicit knowledge, and unique perspectives. An effective integrated map not only captures this diversity but also facilitates its translation into a common language where everyone can understand and contribute. This not only enhances collaboration but also helps avoid the trap of homogenization, where innovative ideas may be lost or overlooked (Nonaka & Takeuchi, 1995).

Finally, it is considered that an integrated map of critical knowledge is more than a tool for KM in interorganizational networks; it is a catalyst for inclusion, collaboration, and innovation. By promoting the integration and effective utilization of diverse knowledge, these maps can help networks operate more effectively, adapt to changes in the environment, and innovate. However, for this to be effective, it is crucial that the mapping process be conducted inclusively, considering the complex dynamics of interorganizational networks.

REFERENCES

Alavi, M., & Leidner, D. E. (2001). Knowledge management and knowledge management systems: Conceptual foundations and research issues. *MIS Quarterly, 25*(1), 107–136.

Alvares, L. M. A. R., & Freire, P. S. (2022). *Frameworks for scientific and technological research oriented by transdisciplinary co-production (Vol. 1)*. London, UK: Anthem Press.

Argyris, C., & Schön, D. A. (1978). *Organizational learning: A theory of action perspective*. Boston, MA: Addison-Wesley.

Bertin, J. (1983). *Semiology of graphics: Diagrams, networks, maps*. Madison, WI: University of Wisconsin Press.

Bessant, J., & Tidd, J. (2011). *Innovation and entrepreneurship*. Hoboken, NJ: John Wiley & Sons.

Bolisani, E., & Bratianu, C. (2017). *Emergent knowledge strategies: Strategic thinking in knowledge management*. Berlin, Germany: Springer.

Börner, K., Chen, C., & Boyack, K. W. (2003). Visualizing knowledge domains. *Annual Review of Information Science and Technology, 37*(1), 179–255.

Boud, D., Cohen, R., & Sampson, J. (2001). *Peer learning in higher education: Learning from & with each other*. London, UK: Kogan Page.

Bresolin, G. G., Souto, B., & Freire, P. S. (2023). Perspectivas de análise da interrelação dos termos governança do conhecimento e colaboração. In *Perspectivas em engenharia, mídias e gestão do conhecimento* (Vol. 4, pp. 167–191). Editora Arquétipos.

Brown, J. S., & Duguid, P. (2001). Knowledge and organization: A social-practice perspective. *Organization Science, 12*(2), 198–213.

Burt, R. S. (2004). Structural holes and good ideas. *American Journal of Sociology, 110*(2), 349–399.

Castells, M. (2011). The rise of the network society: The information age: *Economy, society, and culture* (Vol. 1). Hoboken, NJ: John Wiley & Sons.

Choo, C. W. (2002). *Information management for the intelligent organization: the art of scanning the environment.* Medford, NJ: Information Today, Inc.

Choo, C. W. (2006). *The knowing organization: How organizations use information to construct meaning, create knowledge, and make decisions.* Oxford, UK: Oxford University Press.

Contractor, N., Wasserman, S., & Faust, K. (2006). Testing multitheoretical, multilevel hypotheses about organizational networks: An analytic framework and empirical example. *Academy of Management Review, 31*(3), 681–703.

Courtney, J. F. (2001). Decision making and knowledge management in inquiring organizations: toward a new decision-making paradigm for DSS. *Decision Support Systems, 31*(1), 17–38.

Cronbach, L. J. (1951). Coefficient alpha and the internal structure of tests. *Psychometrika, 16*(3), 297–334.

Cross, R., & Parker, A. (2004). *The hidden power of social networks: Understanding how work really gets done in organizations.* Boston, MA: Harvard Business Review Press.

Dalkir, K. (2011). *Knowledge management in theory and practice.* Third Edition. Cambridge, MA: MIT press.

Date, C. J. (2003). *An Introduction to database systems.* Boston, MA: Addison Wesley.

Davenport, T. H., & Harris, J. G. (2007). *Competing on analytics: The new science of winning.* Boston, MA: Harvard Business Press.

Davenport, T. H., & Prusak, L. (1998a). *Working knowledge: How organizations manage what they know.* Boston, MA: Harvard Business Press.

Davenport, T., & Prusak, L. (1998b). *Conhecimento empresarial.* Rio de Janeiro, Brazil: Campus.

Duhigg, C. (2016). *Smarter faster better: The Transformative power of real productivity.* Westminster, MD: Random House.

Dumas, M., La Rosa, M., Mendling, J., & Reijers, H. A. (2018). *Fundamentals of business process management.* Berlin, Germany: Springer.

Eden, C. (1992). On the nature of cognitive maps. *Journal of Management Studies, 29*(3), 261–265.

English, L. P. (2005). *Improving data warehouse and business information quality.* Hoboken, NJ: Wiley.

Eppler, M. J. (2004). Facilitating knowledge communication through joint interactive visualization. *Journal of Universal Computer Science, 10*(6), 683–690.

Eppler, M. J. (2006). Visualization in knowledge communication. In S. B. Banks (Ed.), *Handbook of visual languages for instructional design: Theories and practices.* Hershey, PA: IGI Global.

Ermine, J.-L., Boughzala, I., & Tounkara, T. (2006). Critical knowledge map as a decision tool for knowledge transfer actions. *The Electronic Journal of Knowledge Management, 4*(2), 129–140.

Few, S. (2006). *Information dashboard design: Displaying data for at-a-glance monitoring.* Berkeley, CA: Analytics Press.

Few, S. (2009). *Now you see it: Simple visualization techniques for quantitative analysis.* Berkeley, CA: Analytics Press.

Foss, N. J. (2007). The emerging knowledge governance approach: Challenges and characteristics. *Organization, 14*, 29–52.

Freire, P. S., Dandolini, G. A., Souza, J. A., Silva, T. C., & Couto, R. M. (2017). Governança do conhecimento (govc): o estado da arte sobre o termo. *Biblios (Peru), 69*, 21–40. https://doi.org/10.5195/biblios.2017.469

Grandori, A. (2001). *Organizing knowledge: beyond knowledge management.* Cheltenham, UK: Edward Elgar Publishing.

Grandori, A. (2008). A rational heuristic model of economic decision making. *Rationality and Society, 20*(4), 415–444.

Gruber, T. R. (1993). A translation approach to portable ontology specifications. *Knowledge Acquisition, 5*(2), 199–220.

Hawkins, D. (1980). *Identification of outliers.* London, UK: Chapman and Hall (CRC).

Helms, M. M., & Nixon, J. (2010). Exploring SWOT analysis–where are we now? *Journal of Strategy and Management, 3*(3), 215–251.

Huxham, C., & Vangen, S. (2005). *Managing to collaborate: The theory and practice of collaborative advantage.* London, UK: Routledge.

Isaacs, W. (1993). Taking flight: Dialogue, collective thinking, and organizational learning. *Organizational Dynamics, 22*(2), 24–39.

Isaacs, W. (1999). *Dialogue and the art of thinking together.* New York, NY: Currency (Penguin Random House).

Jennex, M. E. (Ed.). (2007). *Knowledge management: Concepts, methodologies, tools, and applications (Vol. 1-6).* Hershey, PA: IGI Global.

Jonassen, D. H., Beissner, K., & Yacci, M. (1993). *Structural knowledge: Techniques for representing, conveying, and acquiring structural knowledge.* Mahwah, NJ: Lawrence Erlbaum Associates, Inc.

Kempner-Moreira, F., Freire, P. S., & Souza, J. A. (2022). *Governança Multinível Pública: um novo modelo para a governança pública brasileira* (1a ed., Vol. 1, p. 132). Curitiba: CRV.

Kaplan, R. S., & Norton, D. P. (2004). *Strategy maps: Converting intangible assets into tangible outcomes.* Boston, MA: Harvard Business Press.

Kogut, B., & Zander, U. (1992). Knowledge of the firm, combinative capabilities, and the replication of technology. *Organization science, 3*(3), 383–397.

Levitt, B., & March, J. G. (1988). Organizational learning. *Annual Review of Sociology, 14*(1), 319–340.

Mayer-Schönberger, V., & Cukier, K. (2013). *Big data: A revolution that will transform how we live, work, and think.* Boston, MA: Houghton Mifflin Harcourt.

Marques, D., De Sá Freire, P., Dos Santos, A. V., & Mattar, V. A. (2017). Gestão do conhecimento na documentação de projetos: um método para aperfeiçoar os esforços e a aprendizagem coletiva. *Revista Eletrônica Sistemas & Gestão, 12*, 436–446.

Martins, G. J. T., & Freire, P. S. (2021). Governança Multinível e Comunicação: a inter-relação sobre os termos. In V *Encontro Internacional de Gestão Desenvolvimento e Inovação* (EIGEDIN 2021) (Vol. 1, pp. 5–15). Naviraí: UFMS.

Mell, P., & Grance, T. (2011). The NIST definition of cloud computing. *National Institute of Standards and Technology, 53*(6), 50.

Miles, R. E., Snow, C. C., Meyer, A. D., & Coleman, H. J. (1978). Organizational strategy, structure, and process. *Academy of Management Review, 3*(3), 546–562.

Nielsen, J. (1993). *Usability engineering.* Cambridge, MA: Academic Press.

Nonaka, I., & Takeuchi, H. (1995). *The knowledge-creating company: How Japanese companies create the dynamics of innovation.* Oxford, UK: Oxford University Press.

Norman, D. (2013). *The Design of everyday things: Revised and expanded edition.* New York, NY: Basic Books.

Nooteboom, B., Berger, H., & Noorderhaven, N. (1997). Effects of trust and governance on relationalrRisk. *Academy of Management Journal, 40*(2), 308–338.

Novak, J. D., & Canas, A. J. (2008). *The theory underlying concept maps and how to construct and use them.* Technical Report IHMC CmapTools.

Orr, K. (1998). Data quality and systems theory. *Communications of the ACM, 41*(2), 66–71.

Pearlson, K. E., & Saunders, C. S. (2016). *Strategic management of information systems.* Hoboken, NJ: John Wiley & Sons.

Pipino, L. L., Lee, Y. W., & Yang, R. Y. (2002). Data quality assessment. *Communications of the ACM, 45*(4), 211–218.

Polanyi, M. (1966). *The tacit dimension.* Garden City, NY: Doubleday.

Powell, W. W., Koput, K. W., & Smith-Doerr, L. (1996). Interorganizational collaboration and the locus of innovation: Networks of learning in biotechnology. *Administrative science quarterly,* 116–145. https://doi.org/10.2307/2393988

Powell, W. W., & Grodal, S. (2005). Networks of innovators. In, Fagerberg, J., Mowery, D. C., & Nelson, R. R. (Eds). *The Oxford handbook of innovation* (pp. 56–85). Oxford, UK: Oxford University Press.

Probst, G., Raub, S., & Romhardt, K. (2001a). *Gestão do conhecimento: os elementos construtivos do sucesso.* Porto Alegre: Bookman.

Probst, G., Raub, S., & Romhardt, K. (2001b). *Managing knowledge: Building blocks for success.* Hoboken, NJ: John Wiley & Sons.

Provan, K. G., Fish, A., & Sydow, J. (2007). Interorganizational networks at the network level: A review of the empirical literature on whole networks. *Journal of Management, 33*(3), 479–516.

Quirke, B. (2008). *Making the connections: Using internal communication to turn strategy into action.* Aldershot, UK: Gower Publishing Ltd.

Redman, T. C. (1996). *Data quality for the information age.* Norwood, MA: Artech House.

Redman, T. C. (1998). The impact of poor data quality on the typical enterprise. *Communications of the ACM, 41*(2), 79–82.

Renzl, B. (2008). Trust in management and knowledge sharing: The mediating effects of fear and knowledge documentation. *Omega, 36*(2), 206–220.

Rizzatti, G., & Freire, P. S. (2020). Mecanismos da governança da aprendizagem organizacional (GovA). *E-Tech: Tecnologias para Competitividade Industrial, 13,* 71–86.

Saaty, T. L. (1980). *The Analytic hierarchy process.* New York, NY: McGraw Hill.

Senge, P. M. (2006). *The fifth discipline: The art & practice of the learning organization.* New York, NY: Doubleday.

Shneiderman, B. (1996). The Eyes have it: A Task by data type taxonomy for information visualizations. *Proceedings of the IEEE Symposium on Visual Languages,* 336–343. IEEE.

Snowdon, D. (2002). Complex acts of knowing: paradox and descriptive self-awareness. *Journal of Knowledge Management, 6*(2), 100–111.

Terra, J. C. (2001). *Gestão do conhecimento: o grande desafio empresarial.* São Paulo: Negócio.

Tsoukas, H., & Vladimirou, E. (2001). What is organizational knowledge? *Journal of Management Studies, 38*(7), 973–993.

Tufte, E. R. (2001). *The visual display of quantitative information.* Huntsville, AL: Graphics Press.

Gelder, T. (2001). *How to improve critical thinking using educational technology.* [Sem detalhes adicionais disponíveis para formatação completa].

Wang, R. Y., & Strong, D. M. (1996). Beyond accuracy: What data quality means to data consumers. *Journal of Management Information Systems, 12*(4), 5–33.

Wenger, E., McDermott, R., & Snyder, W. (2002). *Cultivating communities of practice.* Boston, MA: Harvard Business Press.

Wiig, K. M. (1993). *Knowledge management foundations: Thinking about thinking: how people and organizations create, represent, and use knowledge.* Schema Press.

Wurman, R. S. (2001). *Information Anxiety 2.* QUE.

Zack, M. H. (1999). Developing a knowledge strategy. *California Management Review, 41*(3), 125–145.

4

Healthcare Collaboration Frameworks Supporting Inclusion: Including Practitioners, Researchers and Patients in Health Knowledge Management

Deborah E. Swain
North Carolina Central University, Durham, NC, USA

Technology is a queer thing. It brings you gifts with one hand, and stabs you in the back with the other.

— **C.P. Snow,** *The Two Cultures (1959)*

4.1 LITERATURE BACKGROUND

Concerns about AI issues include a study of how medical algorithms fail communities of color (Christensen, et al., 2021). They noted how AI and machine learning (ML) impact decision-making and lead to inequalities mainly because the technology is often built on biased rules and homogenous data sets; for example, kidney transplant decision with non-white patients at the bottom of lists, and National Football League (NFL) use of race norming algorithms to decide brain injury claims. To limit bias, the authors recommend 1) collaboration and patient-centered processes, 2) applying specific processes to evaluate and address bias, and 3) a framework that promotes transparency and accountability in regulations. Both transparency and accountability are aspects of an effective healthcare framework that knowledge managers can recommend.

Earlier in 2019, dissecting racial bias in a commercial algorithm was described in *Science* (Obermeyer et al., 2019) that assigned sicker African American patients the same level of risk as white patients. The authors suggest that use of such an algorithm reduces extra healthcare in the non-white population as health costs are applied as a proxy for need. Overall, how does one know what data or knowledge artifacts to trust?

Clinical decision support systems especially require trustworthy knowledge repositories. As researchers in learning health systems have determined, recommendations from a patient-centered network can be an important part of any knowledge framework for decision support (Richardson, et al., 2019). A team of vendors, clinicians, and policy makers shared suggestions for nine trust attributes which could make up a policy framework for explicitly embedding trust in knowledge objects or artifacts. Thus, researchers and repository knowledge managers or librarians would collaboratively accept and use a collection. As MCBK advocates and researchers explained in a 2018 "manifesto," they strive to promote computable biomedical knowledge, which is the result of an analytic and/or deliberative process about or affecting human health that is explicit, and, therefore, can be represented and reasoned upon using logic, standards, and mathematics. Using the definition from members of the MCBK Trust and Policy (T&P) Workgroup that trust is multidimensional, the recommended object attributes for trusting a technical system in health informatics are:

1. Competency
2. Compliance
3. Consistency
4. Discover-ability and Accessibility
5. Evidence-based
6. Feedback and Updating
7. Organizational Capability
8. Patient-centeredness
9. Transparency

(Richardson et al., 2019)

The mission of the *Learning Health Systems* (LHS) journal demonstrates how collaboration may succeed: "Advance the interdisciplinary area of learning health systems by promoting research, scholarship, and dialog focused on theory, complex issues, conceptual syntheses, models, solution designs, and system evaluations designed to achieve *continuous rapid improvement in health and healthcare and to transform organizational practice*" (Young, K., 2021). Efforts continue to invite researchers to contribute to MCBK and more participation in conferences and the LHS journal show progress. This chapter describes how MCBK frameworks are successful, collaborative applications of Knowledge Management (KM) theories with evidence from research presentations, education resources, systematic reviews, and case studies on how to apply KM practices to support inclusion through collaboration and communities of practice (CoP). There are three sections demonstrating healthcare collaboration frameworks that support inclusion:

Section 4.2. Saving time to implement healthcare informatics with CBK;

Section 4.3. Using SECI to promote collaboration and knowledge sharing;

    Section 4.3.1. Systematic Reviewing, PRISMA, PICO, and Scoping Reviews,

    Section 4.3.2. Collaboration between knowledge managers of repositories and healthcare researchers.

Section 4.4. Community frameworks and examples of KM impacting health disparities.

4.2 SAVING TIME TO IMPLEMENT HEALTHCARE INFORMATICS WITH CBK

Historical evidence suggests that there can be a 17-year gap between published research and application of treatment or new procedure in medical practice (Friedman, 2021; Morris, et al., 2011). The *Learning Health Systems (LHS) Journal* supports open access publications that reduce the years to months. That is, the time to review and/or verify a theory or data collection presented as explicit knowledge is reduced if reviewers can access the system, software, or data and run the research or device sample in "real time" using open access journals or web-based tools. As quoted in the October 2018 manifesto for MCBK, "Computable Biomedical Knowledge is the result of an analytic and/or deliberative process about human health, or affecting human health, that is explicit, and therefore can be represented and reasoned upon using logic, formal standards, and mathematical approaches."

The consequences of open access publications are an increase in inclusion for practitioners, researchers, and patients due to a learning cycle. See

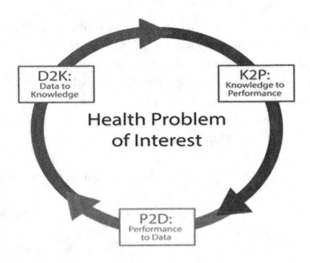

FIGURE 4.1
LHS Cycle and MCBK Open Access.

Figure 4.1: LHS Cycle and MCBK Open Access describing the cycle for a health problem of interest. The cycle for a healthcare learning community begins with the capture of healthcare practice research or application performance as data or P2D (performance to data). Then the external evidence of data is assembled and analyzed as "knowledge" D2K (data to knowledge). Traditionally in published literature, the human-readable knowledge is presented as words, pictures, or equations in articles or conference paper (or posters). The result is a "knowledge gap" blocking sharing and final verification up to 17 years. Then results are interpreted and shared during the next stage when the new knowledge becomes part of healthcare practice or performance, that is, K2P (knowledge to performance). During this stage of the cycle, design intervention by added practitioners, researchers, and patients occurs and they may take action starting a new cycle capturing additional practice as data or P2D in the continued cycle of study and change (Friedman, 2020).

The gap, however, can be reduced if knowledge, which acts as a "keystone" at the top of the cycle can be part of a mass action to be dynamic knowledge on an unlimited scale through the mobilizing of computable biomedical knowledge (MCBK). If knowledge is represented as computable, machine executable code, knowledge artifacts, or as a "model" in an open access publication, the gap may become days or weeks with teams in the learning community of practice verifying the data-based knowledge

(Friedman, 2020). Note that the continuous cycle of learning in MCBK is based on David Kolb's experiential learning cycle (concrete learning, reflective observation, abstract conceptualization, and active experimentation); effective learning can be reached by progressing through each stage (Kolb, 1984; 2015).

A multi-stakeholder effort to mobilize computable knowledge began in 2018 with first annual US meeting of the MCBK in-person and then included a UK meeting in October, 2019. The MCBK Conference grew to attract 240 participants virtually during the COVID-19 pandemic in 2020. All materials from worldwide meetings and the manifesto are available at www.mobilizecbk.org. Examples and demos are available for prevention efforts and clinical pharmacogenomics. The drive for "mass access" early on included the international Clinical Pharmacogenetics Implementable Consortium (CPIC) guidelines in human-readable table format and has grown to guidelines for fully computable knowledge object format available in PubMed as clinical guidelines (Crews et al., 2014). Next computable objects are becoming publicly available through a trusted digital library. "Activation" services will use the objects to generate advice in the future through applications (apps) or electronic health records (EHRs).

The persistent challenges in healthcare, such as patient safety, outdated public health infrastructures, less necessary care, more inappropriate care, and the 17-year latency from bench to bedside, inspires calls for system-level improvements worldwide (Friedman et al., 2017). Since suggested at the Institute of Medicine in 2007, Learning Health Systems or LHSs have grown and recommended this 5-point framework for collaboration:

1. The characteristics and experiences of every patient are securely available as data for learning.
2. Best practice knowledge from the data is available to individuals, care providers, and knowledge managers or planners of health services.
3. Continuous improvement from ongoing study addresses health improvement and related goals.
4. Enabling a socio-technical infrastructure will support routine sharing of health knowledge by applying automation and economy of scale.
5. Within the health system, stakeholders view these steps as part of their learning culture.

(Friedman et al., 2017)

Examples of learning health systems worldwide include endorsement from the Precision Medicine Initiative of the National Institutes of Health in the United States, the TRANSFoRm project for continuous learning supported by the European Commission meeting in 2015 (Delaney et al., 2015), the Farr Institute in the UK (www.farrinstitute.org), and an infrastructure collaboration in Asia between Taiwan and the Tohoku region of Japan (www.megabank.tohoku.ac.jp/english/timeline/20160527_01/). Thus, the LHS Journal strives to provide continued support in an open access format to promoting LHS and encouraging MCBK globally.

4.3 USING SECI TO PROMOTE COLLABORATION AND KNOWLEDGE SHARING

As healthcare data is collected more and more, efforts by knowledge managers and librarians to sustain repositories for researchers' performance data and knowledge objects becomes significant. In this section, the chapter will cover best practices for collaboration and knowledge sharing. Starting January 25, 2023, the National Institutes for Health (NIH) officially began requiring researchers to have data management and sharing of plans for data sharing. Building on the KM concept of a Community of Practice (CoP), it has been proposed that partnerships from libraries and research labs collaborate in sharing healthcare data and software. Also, it is recommended that sharing knowledge and working in a "commons" environment can promote growth in healthcare and enhance experiences for both professional librarians and biomedical researchers (Swain, 2023). Applying the SECI (Socialization, Externalization, Combination, and Internalization) Model to the collaboration framework may improve use of both tacit and explicit knowledge (Nonaka and Takeuchi, 1995). However, communication and conversations are required for the framework to succeed when applied.

4.3.1 Systematic and Scoping Reviews

One of the major contributions that knowledge managers and librarians can make to research is guidance in completing thorough systematic and scoping reviewing when developing literature reviews (Tu-Keefner, 2021). Systematic reviews, which are in-depth, professional reviews of research literature, can be considered the top level of evidence-based research helping to

- answer specific clinical questions about therapy or treatment;
- define a specific search strategy by listing what to include or exclude in article selection;
- include a meta-analysis within the literature review (optional; to combine studies for statistical analysis).

Most or all of the data should be available for examination including journals or clinical trials not in PubMed or Medline; therefore, complex, sensitive search strategies are needed for identification and experienced knowledge managers and librarians can help. For example, for covering multiple sources, sizing any backfiles, and providing database management to remove duplicate data and to develop policies on adding new records.

A Patient (or Problem) Intervention (or indicator) Comparison Outcome of Interest (PICO) approach is recommended. Sample PICO healthcare subjects could include hospital-acquired infections, hand-washing and masks, and reduction in infections. Knowledge managers and librarians can use as search tools MeSH (medical subject heading) tags for subject indexing and CINAHL (index for nursing, allied health, biomedicine, and healthcare journals in English).

The Preferred Reporting Items for Systematic Reviews and Meta-Analyses (PRISMA) guidelines help ensure transparent and comprehensive health research. PRISMA provides checklists for literature reviews and abstracts, and workflow diagrams for systematic reviewing. Details from the 2020 guideline updates are available from the *British Medical Journal* (BMJ) at www.bmj.com/content/372/bmj.n71. Knowledge managers and librarians can help researchers, peer reviewers, authors, and editors complete detailed systematic reviews using PRISMA tools as described at www.prisma-statement.org or www.campbellcollaboration.org.

In comparison to a systematic review, a scope review can help researchers to synthesize evidence or to categorize and group existing literature in terms of nature, features, and volume (Tu-Keefner, 2021). Using a scope review, knowledge managers and librarians can provide preliminary assessments of size and scope of available literature, and also include ongoing, current research. Considering a low to high confidence level, scoping reviews can start as narrative reviews, grow into quick scoping reviews, become rapid evidence assessments, or finally be full systematic reviews (Peters et al., 2015).

Thus, a scoping review can be considered exploratory as it supplies answers to broad research questions and assesses existing research. It would be valuable in the collaboration process for researchers to involve knowledge managers and librarians early. Especially if the research is complex, large, or heterogeneous, a scoping review is recommended to map the literature volume, to clarify definitions and topic boundaries, and to identify gaps in literature and research (https://libraryguides.missouri.edu/c.php?g=28397&p=6022220). Note that a scoping review is not necessarily easier than a systematic review as there are more citations and it may take longer. Sometimes the results may be too broad and multiple, refined searches may be needed, which experienced knowledge managers and librarians can do. For training, see https://training.cochrane.org/resource/scoping-reviews-what-they-are-and-how-you-can-do-them.

4.3.2 Collaboration between Knowledge Managers of Repositories and Healthcare Researchers

What seems to hinder knowledge managers/librarians and healthcare researchers from forming partnerships? Many in the USA thought that the 2023 NIH requirement to share data would increase collaborations and partnerships with knowledge managers or librarians. Some researchers have said informally that they just are not comfortable sharing their data during the research, and it is not part of their practices or long-term procedures. However, knowledge managers and librarians can provide valuable, professional assistance as noted concerning systematic and scoping reviews of medical and healthcare research. The following summary of a pilot survey and a cross-disciplinary publication suggests that barriers might be reduced based on a KM framework for collaboration applying SECI to uncover tacit knowledge and share in the creation of explicit knowledge.

As the SECI adapted model in Figure 4.2 shows tacit knowledge is part of socialization at first. Then in a repeating cycle, tacit becomes explicit during externalization phase, explicit is shared during the combination phase, and completing a cycle, explicit becomes tacit during internalization. The proposed framework for collaboration applies the SECI model phases while partnerships between researchers and knowledge managers/

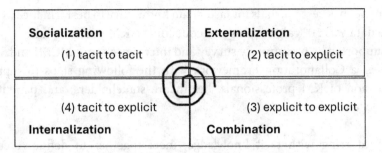

Socialization (1) tacit to tacit	Externalization (2) tacit to explicit
(4) tacit to explicit **Internalization**	(3) explicit to explicit **Combination**

FIGURE 4.2
SECI Model.

librarians occur as data is collected or performance information is collected as data. The phases are repeated iteratively during collaboration.

The hypothesis is that sharing knowledge and working in a "commons" environment can promote growth in healthcare and enhance experiences for professional librarians and biomedical researchers as part of learning health systems. In a pilot survey and semi-structured interview with about 10 professionals and researchers, social research methods (Wildemuth, 2017) were applied to define and analyze tacit and explicit ideas. Knowledge was described as capable of moving in the SECI model cycles, and participants defined a collaboration framework (Swain, 2023) for the future by looking back at communications. Ways for data librarians and KM to collaborate could mean effective CBK analysis and abbreviated periods of time to bring new healthcare diagnosis techniques, data-based programs, evidence-based prescriptive solutions, and useful devices into learning health systems. In the future, library and clinical professionals may collaborate more to create digital libraries that store collections of computable knowledge objects (code) and data in addition to human-readable knowledge.

The proposed collaboration framework takes the 5% of knowledge that is explicit (data, records, and files) incorporates it with the 95% of tacit knowledge (experience, thoughts, competence, commitment, and unshared deeds) into open access articles and repositories for human and machine-readable analysis. From pilot survey with four librarians and two researchers, most library/knowledge professionals do work with researchers. About one-third sometimes collaborate on systematic reviews. But only one partnership on sharing computable biomedical data for a repository was found. Few librarians and no researchers had yet validated data from open access journals for faster data knowledge to performance (K2P). The data was 50% algorithms and code for the KM professionals.

Supported by preliminary survey and interviews about MCBK and SECI cycles, a Collaboration Framework with the following steps to support inclusion of KM professionals, healthcare stakeholders, and patients is proposed:

1. Starting with tacit knowledge, meet together to define research question(s) during socialization phase.
2. Use scope reviews for early partnership communication to make tacit knowledge explicit to refine research question(s) as externalization phase in first SECI cycle.
3. Assign knowledge managers/librarians to complete and report systematic reviews on the question(s) for the combination of explicit ideas and planned research findings.
4. Apply early research data or qualitative observations in the internalization phase for researchers to validate open access data where available and to turn explicit knowledge into new tacit knowledge, which in next cycle can provide feedback to researchers.
5. Partner more in second cycle to socialize tacit-to-tacit knowledge culled from both knowledge manager/librarians and healthcare researchers.
6. REPEAT steps as needed for more externalization, communication, and internalization as healthcare solutions are prepared for K2P (knowledge to performance) applications in an LHS.

Recommendations for the future based on brief SECI interviews with subjects in follow-up semi-structured questions are:

- Encourage Systematic Reviews designed together by teams (using tools like EndNote and Covidence).
- Share more tacit knowledge in personal conversations by KM/library and health research team members on all levels during a research project (colleagues, interns, practicum students, and patients/subjects).
- Ensure that accessible assets and repositories are "advertised" to research teams and organizations (academic and corporate).

Thus, there are real opportunities to improve LHS with collaborations.

4.4 COMMUNITY FRAMEWORKS AND EXAMPLES OF KM IMPACTING HEALTH DISPARITIES

Harnessing technology to help both healthcare providers and knowledge managers is a shared goal. However, forming collaborative partnerships, as has been discussed previously, has barriers that hopefully knowledge-based tools like the SECI model and computer-based strategies and metadata infrastructures for MCBK can resolve. This final section of the chapter introduces examples of community frameworks and use cases reducing health disparities. First, separately a humanities and KM community partnership and then a computable biomedical research infrastructure framework for sharing are described. These communities are not examples of integrated science and humanities per se, but the health cases that follow may be.

4.4.1 Community Frameworks in Humanities and Technology

4.4.1.1 Humanities-Based Technology

A research article on joint-use, collaboration (Swain and Roughen, 2021) for a facility serving theater and library users attempts to answer the question: How might innovation be sustained by KM when organizations from different cultures are merged? The specific facility was ImaginOn in Charlotte, NC. Two diverse organizations from different cultures joined as one organization to benefit their community and state. The organizations were a children's theater and a public library for youth and the joint facility has functioned successfully for about 20 years. The ImaginOn effort was defined by an innovative, shared mission to bring stories to life for children and young adults, and innovative solutions seemed to continue with coordinated teamwork (Swain and Roughen, 2021). Growth of intellectual capital (IC) seemed to stem from the application of tacit knowledge and the operationalization of collaboration among teams in the combined organization (Liebowitz, 2012; Dalkir, 2017).

The case study of ImaginOn used documents, surveys, and interviews for analysis. A framework of KM practices based on the ImaginOn's sustained history of knowledge sharing and collaboration planning for a hybrid, joint-use facility suggested that knowing cognitive modes might support collaborating. That is, knowing how a group's cognitive modes occur in three basic collaborative thought-processing sequences can help members determine where they are and what to do next to collaborate successfully on a project. The modes are:

1. Discussion or brainstorming to externalize information and resolve conflicts.
2. Presentation, summary, or demonstration of prototypes to introduce information to team members.
3. Delegation and decision-making to assign appropriate tasks or evaluations (acting on knowledge).

As an English scholar and computer scientist, John Smith (1994) merged art and science to research collaboration and produced a model about collective intelligence and cognitive modes as a way of thinking, which also identifies collaborative group tasks. Smith's framework was centered on computer-aided collaboration tools.

The use case researchers proposed that by integrating the evidence-based models that were collected from qualitative data and analyzed, a resulting KM framework might be used both to study collaboration in joint-use efforts and to understand how to promote sustained innovation. Also, perhaps an integrated KM framework might have prescriptive uses within and between organizations (Dalkir, 2017). The ImaginOn research team found that through model-based analyses of qualitative data, an integrated framework for KM in a joint-use facility emerged.

The proposed KM Practices framework (Swain and Roughen, 2021, figure 4) requires (1) knowledge development as provided by the SECI model (and interaction during knowledge sharing); (2) knowledge sharing as provided by IC model analysis and post-project reviews; and (3) collaboration enablers surpassing a matrix of barriers and applying cognitive modes of model analysis during project activities.

This framework may help others in healthcare plan successful collaborative operations that also build on KM. For sustaining a business and managing with innovation, the examples from ImaginOn's creative staff, volunteers, children and parents, and an involved community suggest how transparency and accountability can be aspects of an effective healthcare framework that knowledge managers can recommend.

4.4.1.2 CBK-Based Technology

As an important framework for data sharing of computable biomedical data or knowledge objects, CBK needs to be in an accessible or standard format for collaboration by healthcare clinicians and data scientists. Using real-world data, a team of data scientists produced guidelines for using EHR raw medical data for data analytics (Bastarache, L., et al., 2021). They suggest that using such practice-based evidence may lead to more effective evidence-based medicine. But how can the volumes of information about patients (for example, body measurements, diagnoses, health history markers) be used to create decision-making algorithms for risk analysis and exposure knowledge for intervention and the prediction of outcomes? As noted by the researchers, EHR data is rarely neutral since it depends on the human healthcare team inputting data. Furthermore, transforming raw data into analytical data sets requires multiple decisions and, therefore, a collaborative process. However, the data scientist may often have to work without a clinician's input. The results are challenges to accuracy and non-bias data creation due in part to the timing (temporality) and shifts in context.

Sometimes supporting information can be applied to improve accuracy, and such redundancy may help to refine a phenotype since, for example, phenotypes based on diagnostic codes may require multiple codes on different dates to be more accurate (Verma and Ritchie, 2017). Furthermore, supporting evidence from orthogonal data sources, such as lab reports, and clinical interventions may help refine phenotypes. Thus, obtaining accurate data can be complex and not foolproof (Bastarache L. et al., 2021). Issues of laboratory results names and secular trends have impacts, too. Vital signs and medications also impact efforts to develop computable phenotypes and analytical strategies. Research networks and common data models have offered some support with standardizations. Observational Medical Outcomes Partnership (OMOP) is one common data model that helps institutions convert and then share EHR data (Bastarache, L., et al., 2021). Additional initiatives such as the national eMerge program provide standards to help in computable phenotype applications, and the informatics community "has grown more adept at harmonizing EHR data" (Bastarache, L., et al., 2021).

The researchers recommend that the guiding framework for developing high-quality, evidence-based knowledge from real-world clinical data be based on collaboration, communication, and iterations during development by data scientists and clinicians. Data scientists will require some training on the idiosyncrasies of clinical data and interpretations, and healthcare clinicians might be involved in phenotyping and work with data scientists on data-driven decision-making (Bastarache L. et al., 2021).

They noted the importance of recognizing the complexities of EHR data, but also noted how well-conducted EHR-based studies report critical and reproducible findings. Collaboration can lead to success.

4.4.1.3 Community Frameworks Reducing Health Disparities

Community frameworks and KM practices can have impact on health disparities. As this section will describe, a framework can be designed to integrate health equity into LHS to overcome racial and ethnic disparities in the USA. Through patient-centered design, data analytics, and continuous improvement, communities can benefit from targeted efforts as a case study will show (Brooks D. et al., 2017). In comparison, national health systems, such as those in the United Kingdom, have different issues and may provide community projects to address health disparities, such as access to digital information. As a knowledge manager in England, Sue Lacey-Bryant, Chief Knowledge Officer, National Health Service (NHS) England and Chair Health and Digital Literacy Partnership (sue.lacey-bryant@hee.nhs.uk) has observed and collected data on others' projects in her country. Her information about a national initiative concerning digitalization of information post-COVID-19 was led by knowledge managers, librarians, and health information scientists and shared with the Global MCBK Conference (October 3-5) and the Sustainability and Inclusion (S&I) MCBK Workgroup in 2023. The cases studies and projects are summarized here.

4.4.2 HS Framework in USA

A framework for integrating healthcare equity into community learning health systems has been proposed in the USA. A team of researchers (Brooks, D., et al., 2017) has suggested that patient-centered design, data analytics, and continuous improvement based on LHS can reduce racial and ethnic health disparities. Through a practical framework equity can be incorporated into a developing LHS. Reviewing two projects, the team applied the proposed framework as a case study.

According to the World Health Organization (WHO), health inequities are avoidable for population groups where differences seem to be based on social and economic conditions. Individual factors can include race, gender identity, and disability, too. In the USA, life expectancy between rich and poor counties in the United States can vary as much as 30 years (Powell, A., 2016).

The LHS mission has been described as a truly integrated system "in which progress in science, informatics, and care culture align to generate new knowledge as an ongoing, natural by-product of the care experience, and seamlessly refine and deliver best practices for continuous improvement in health and health care" (Friedman C. et al., 2014).

The "PETAL Framework" is practical and grounded in community partnership, incorporates technology, and is sustainable (Brooks D., et al., 2017, figure 1). PETAL stands for Prioritize health equity; Engage the community; Target health disparities; Act on the data, and Learn to improve. It is a community driven framework that aligns with the 10 core values of LHS (person-focused care, privacy, inclusiveness, transparency, accessibility, adaptability, governance, cooperative and participatory leadership, scientific integrity, and value). Case studies of the PETAL framework have focused on African American communities; however, it applies across many domains (Brooks, D., et al., 2017, table 2).

Another case study used Patient-Centered Outcomes Research Institute (PCORI) for multi-institutions and academic communities and is called CEERIAS, for community engagement for early recognition and immediate action in stroke. This study addressed early identification and treatment for strokes, which has racial and ethnic disparity issues. The research principal investigators prioritized health equity by using funds for patient, family, caregiver, and community-centered projects to provide robust support (Brooks D. et al., 2017).

Another case study looked at THRIVE, a project of the Morehouse School of Medicine. It seeks to reduce mental health disparities through a culturally centered integrative healthcare model. THRIVE targets African American populations at risk for three co-occurring health problems (depression, cardiovascular disease, and diabetes). Three community health clinics in Atlanta, Georgia participate in applying LHS initiatives and providing kiosks as spinoffs on telemedicine technology to help screen for mental health issues.

Overall, the case studies in this research analysis supported LHS as a strong model to help confront health disparities. However, the authors noted that LHS requires strategic alignment with health equity principles to achieve true equity (Brooks D. et al., 2017).

4.4.3 Collaboration Efforts Using KM in the UK

In comparison, initiatives in England have been shown to focus recently on digital health inequities (Lacey-Bryant, S., 2023). Health literacy is the ability to access, assess, and use health information. Applying information literacy means:

- Using health information to make choices about self-care,
- Having informed discussions with health professionals, and
- Making shared decisions as patients, knowledge managers, and clinicians.

The shift to online health information and health service interactions has increased the importance of digital access and internet skills resulting in growth of the need for digital health literacy (Lacey-Bryant, S., 2023). A national English initiative was launched working with partners to establish a sustainable approach to incorporating or building digital (online) health literacy into existing healthcare services. One in six adults struggle with health literacy in the country. When health providers, patients, and the public have access to health information, better health-related outcomes occur. Librarians and knowledge managers in England and parts of the UK want to partner with professionals and family carers to meet health and literacy challenges successfully. The initiative workers were health informatics practitioners and administrators in the information and healthcare industry with access to evidence of concerns and also examples of solutions they have seen working.

The COVID-19 pandemic accelerated the adoption of online services through which patients in England were asked to interact with the National Health Service (NHS) including e-consultants. This increase in the use of online health information and health apps (phone applications) as a new health technology changed accessing information risks, increased health inequalities, particularly where people have low health literacy skills alongside low digital skills and poor digital connectivity and bandwidth. Patients, care givers, and members of the public who access, understand, appraise, and use health information are challenged in England (Lacey-Bryant, S., 2023). It was reported that one in six adults struggle with digital literacy. Furthermore concerning health literacy, 43% of adults aged 16–65 cannot understand word-based health information sufficiently well to make health decisions, and if numbers are added, 61% of adults are unable to understand and act on the information. Specifically, as data from the University of Southampton indicated (http://healthliteracy.geodata.uk/), in isolated rural and coastal areas the percent of those struggling with words and number in health information ranges from 46% to almost 82%, and it is where download speeds can be very slow. However, in England some of the worst local communities with low health literacy are concentrated in many urban areas (Lacey-Bryant, S., 2023). Thus, low digital literacy and digital connectivity often overlap.

Since 2021, hands-on activities were part of an initiative for knowledge managers, librarians, and information scientists to work with partners to establish a sustainable approach to building digital/online health literacy into existing services in England. Collecting data about local pilot projects in 2022, produced reports on health progress, training projects (cascades for training the trainer), and tool development led by the national NHS knowledge and library services team. There are in England financial challenges to patients, care givers, and the public, and technology implications for the NHS in 2023 when six million people in the UK cannot access the internet without assistance.

Solutions at the borough level were contextualized by the strategic national perspective. Details, for example, of borough-level geodata from the University of Southampton illustrated health literacy issues in rural and coastal areas of England. With NHS librarians leading skills development across the sector, libraries and community information services began providing support. Enabling the public to build skills and use health information in trusted spaces throughout England is a goal of the initiatives.

At the MCBK Global 2023 conference attendees were introduced to new data analysis as well as tools and techniques, and "digital by stealth" strategies with solutions to health knowledge gaps. In 2021, 93% of the public expressed trust in librarians. Libraries and community information centers provide neutral spaces and trusted staff who can build information/health literacy and digital navigation skills. Public libraries may act as digital hubs in communities with low access and poor downloading speed. In addition, health literacy is sometimes embedded in existing community organizations, such as prison libraries and community pharmacies, and into digital skills training to build health digital and data literacy (Lacey-Bryant, S., 2023).

In 2022 (April and October), two cohorts established pilot sites in communities, first such as Lancashire, Leeds, and Norfolk, and secondly Scarborough, Oldham, and Essex. Working with partners to plan, recruit, educate, and train, positive changes in health literacy occurred. It was noted and nicknamed "digital by stealth" when people who needed health information were taught relevant digital skills for accessing online information. The terms "online" or "internet" were preferred over "digital." Integration activities included using iPads for job seekers to also find health information. In the future, partnership with care givers to reduce "care leavers" is recommended. Increased confidence among knowledge managers and library staff was noticeable (Lacey-Bryant S., 2023).

As a representative of the National Healthcare Inequalities Improvement team for NHS in England, Ruth Carlyle proposed a local pilot site testing mechanisms to embed digital health literacy into existing provisions (Lacey-Bryant, S., 2023). NHS KM contacts on activities and research into digital health disparities include: Sue Lacey-Bryant, Chief Knowledge Officer, NHS England and Chair Health and Digital Literacy Partnership (sue.lacey-bryant@hee.nhs.uk); Ruth Carlyle, Head of NHS Knowledge and Library Services - Midlands, East and North of England Workforce, Education and Training Directorate (Ruth.Carlyle@hee.nhs.uk); Susan Smith (RBT) Mid Cheshire Tr (susan.smith2@mcht.nhs.uk); Coral Pepper, NHS, UK (coral.pepper@uhl-tr.nhs.uk); Ania Matuszewsk, Lanarkshire, NHS, UK (ania.matuszewska@lanarkshire.scot.nhs.uk); Emily Hopkins (Emily.Hopkins@hee.nhs.uk); and Louise Goswami (Louise.Goswami@hee.nhs.uk).

4.5 CONCLUSION

Both transparency and accountability are aspects of an effective healthcare framework that knowledge managers and librarians can follow for collaboration and participation early in research with healthcare, biology, and medical researchers who collect data and develop computable, biomedical knowledge. MCBK has provided a framework cycle for learning and development. Experts in scoping and systematic reviews from among KM and library professionals can contribute to research problem definitions and literature review verifications. In addition, repositories of knowledge objects and data can be administered and managed for healthcare researchers required to share data by the NIH beginning in 2023. Together, both sides of KM and development can develop policies and frameworks for sustaining research and development in healthcare including tacit knowledge with explicit documents during projects. What this chapter offers are examples of research in "lost" literature from conferences, presentations, and varied open access articles as well as traditional publications. In conclusion, although collaboration barriers to improving healthcare can be lowered and removed by cooperation among knowledge managers/librarians and clinical healthcare practitioners and researchers, issues of health literacy and digital disparities may remain to be solved for low-income and some ethnic populations. Hopefully the frameworks and examples described will encourage continued sharing of healthcare data and knowledge in open publications, talks, and conferences and producing progress in health inclusion.

Some further questions that remain to be addressed by KM researchers, educators, and practitioners include:

1. How might knowledge managers and librarians test MCBK
   a. Open access documents?
   b. Metadata infrastructure?
2. What policies would be good for a library or KM center concerning helping researchers with Systematic Reviews and Scoping Reviews?
3. What barriers prevent knowledge managers/librarians and healthcare researchers from collaborating to create repositories of data for sharing?
4. How do cognitive modes support collaboration?
5. Why should data scientists and clinicians collaborate on real-world data analytics?
6. How can frameworks in communities in the United States be integrated into healthcare and impact health disparities?
7. What types of KM projects in England might improve access to healthcare information in digital formats?

ACKNOWLEDGMENTS

Amrit Vastrala, MIS research assistant, NCCU

Student graduate assistants for MLA and SLA presentation: Rosalyne Galloway, Janelle Collins, Charlene Raiford, and Tracy Smith.

REFERENCES

Bastarache, L., J. Brown, J. Cimino, D. Dorr, P. Embi, P. O'Payne, A. Wilcox & M. Weiner 2021. "Developing real-world evidence from real-world data: transforming raw data into analytical datasets," *Learning Health Systems*, October, 6(1). https://doi.org/10.1002/lrh2.10293

Brooks, D., M. Douglas, N. Aggarwal, S. Prabhakaran, K. Holden & D. Mack (2017). "Developing a framework for integrating health equity into the learning health system," *Learning Health Systems*, October 17, 2017, 1(4), e10043.

Christensen, D., J. Manley & J. Resendez (2021). "Medical algorithms are failing communities of color," *Health Affairs Forefront* (September 9, 2021). https://doi.org/10.1377/forefront.20210903.976632

Crews, K.R., A. Gaedigk, H.M. Dunnenberger, J.S. Leeder, T.E. Klein, K.E. Caudle, C.E. Haider, D.D. Shen, J.T. Callaghan, S. Sadhasivam & C.A. Prows (2014). "Clinical Pharmacogenetics Implementation Consortium guidelines for cytochrome O450 2D6 genotype and codeine therapy," *Clinical Pharmacology & Therapeutics.* April 1, 2014, 95(4), 376–382.

Dalkir, K. (2017). *Knowledge Management in Theory and Practice.* Cambridge, MA: The MIT Press.

Delaney, B.C., V. Curcin, A. Andreasson, et al. (2015). "Translational medicine and patient safety in Europe: TRANSFoRm-architecture for the Learning Health System in Europe," *Biomed Research International,* 1. https://doi.org/10.1155/2015/961526

Friedman, C., J. Rubin, J. Brown, et al. (2014). "Toward a science of learning systems: a research agenda for the high-functioning Learning Health System," *Journal of American Medical Information Association,* 22(1), 43–50. https://doi.org/10.1136/amiajnl-2014-002977

Friedman, C. (2020). *Keynote Speaker Presentation at International Conference for Knowledge Management (ICKM),* Durham, NC. Dec. 3, 2020.

Friedman, C. (2021) *Presentation to MCBK Pilot Class,* NCCU, Durham, NC. Dec. 15, 2021, Introductory Speaker. Retrieved February 24, 2024 from IMLS Grant's MCBK Pilot Training Homepage | North Carolina Central University (nccu.edu) and MCBK module in NCDOCKS at https://libres.uncg.edu/ir/nccu/clist.aspx?id=41690

Friedman, C.P., N. Allee, B.C. Delaney, A.J. Flynn, J.C. Silverstein, K. Sullivan & K.A. Young (2017). "The science of learning health systems: Foundations for a new journal," *Learning Health Systems,* January, 2017 1(1), first published online, November 29, 2016. https://doi.org/10.1002/lrh2.10020

Kolb, D. (1984, 2015). *Experiential Learning: Experience as the Source of Learning and Development* 2nd edition, Upper Saddle River, NJ: Pearson Education.

Lacey-Bryant, S., (2023). "Health and digital literacy to underpin CBK: NHS England data + experience", *Presentation 2023 Global MCBK Meeting,* October 3–5, 2023.

Liebowitz, J. (2012). *Beyond knowledge management: What every leader should know.* Boca Raton, FL: CRC Press.

Morris, Z.S., S. Wooding & J. Grant (2011). "The answer is 17 years, what is the question: understanding time lags in translational research," *Journal of Research in Social Medicine,* 104(12), 510–520. https://doi.org/10.1258/jrsm.2011.110180

Nonaka, I. & H. Takeuchi (1995), *The Knowledge Creating Company: How Japanese Companies Create the Dynamics of Innovation,* New York, NY: Oxford University Press.

Obermeyer, Z., B. Powers, C. Vogell & S. Mullainathan (2019). "Dissecting racial bias in an algorithm used to manage the health of populations," *Science,* October 25, 2019, 366, 6464, 447–453. https://doi.org/10.1126/science.aax2342

Peters, M.D., C.M. Godfrey, H. Khalil, P. McInerney, D. Parker & C.B. Soares (2015). "Guidance for conducting systematic scoping reviews," *International Journal of Evidence-based Healthcare,* 13, 141–146. https://doi.org/10.1097/XEB.0000000000000050

Powell, A. (2016). "The cost of inequality: money = quality health care = longer life," *Harvard Gazette,* February 22, 2016.

Richardson, J., B. Middleton, J. Platt & B. Blumenfeld (2019). "Building and maintaining trust in clinical decision support: recommendations from the patient-centered CDS learning network," *Learning Health Systems* (October, 2019). https://doi.org/10.1002/lrh2.10208

Smith, J. (1994). *Collective Intelligence in Computer-Based Collaboration.* Hillsdale, NJ: Lawrence Erlbaum Associates, Publishers.

Swain. D. & P. Roughen (2021). "Applying Knowledge Management to Planning Joint-Use Facilities: The ImaginOn Library and Theater," *Journal of Knowledge Management*, December 7, 2021, ISSN: 1367-3270.

Swain, D. (2023). "Partnering for Research in Healthcare and Computable Biomedical Knowledge," *Presentation, Medical Library Association (MLA)-Special Library Association (SLA) Joint Conference*, May, 2023, Detroit, MI.

Tu-Keefner, F. (2021) *Presentation to MCBK Pilot Class*, NCCU, Durham, NC. Dec. 28, 2021, on Systematic Reviews and Scoping Reviews. Retrieved February 24, 2024 from IMLS Grant's MCBK Pilot Training Homepage | North Carolina Central University (nccu.edu) and MCBK module in NCDOCKS at https://libres.uncg.edu/ir/nccu/clist.aspx?id=41690

Verma, A. & M. Ritchie (2017). "Current scope and challenges in Phenome-wide association studies," *Current Epidemiology Report*, 2014, 4(4), 321–329.

Wildemuth, B., (Ed.) (2017), *Applications of Social Research Methods to Questions in Information and Library Science*, 2nd ed, Westport, CT: Libraries Limited.

Young, K. (2021) *LHS* Editorial Assistant, *Presentation on journal manuscript submission process to MCBK Pilot Class*, NCCU, Durham, NC. Dec. 20, 2021. Retrieved February 24, 2024 from IMLS Grant's MCBK Pilot Training Homepage | North Carolina Central University (nccu.edu) and MCBK module in NCDOCKS at https://libres.uncg.edu/ir/nccu/clist.aspx?id=41690

5

Inclusiveness in Knowledge Management Education: Empowering Future Professionals for a Diverse World

Kendra S. Albright
Kent State University, Kent, Ohio, USA

Andreas Brandner
Knowledge for Development Partnerships, Vienna, Austria

Annet K. Nabatanzi-Muyimba
Makerere University Business School, Kampala, Uganda

5.1 INTRODUCTION AND BACKGROUND

The research literature specifically recognizes knowledge as an indispensable resource for the achievement of sustainable development (Caniglia et al., 2021). Knowledge is a competitive advantage especially for multinational companies and academia (Miminoshvili & Cerne, 2022). Its relevance is mainly felt in the knowledge-based economy, where companies can only develop and compete through constant growth in innovative and collaborative knowledge. The management of knowledge as an organizational and strategic asset is underpinned by the resource-based view of the firm (Tiwari, 2022). The resource-based view/theory of a firm argues that sustainable competitive advantage and superior performance derive from possession of superior resources and capabilities (Barney, 1991). This view assumes that an organization's resources and capabilities foster competitive advantage, which in turn generates superior performance. In other words, an organization that achieves a competitive edge over others, is

DOI: 10.1201/9781003407966-5

one that is able to develop valuable, rare, imperfectly imitable and non-substitutable resources and capabilities. In this chapter, it should be understood that knowledge is a resource and/or a competitive advantage while knowledge management (KM) is a superior capability or competence that individuals, organizations and nations can capitalize on to attain superior performance and sustainable development.

Knowledge resources exist in mainly two forms namely tacit or implicit and explicit. Tacit knowledge refers to the invisible, informal or intangible "knowhow" located in the minds of individuals acquired through learning from education, training and research, practice and intuition or reflection while explicit knowledge refers to the formally documented or codified knowledge which is visible, tangible and available in forms that can be easily accessed even when the creators of the knowledge are unavailable (Fombad, 2018). However, it is important to note that not all people have equal access to both types or either type of knowledge resources; individuals or groups of people may be specifically denied access to knowledge and information resources and/or may be excluded from fully participating, contributing and benefiting in knowledge processes and systems due to disparities in social-economic status, age, gender, sexuality, race, religion, ethnicity, location, education, language, skills, etc. This phenomenon is referred to as knowledge exclusion, which is a component of social exclusion. We define knowledge exclusion as

> the act of hindering someone to take part in a knowledge process related to a specific domain. Knowledge processes can include—but are not limited to—finding, accessing, acquiring, creating, commenting, transforming, sharing, applying, capturing, and managing knowledge. Hindrances can include legal barriers, financial, language, information, skills, time, distance, motivation, and other barriers.

Equally, we define knowledge exclusion as

> the act of hindering someone to take part in a knowledge process related to a specific domain. Knowledge processes can include—but are not limited to—finding, accessing, acquiring, creating, commenting, transforming, sharing, applying, capturing, and managing knowledge. Hindrances can include legal barriers, financial, language, information, skills, time, distance, motivation, and other barriers.

An exclusive knowledge society hinders citizens to take part in societal knowledge processes and thereby excludes them from citizen rights and from the achievement of their potential, whereas an inclusive knowledge society enables all citizens to take part in the societal knowledge processes to avail themselves of all citizen rights and to achieve their potential.

These definitions reflect the general view that inclusion and exclusion are an act rather than a phenomenon (Cambridge dictionary) and the recent view in the development context, that not only access to knowledge is required to create inclusive knowledge societies, but also the active participation in process of a knowledge society (e.g., UNESCO 2005).

In practice, knowledge exclusion manifests in many various ways, including limited access to education and information technology, restricted entry for certain people to information or knowledge networks, barriers due to language or cultural differences, stereotypes and biases or prejudices within knowledge-sharing environments. Hence, it results in certain individuals or groups of people being disempowered and/or deprived of the ability to participate, contribute to or benefit from knowledge exchange. One of the widely spread ways to exclude stakeholder groups is to consider them not knowledgeable enough to be a speaker on a panel, a lecturer in a course, a contributor to a law, etc. due to their social background.

Social exclusion on the other hand is described as a broader and multidimensional phenomenon that pertains to the systematic marginalization or segregation of individuals, households, groups, neighborhoods or communities from full participation in social, economic, political and cultural activities, spaces and decision-making processes within a society usually characterized by denial of rights and access to resources, services and opportunities. According to the World Bank (n.d.), individuals and groups may be excluded not only through institutional or legal systems but also through discriminatory or stigmatizing attitudes, cultures, beliefs or perceptions. People are disadvantaged, isolated or discriminated against based on disparities in gender, sexuality, age, race, ethnicity, origin, class, location, occupation, citizenship, religion, disability, health, criminality or other status. Poverty also inhibits access to education, healthcare and decent living, hence perpetuating social exclusion. Social exclusion is the cause of social divisions and inequalities, poverty, disempowerment and alienation of certain individuals and groups in society (Muddiman, 2000). Usually excluded individuals do not have access to education, work, healthcare; lack power and political participation; and are hence deprived of their political and social rights. For instance, failure to get a paid job leads to unemployment which consequently results in low income, poor living standards, family breakdown and single parenthood, causes physical and mental health problems, increased crime and unrest, narrows down one's social networks, leads to a decline in one's social status, and ultimately stigma and isolation (Muddiman 2000. Kissová and Rapošová, 2017). Thus, social exclusion is a widespread societal problem affecting all regions, areas and people in the world. It can be caused by different factors, experienced at different levels in society and in different ways. It is also a dynamic process and not a static state, and hence, a context-based phenomenon dependent on the historic and current particulars of a given society or country.

Although social exclusion and knowledge exclusion are related phenomena that both regard the denial of rights, participation, and access to resources, services or opportunities within a society, they operate and impact people in slightly different ways. Social exclusion often perpetuates knowledge exclusion. For instance, if certain individuals or groups face economic barriers or discrimination that prevents access to education or training, they experience knowledge exclusion. Similarly, cultural or linguistic barriers within a society that segregate specific groups can lead to restricted access to knowledge-sharing platforms and networks, which perpetuates knowledge exclusion. Therefore, unless social exclusion is addressed, knowledge inclusion may not be achieved. To address social exclusion, which can consequently lessen knowledge exclusion, it requires measures and policies such as providing equal access to education and information technology, enforcement of equal opportunity to end discrimination and poverty and empowerment to maximize the potential of all human beings (United Nations, 2016). In particular, the creation of more inclusive educational systems and opening up of opportunities for knowledge-sharing, collaboration, networking and participation can reduce the barriers that contribute to knowledge exclusion for disadvantaged groups (U.S. Department of Education, 2022).

Consequently, social inclusion and knowledge inclusion are forwarded as counter actions to social exclusion and knowledge exclusion, respectively, as enshrined in the general principle of the United Nations 2030 global development agenda (United Nations, 2015) of leaving no one behind and ensuring that all people in all nations enjoy their fundamental human rights and get access to goods and services, resources and opportunities such as jobs and finances, education and information, food, clothing, shelter, healthcare and other resources and necessities to fully participate in the economic, civil, political, social and cultural processes in order to prosper and enjoy minimum standards of living. Social inclusion is particularly defined by the World Bank as the process of improving the terms on which individuals and groups participate in societal activities and processes, in particular improving the ability, opportunity and dignity of people disadvantaged on the basis of their identity (World Bank n.d.). In other words, it targets barriers that lead to the exclusion of people within a society based on factors like race, gender, age, socioeconomic status, disability or cultural background. It creates a cohesive society in which there is a sense of belonging, understanding, empathy and interaction, respect, tolerance and equity among individuals from diverse backgrounds. According to Gidley, Hampson, Wheeler and Bereded-Samuel (2010), social inclusion can be practiced in three broad perspectives, namely enhancing access to resources and opportunities, improving participation in societal activities and processes and empowerment of individuals and groups with the mindset, knowledge and skills through education and training to maximize their potential. Thus, organizations and communities that embrace diversity and inclusion harness a wide range of innovative ideas and create environments that boost morale and productivity. Knowledge inclusion specifically ensures that all individuals and groups have equal access to actively participate in and benefit from knowledge resources, knowledge sharing, and creation processes (Bodla et al., 2018). It involves breaking down barriers to accessing information, education and training, information and communication technology and participation in knowledge networks that allow a multiplicity of perspectives, insights, skills, expertise and experiences to be shared that contribute to creation, dissemination and utilization of knowledge in planning, decision-making and in bettering their lives (United Nations, 2016). However, achieving both social and knowledge inclusion requires collective efforts. Governments, NGOs and communities must collaborate to dismantle systemic barriers hindering inclusion (United Nations, 2016). Policies promoting equal opportunities, anti-discrimination laws and initiatives fostering diversity in various spheres are vital steps toward a more inclusive society.

It is further important to note that social inclusion and knowledge inclusion are intertwined processes that complement each other. For instance, by breaking down social barriers and promoting equality in access to resources, opportunities and knowledge in particular, societies can become more inclusive, knowledgeable, innovative and conducive to the development of all individuals (Qureshi, Sutter, and Bhatt, 2018). Successful efforts in social inclusion, such as reducing discrimination and providing equal opportunities, facilitate knowledge inclusion by creating an environment where diverse knowledge is valued and shared (Sutz and Tomasini, 2013). Similarly, knowledge inclusion contributes to social inclusion by empowering individuals with the knowledge and skills needed for effective participation in society (Tsiplakides, 2018). Thus, understanding the dynamics of social exclusion is crucial in effectively defining and constructing social problems especially those concerning the poor and disadvantaged people whereas social inclusion is essential in the development of effective social policy responses, funding and strategic solutions (Kissová and Rapošová, 2017). The application of social inclusion theory to the KM discourse highlights the need to design, promote and employ specific KM practices that directly impact the lives and work of individuals and groups experiencing knowledge exclusion. Therefore, this chapter familiarizes KM professionals with the key concepts and dynamics of social exclusion and inclusion, and introduces theoretical and practical approaches that help to solve knowledge exclusion in society and in particular those approaches that promote inclusiveness in KM education. Consequently, educating KM professionals about social inclusiveness is crucial for several reasons including:

1. **Creating Inclusive knowledge systems**. Knowledge professionals are instrumental in structuring knowledge systems within organizations. Educating and equipping them with knowledge, skills and attitude about social inclusiveness ensures that these systems are designed to accommodate diverse perspectives and contributions.

2. **Facilitating knowledge sharing and learning**. KM professionals that are sensitive and aware of social inclusiveness are better equipped to encourage and facilitate knowledge-sharing practices that are inclusive and respectful of diverse voices and experiences. When people feel included, they open up and are more willing to share and learn from others, resulting in a more knowledgeable and skilled workforce.

3. **Enhancing knowledge collaboration**. Educating and skilling KM professionals in social inclusiveness can help them understand the value of collaboration among diverse teams. They are able to create environments that foster knowledge collaboration and ensure that all team members' contributions are heard and valued. This encourages more participation in knowledge sharing activities, leading to a more robust knowledge repository.

4. **Promoting diversity and innovation.** If KM professionals are educated on social inclusiveness, they begin to appreciate the role of diversity in fostering innovation. By understanding the importance of social inclusiveness, they can encourage diverse thinking, which in most cases results in more innovative solutions that address complex problems.

5. **Improving decision-making and problem solving.** When KM professionals are sensitized on social inclusiveness, they are more likely to consider a wide range of perspectives and insights when making decisions. This results in more informed, inclusive and comprehensive decision-making processes.

6. **Developing inclusive knowledge policies and strategies.** KM professionals that are educated about social inclusiveness are able to contribute to developing inclusive KM policies, strategies and practices within an organization or community. These policies can ensure fair representation, access to knowledge resources and participation for all members.

7. **Cultivating inclusive and adaptive work cultures.** Education and training on social inclusiveness help in creating inclusive work cultures and building teams that easily adapt to diverse, new and challenging environments. Awareness of social inclusiveness allows KM professionals to promote values of respect, empathy, openness and inclusivity of different groups of workers and stakeholders at their workplaces or communities, fostering a welcoming and nurturing environment for diverse teams to thrive.

8. **Employee engagement and satisfaction.** When individuals and groups working with knowledge professionals feel included and appreciated, they are more motivated to share and contribute their expertise and experiences, which eases the work of knowledge professionals and boosts knowledge production, sharing and utilization, resulting in higher productivity and job satisfaction.

In summary, educating KM professionals about social inclusiveness equips them with the mindset, knowledge, skills and strategies necessary to create and manage knowledge systems and environments that embrace diversity, encourage collaboration and leverage the strengths of a diverse workforce relevant in the generation of sound decisions, quality knowledge and sustainable innovations.

5.2 SOCIAL ISSUES OF KM INCLUSIVENESS

Several social issues need to be addressed to promote diversity, equity and inclusiveness in KM. Key issues include:

- Access to Knowledge
- Diverse Perspectives
- Collaboration and Participation
- Learning from Each Other/Knowledge Flows
- Organizational Culture
- Innovation and Adaptability
- Ethical Considerations

Knowledge management, as a discipline, can become more inclusive and equitable, enabling organizations and communities to leverage diverse perspectives and knowledge for the benefit of all stakeholders. It raises questions, however, of how we prepare KM professionals for meeting these goals. Few formal degree programs in the world focus solely or partly on KM. Are the social issues described above woven into the current KM curricula of these programs? In what ways? How are they assessed?

5.3 INCLUSIVE COMPETENCIES IN KM THAT NURTURE A DIVERSE KNOWLEDGE ECOSYSTEM

Turning to inclusive competencies in knowledge management, this section describes the important role of inclusive competencies within KM. Acknowledging the evolving landscape of KM and the dynamic nature of knowledge ecosystems, a comprehensive set of competencies is necessary for fostering inclusivity. From cultural competence to continuous learning, this section provides insights into each competency's significance and practical applications in the KM domain. It also offers guidance on how educators and practitioners can cultivate and integrate these competencies into their approach to KM.

The first competency focuses on exploring the importance of understanding and respecting diverse cultural perspectives in KM. This is termed **Cultural Competence** and involves strategies that foster a global mindset and create an inclusive knowledge environment that encourages participation by all and transcends cultural boundaries.

The second competency is necessary to facilitate the first: **Empathy and Active Listening** are important to facilitate effective knowledge sharing and collaboration. Learning about these competencies and practicing them helps develop these skills which build trust and understanding within a diverse KM team.

Communication Skills are also necessary to facilitate collaboration, trust and understanding in a diverse workplace. Effective communication reduces misunderstanding, promotes collaboration and ensures that knowledge is shared throughout the workplace and across diverse stakeholders.

Being aware of **Unconscious Bias** and its potential impact on decision-making is also important in building inclusive competencies in KM. Suveren (2022, p. 414) defined unconscious bias as "the systematic error experienced in decision-making." Unconscious bias has also been labeled as "implicit bias" (Greenwald and Banaji, 1995), and is defined as "the unconscious attitudes and stereotypes that impact our understanding, actions, and decisions in an oblivious way" (Suveren, 2022, p. 415), which reveals the nature of personal biases that we all hold without necessarily being aware of it. In other words, unconscious bias refers to individuals' unintentional mental associations or attitudes toward certain groups of people. They are based on personal experiences, cultural conditioning and societal stereotypes and can influence decision-making, behavior and perceptions in various contexts, including the workplace, education and social interactions.

Unconscious bias can manifest itself in various ways including the following:

Affinity Bias: Preferring individuals who are similar to us in terms of background, interests or experiences.

Confirmation Bias: Favoring information from others that confirms our pre-existing beliefs or stereotypes.

Halo Effect: Allowing a positive impression of a person in one aspect to influence perceptions in other unrelated areas. First identified by Thorndike (1920), he reported that employees in two different companies reported the same traits for one man including intelligence, reliability, technical skill, etc. But he also noted that everyone could not know the specific performance for each of those skills individually.

Thorndike summed it up by saying "Their ratings were affected by a marked tendency to think of the person in general as rather good or rather inferior and to color the judgments of the qualities by this general feeling" (1920, p. 25).

In the context of KM, an example of the halo effect might be when individuals or teams are working on a successful knowledge initiative. The positive outcomes of this project could create a favorable impression that extends beyond the specific achievements of that specific initiative. This positive halo effect might influence perceptions of the individuals or teams involved, potentially leading to overestimating their competence or success in other areas of KM or on future projects.

The halo effect in KM can have an impact on decision-making processes; examples include the allocation of resources, project assignments or leadership roles. Organizations need to be mindful of this bias and ensure that evaluations are based on a comprehensive understanding of individuals' or teams' actual work, rather than being overly influenced by the success of a single project. In addition, recognizing and addressing the halo effect is crucial for promoting fairness and preventing the exclusion of other capable individuals or teams within the organization.

Stereotyping: Assignment of certain characteristics or traits to individuals based on their membership in a particular group, without considering their individual differences.

In-group Bias: Favoring individuals who belong to the same social, cultural or professional group.

It is important to be aware of unconscious bias because it can lead to unfair treatment, discrimination and exclusion of certain individuals or groups. I can also affect hiring decisions and performance evaluations, as well as hinder opportunities for career development and advancement. Recognizing and addressing unconscious bias will promote an inclusive environment and promote fair and equitable practices throughout the organization. Education, training and implementing objective decision-making practices can help reduce the likelihood of unconscious bias in an organization.

Another inclusiveness competency pertains to **Collaboration and Teamwork** in knowledge creation, sharing and management. Through building inclusive teams and leveraging diverse strengths, perspectives and experiences, team members can feel that their contributions are valued. Collaboration and teamwork can build inclusiveness in KM in several ways.

Collaboration and teamwork bring together individuals with diverse backgrounds, perspectives, and expertise. This diversity of thought is important for generating innovative ideas, problem solving and creating a more comprehensive knowledge base that reflects the richness of the varied experiences on the team. In addition, collaboration and teamwork can build a culture where members can express their ideas without fear of judgment or reprisal. When individuals feel included and respected, they are more likely to collaborate in addressing challenges. Diverse teams can approach problems from multiple angles, leading to more innovative and novel solutions.

Knowledge sharing becomes a routine part of the workday in inclusive teams. Team members are more likely to share their expertise openly, leading to better knowledge transfer within and across their team and organization. This collaborative knowledge-sharing process ensures that insights from different team members contribute to a collective understanding. It is important to create and use platforms that facilitate open and equitable sharing of information and knowledge to ensure that diverse perspectives are embedded in the organizational knowledge repository.

Collaboration and teamwork build trust among team members. In an inclusive environment, trust is established through open communication, mutual respect and a shared commitment to common goals. A trusting culture is essential for creating a safe space where individuals feel comfortable sharing their knowledge. An inclusive culture that includes trust, collaboration and learning, and is led by supportive and participative management, will "eventually lead to enhanced innovation capability of the firm" (Lam et al., 2021, p. 66).

Collaboration involves recognizing and celebrating the contributions of all team members. When individuals are recognized and rewarded for their contributions and sharing their perspectives, they are more likely to engage in collaborative efforts, furthering an inclusive organization.

Inclusive collaboration supports an organization that is adaptable to change. Inclusive teams are more flexible and able to respond to new opportunities and threats, emerging trends and evolving challenges. This adaptability is crucial in the dynamic landscape of KM. Inclusive leaders are better able to enlist "people in change and keeping them committed throughout, in the face of uncertainties, fears, and distractions" (Dinwoodie et al., 2015).

In sum, collaboration and teamwork are important for building a culture of inclusion within an organization. An inclusive approach can maximize the potential of diverse teams while contributing to the creation of a knowledge ecosystem that reflects a wide range of perspectives and experiences, promoting values of diversity, equity and respect for all individuals.

Conflict Resolution is another important competency in developing an inclusive environment. Conflicts are inevitable in knowledge-intensive environments. An effective strategy is to emphasize the role of conflict resolution in maintaining a healthy and inclusive knowledge-sharing environment. Al-Hawamdeh (2003) also considers:

> When trying to change one's culture in a new organization, conflicts are bound to arise. Norms and practices within the organization can help in dealing with the problem to a certain extent, but the challenge remains when the avenues of knowledge sharing and dissemination are explored within an organization where cultural diversity is evident...The success of any knowledge management practices will depend to a large extent on the successful integration of different skill sets across different cultures with a common goal in mind.
>
> (p. 103)

Knowledge Transfer and Mentoring are important in fostering inclusivity. Mentorship programs can be designed and implemented to promote the transfer of knowledge across the diverse backgrounds of individuals in the organization.

Inclusive Leadership is a necessary competency in the context of KM. Identifying and training the characteristics of inclusive leadership can set the tone for an inclusive organizational culture that values diversity and promotes equitable knowledge practices. According to Bourke et al. (2020), there are six "signature traits" of inclusive leadership that include:

1. Visible commitment: a commitment by leadership to support diversity, challenge others and hold them accountable, and make this commitment a "personal priority."
2. Humility: an attitude of modesty, admission of mistakes and giving others a chance to contribute their ideas.
3. Awareness of bias: leadership demonstrates awareness of their own biases, awareness of biases in the system and working toward building strengths based on the abilities of team members rather than on their own internal biases.

4. Curiosity about others: an effective leader demonstrates active listening and is authentic about their interest in others; they are open-minded and non-judgmental.
5. Cultural intelligence: leadership demonstrates an awareness of others' culture and is considerate of those values and practices.
6. Effective collaboration: leadership focuses on team building while fostering a diversity of ideas and the emotional safety of team members.

Bourke et al. (2020) report the single most important characteristic of inclusive leadership is awareness of their own biases, as well as those of the organization. An effective leader challenges their own and encourages others to do the same.

A **User-Centric Approach** is also important in developing an inclusive workplace. Strategies in the organization should be incorporated that reflect the needs and perspectives of KM stakeholders to ensure systems and processes are accessible and relevant to diverse audiences.

Being **Flexible and Adaptable** in responding to the evolving nature of knowledge ecosystems within the organization. Cultivating these competencies allows KM professionals to navigate change and embrace emerging opportunities.

One of the increasing areas of importance in KM inclusiveness is **Data Ethics and Privacy**. It is imperative to recognize and uphold privacy standards, ensure data integrity, and incorporate ethical principles into KM practices.

Assessment of Inclusive Practices should be conducted regularly to ensure continuous improvement strategies and to evaluate and enhance inclusiveness practices within KM processes. Assessment can include feedback from stakeholders, metrics, case studies, as well as stories.

Advocacy for Inclusion by all stakeholders to champion diversity, equity and inclusion initiatives within their organizations and broader communities will continuously support and expand existing practices.

Finally, the importance of **Continuous Learning** in KM cannot be over-emphasized. Encourage stakeholders to stay abreast of evolving trends, foster a culture of learning within KM teams and adapt knowledge practices to align with emerging inclusivity considerations.

This section identifies and describes competencies for fostering inclusivity in KM practice. It serves as a useful guide for educators, practitioners and students who wish to cultivate and integrate these competencies into their approach to KM. These competencies help create a more resilient, innovative and equitable knowledge ecosystem.

5.3.1 Summary

Knowledge is a driving force for the social and economic development of societies, of organizations and companies, as well as for the individual citizens, both in modern knowledge societies as well as in developing and emerging countries. Therefore, the concepts of knowledge inclusion/exclusion and social inclusion/exclusion are highly overlapping and interrelated.

KM can play a vital role in the advancement of knowledge inclusion, as it can create the frameworks, structures of processes, which enable and facilitate knowledge inclusion. Thereby, Knowledge Managers have a high potential to contribute to knowledge inclusion and social inclusion in their respective context. This includes all types of knowledge, including tacit and explicit knowledge as well as all different knowledge processes, spanning from searching and finding, to accessing and acquiring, creating, sharing, applying, capturing and managing knowledge.

Whereas in private companies, the limitation of access to knowledge can be a competitive advantage and thereby be legitimate, the access to knowledge of public bodies or knowledge financed through public funds is a matter of social equity and inclusion. Open access to knowledge as well as the possibilities to participate in all knowledge processes of a knowledge society are fundamental demands to achieve inclusive knowledge societies, as for example, articulated by UNESCO.

Social exclusion is a broader phenomenon, involving systematic marginalization from societal activities, with factors like gender, age, race, ethnicity and socioeconomic status playing a role and often perpetuating knowledge exclusion, which again reinforces social inclusion. To address these issues, measures such as equal access to education, anti-discrimination laws and inclusive educational systems are recommended, but also the inclusion in participative knowledge processes, such as consultative processes for laws as well as economic and social initiatives. Knowledge inclusion is finally a key component in achieving the objectives of the United Nations 2030 global development agenda which articulates clear objectives for inclusion and participation and the overall vision of leaving no one behind.

Educating KM professionals on social inclusion and knowledge inclusion will therefore make a big difference, as they can influence the development of inclusive knowledge systems, the facilitation of societal knowledge sharing mechanisms, the enhancement of collaboration, the promotion of diversity and social innovation, the improvement of decision-making and cultivation of inclusive work cultures. If KM education excludes certain stakeholders or societal groups, it already lays the foundation for further knowledge exclusion.

KM educational programs can contribute a lot in strengthening the inclusive competencies in KM, like cultural competence, empathy, active listening, communication skills, awareness of unconscious bias, collaboration and teamwork, conflict resolution, knowledge transfer, inclusive leadership, user-centric approach, flexibility and adaptability, data ethics and privacy, assessment of inclusive practices, advocacy for inclusion and continuous learning.

Sustainable knowledge societies cannot exist without knowledge inclusion. It is therefore paramount that all educational institutions offering programs in KM emphasize the importance of social and knowledge inclusion and thereby contribute to more resilient, innovative, and equitable knowledge ecosystems.

5.4 CURRICULAR ELEMENTS OF INCLUSIVENESS

From the above list of curricular concepts above, it is possible to develop specific curricular elements and examples that are important to consider in building course content. Examples for each are provided in the list below.

Diverse Course Content
Diversity scholars (Cumming-Potvin, 2013; Falicov, 2014) encourage instructors to reflect on their own sociocultural backgrounds and positions and ways in which they may influence how they address inclusion efforts in their syllabi and course. This includes the scope of topics, perspectives and case studies included in the curriculum, ensuring a wide representation of diverse voices and experiences. Multiple cultural, social and industry perspectives should be included. A focus on reflexivity in syllabus design and course assessments is advised (Fuentes, Zelaya, and Madsen, 2021).
Inclusive Teaching Methods
This includes the kinds of approaches used by instructors to engage students with consideration of their diverse learning styles and backgrounds. A variety of teaching methods/techniques should be used,

including group and peer discussion (Ginsberg and Wlodkowski, 2009), experiential learning and the use of technology. Freire (1996) advises instructors to encourage critical thinking through active listening, discourse and taking action. Active learning methodologies facilitate collaboration, with students working together in small groups to attain specific objectives and engage in discussions (Johnson and Johnson, 2008). The benefits of active learning demonstrate particular effectiveness among those who identify as Black or first-generation (Fuentes, Zelaya, and Madsen, 2021).

Diverse Faculty, Guest Speakers and Industry Experts

Participating speakers should represent diverse backgrounds, ethnicities, genders and experiences. They should also be encouraged to read the syllabus and diversity statement in the syllabus and use inclusive language in their talks.

Bias and Stereotypes

Biases should be addressed through course materials selection, discussions and assessments. The curriculum should acknowledge the existence of biases and actively work to address and eliminate them to promote a fair and inclusive learning environment. In addition, however, Vaccaro (2019) recommends devoting one class session to the topics related to inclusion to emphasize the importance of these topics. Otherwise, it could be viewed as "tokenism" and exclusionary.

Cultural/Intercultural Competence

Overall (2009) suggests that cultural competence is the ability to understand the importance of culture in our lives and those of others while respecting the differences between us. As teachers, we want to cultivate an awareness in our students of the importance of culture in personal and collective experiences. It involves understanding and valuing diverse cultural and background traits through meaningful interactions with individuals from cultures and backgrounds. This awareness extends to seamlessly integrating the richness of diverse cultures into services, work and institutions, to enhance the lives of all within the knowledge professions.

Foster an understanding and working with different cultures while developing intercultural communication and collaboration. Integrate content and activities to enhance cultural awareness and competence.

Collaborative Projects

Provide opportunities for students to work together on projects, promoting teamwork and leveraging diverse perspectives. Effective collaborative projects should encourage interaction among students with different backgrounds.

Inclusive Language and Communication

Language in the curriculum should be respectful and inclusive and avoid reinforcing stereotypes or exclusionary norms. Materials should be evaluated, and appropriate communication channels selected to ensure they are inclusive and free from discriminatory language. One way to support inclusiveness is by acknowledging and recognizing different holidays, both in the syllabus and verbally in the classroom (online or face-to-face).

In many countries, the access to education is limited as the courses are not available in the mother tongue or even the second language. The predominance of English language on a global level excludes millions of people whose native language may be a local, tribal language; the second language may be a colonial one, like French or Portuguese; while English is a third or fourth language (if at all) and the ability to fully benefit from a course may be highly limited.

Accessibility

All course materials, technologies and learning environments should be accessible to all students, including those with disabilities. Consider accommodation options and technology support for everyone.

Power Dynamics

Power imbalances within the learning environment should be acknowledged and addressed, fostering an environment that encourages participation from all students. Historically, power dynamics have been entwined with colonization, involving the acquisition of indigenous lands by Western forces and subsequent use to reinforce Western values while exploiting people of color (Stein and de Oliveira Andreotti, 2016). Recognizing this historical context is crucial, along with subsequent endeavors to decolonize, such as those undertaken by Indigenous communities (Dei, 2006) and the efforts of Black slaves striving to liberate themselves from the shackles of slavery (Stein and de Oliveira Andreotti, 2016).

Instructors may consider designing questions for students where they should analyze impacts on various ethnic/cultural groups as part of course discussions or assignments. Instructors may also want to include readings highlighting the lack of representation in relevant research related to the topics—whose voices are excluded/missing/absent/silent?

Inclusive Leadership

Foster inclusive leadership skills to recognize and leverage the strengths of a diverse team. The curriculum should integrate content related to inclusive leadership and prepare students to lead diverse teams effectively. Inclusive leadership can be demonstrated by embedding commitment to inclusionary language in the course learning outcomes as stated in the syllabus. It can also be demonstrated by including a diversity statement or statement of inclusion in the syllabus (Armstrong, 2011; Branch et al., 2018).

Research on Inclusiveness

Encourage and support research that explores and contributes to the field of KM with an emphasis on inclusiveness. Include the availability of diverse resources and support for student research projects.

Inclusive Assessment

Educators can recognize the varied learning abilities of their students and utilize new and creative approaches, such as flipped classroom models, interactive activities and technology (Bishop and Verleger, 2013). Combined with group-based projects, these will provide fairer measures of intelligence for grading purposes than standardized tests, which have been shown to be biased. Emphasizing these strategies in the grading rubric can also contribute to fostering inclusiveness within the classroom. Thus, instructors should design assessments that are fair, unbiased and considerate of diverse learning styles and backgrounds. Ensure assessments do not inadvertently disadvantage any particular group.

5.5 CASE STUDY 1: KENT STATE UNIVERSITY— MASTER OF SCIENCE (M.S.) IN KNOWLEDGE MANAGEMENT

The Kent State University located in Kent, Ohio, offers the M.S. in Knowledge Management degree, one of five master's degree programs in the School of Information (iSchool, https://www.kent.edu/iSchool). One of three master's degree programs in Knowledge Management in the United States, it was initially part of the Information Architecture and Knowledge Management (IAKM) master's degree program, launched in fall 2001. The IAKM M.S. degree also included information architecture and information use as core concepts in the program. There were eight core course requirements and IAKM courses were taught by faculty across the campus from different academic programs (e.g., communication studies, journalism, computer science). In 2005, the M.S. online program was launched and soon became online only. In 2008, an 18-credit hour graduate certificate in KM was launched as part of the online program. It was designed to assist in strengthening the KM concentration in the IAKM program. A full KM curriculum was available the following year and reduced the required credits from 48 to 42 with only two core courses in all IAKM concentrations and allowed students to focus more specifically on their chosen concentrations. In 2011, thanks to a generous endowment from the Goodyear Corporation, an endowed professorship was established in the area of KM and the first holder of this position was hired. The following year, through a partnership with George Washington University, a forum was held to discuss important aspects of KM education. They engaged with people from government, business and education to determine employers' needs for knowledge workers to help inform curriculum development. This work resulted in a major revision of the KM curriculum. In 2017, the KM program became its own major, and the M.S. in Knowledge Management was launched with a reduced credit requirement of 36 credit hours. In 2020, a new Goodyear Endowed Professor of KM was hired to revise the curriculum and address what appeared to be an increasing interest in knowledge workers in the United States. A KM Advisory Board was established of renowned practitioners, scholars, and Kent State students in KM. In the spring of 2021, the Board established a set of core competencies in the field, from which programmatic learning outcomes were identified. These outcomes served as the framework for the course review process and all but one course was either revised or dropped. A new set of five core courses were established, moving away from the heavy focus on organization in the previous curriculum, and offering a broader focus on the "people" aspects of KM. This resulted in the addition of five new core courses, including a general management course (taught by the Management Department in the Ambassador Crawford College of Business and Entrepreneurship at Kent State), a KM "thought leadership" course (KM 60306), a theoretical foundations course (KM 60301), a "how-to-do KM" practice course (KM 60302) and a course on "Semantic Analysis Methods and Technologies" (KM 60370). Besides the new core, additional new courses included "Knowledge Metrics and Assessment,"

"Communities of Practice," "Emerging Technologies in KM," "Strategic Intelligence" and "Organizational Culture Assessment."

Finally, in the process of this extensive curricular revision, much of the overlap between the classes was removed, except where necessary to link topics together. As a result of this streamlining, in 2023 the required credit hours for the M.S. in KM program dropped from 36 to 30, making it possible to complete the M.S. program in one year full-time (https://catalog. kent.edu/coursesaz/km/). Similarly, the 18-credit hour requirement for the master's certificate in KM was reduced to 12 credit hours, accounting for the required core courses in the newly revised M.S. program. Students who pursue the certificate are required to take the core courses that give them a solid foundation in KM work. All 12 credit hours are directly transferable into the M.S. program, where they can build their program in their areas of interest if they choose to continue. Electives can be taken from the iSchool's other programs in Library and Information Science, User Experience and Health Informatics. They can also take courses from sister schools in the College of Communication and Information including the School of Communication Studies, the School of Emerging Media and Technology, the School of Journalism and Media or the School of Visual Communication Design (https://www.kent.edu/cci/about). In addition, students may also take courses in the Ambassador Crawford College of Business and Entrepreneurship. As more students come to the KM program from outside, a new dual degree (MBA/M.S. in Knowledge Management, https://www.kent.edu/business/mba-dual-degree-programs) was launched in fall 2023 to accommodate the interest and growing number of students from this College. At the time of this writing, the M.S. in Knowledge Management is offered online only and is asynchronous (i.e., does not meet in real-time) so students are able to take the course at their own pace within the semester structure.

There are two options for reviewing KM curriculum for inclusiveness. The first is to review each course individually using the established criteria. The second is to apply the criteria to the curriculum as a whole, with examples of each criteria from different courses. This second option gives a broader overview of the program, which is useful in evaluating a program rather than a course. This is the process used in the following analysis of a case study, using Kent State University's Master of Science in Knowledge Management core courses, which are required for all master's and certificate program students (Table 5.1).

TABLE 5.1

Elements of Inclusion Applied to Core M.S. in KM Courses at Kent State University

Criteria of Inclusion	Elements of Inclusion in the Core Courses in the M.S. in Knowledge Management at Kent State University
Diverse Course Content	Demographics of the US population help to understand the knowledge economy (KM 60301).
	Overview of people in the overall knowledge management process (KM 60302).
	This course focuses on personal development and soft skills in KM. The focus, therefore, is on the student and what they see as their strengths and/or areas they want to strengthen (KM 60306).
	Course content focuses on technical aspects of knowledge organization (KM 60370).
Inclusive Teaching Methods	Peer discussions (KM 60301)
	Opportunities to interact with instructor outside of classroom hours (Note: office hours are not always held in the online environment). (KM 60302)
	Regular meetings are held with an instructor. Additional appointments can be made to talk with the instructor. (KM 60306)
	The instructor holds office hours to meet with students. (KM 60370)
Diverse faculty, guest speakers, and industry experts	Guest speakers with differing opinions to give multiple perspectives. (KM 60301)
	Numerous guest speakers participate but do not yet represent a wide representation of either the students or the population as a whole. (KM 60306)
Bias and stereotypes	Discussions of economics provides perspectives on underrepresented populations and political aspects. (KM 60301)
	Focus on communication and collaboration to facilitate knowledge sharing. (KM 60302)
	Some bias is represented by the selection of guest speakers all being white men. Course materials, however, are selected to be more representative of the wider population. (KM 60306)
	The instructor is from an underrepresented group and is very calm and takes time with each student. (KM 60370)
Cultural/Intercultural competence	Papers in the class must address aspects of exclusion in society. (KM 60301)
	Implicit in the course subject matter of knowledge facilitation and sharing. (KM 60302)
	One of the instructors who teaches this class is from an underrepresented group. The other has lived in multiple countries and recognizes and values intersectionality. (KM 60306)
	The instructor has taught for many years and has developed an open and nurturing environment for students. (KM 60370)

Collaborative projects	Discussion board postings and responses include everyone in the course. (KM 60301)
	From the course overview: "Two broad areas of focus will include 'purposeful collaboration' and 'effective networking;'" "Rewards and recognition of people. (KM 60302)
	Due to the nature of this course being individually focused, there are no group projects. Introductions are made to each other on the discussion board, including some personal information to facilitate cohesion. Reflexive exercises may be shared. (KM 60306)
	Discussion posts are shared among the students for comments by others. This builds collaboration and cross-student learning. (KM 60370)
Inclusive language and communication	Challenges exist when using terms like "developed countries, lesser developed countries." "Global North" and "Global South" are better, although not as precise and do not align with the economic divisions used by data sources (e.g., U.N., World Bank, etc.). (KM 60301)
	Diversity statement included in the syllabus. (KM 60302, KM 60306, KM 60370)
Accessibility	All course websites in Canvas are designed to meet accessibility standards. (KM 60301, KM 60302, KM 60306, KM 60370)
Power dynamics	Debate on power and control in the knowledge economy is presented. (KM 60301)
	There is an option to participate in a personal quiz about KM and social skills. The course is quite structured but focused on individual interpretation of course materials. (KM 60306)
	By its nature, this course on technology recognizes bias in system design so this is discussed throughout the course. (KM 60370)
Inclusive leadership	Stating instructor bias toward the knowledge economy (KM 60301)
	Instructor goes through projects with students and reviews their steps alongside their work. (KM 60302)
	Instructor shares past experiences with different cultures at beginning of the course during introductions (KM 60306)
	The instructor is by their own nature very approachable, welcoming, and enthusiastic about student ideas. (KM 60370)
Research on inclusiveness	Students are exposed to research that is not directly related to inclusiveness; however, discussions of the "haves" and "have-nots" in society is relevant to who is included and who is left out. (KM 60301)
Inclusive assessment	Asynchronous online programs offer some anonymity in grading because there is no real-time interaction with students required. (KM 60301, KM 60302, KM 60306, KM 60370)
	Case studies are used in assessment, along with individualized exercises. (KM 60302)

By incorporating these and other inclusive practices and curricular ideas into a master's degree program in KM, educators can foster an inclusive learning environment that prepares students to be more inclusive and culturally competent KM professionals. Through an inclusive KM education, a new generation of knowledge management professionals will be better equipped to address diversity, equity and inclusiveness challenges in their future roles.

5.6 CASE STUDY 2: THE KNOWLEDGE MANAGEMENT CERTIFICATION COURSE OF THE KNOWLEDGE MANAGEMENT ACADEMY, VIENNA, AUSTRIA

The Knowledge Management Academy (KM Academy) is the educational program of KMA Knowledge Management Associates GmbH, a private company established in Vienna, Austria, in 2001. Since its foundation, the KM Academy has offered Knowledge Management Trainings to individuals—funded mostly by their employers, private and public organizations—in open courses and to organizations through tailored inhouse courses. At least two certification courses have been offered every year since its foundation; additional special training modules complement the core certification course, whereas the topics have changed and further developed throughout the years. The Certification Course started in 2002 with six modules of two days each (12 days of classroom training altogether), plus various assignments and specifically the task of developing a case study in KM or a comparable practical work, demonstrating the ability to apply the learned in real context. Supervision and coaching has been part of the training program ever since. Due to the steadily growing limitations of companies participating in classroom courses for more than a few days per year, the number of classroom training days has decreased and have resulted in 5 days since 2019. The reduction of days has therefore been a matter of customer-orientation as well as of inclusion, as a longer course duration would have excluded a significant number of interested participants.

In 2020, the pandemic opened a new chapter for the KM Academy, as all the training then had to be provided online. Although the quality and impact of the training was expected to go down, the inclusion aspect benefited, because a significant number of participants could join online much easier, once for cost reason—no travel and accommodation—as well as for time reasons and the ease of integrating the learning modules into daily business. Since the Certification Course at that time had been offered not only in German language, but also in English language, the accessibility to the courses has dramatically increased. Due to the vast engagements of KMA in Africa and the development context—as an initiator of the Knowledge for Development Partnership—the interest of the African market in the Certification Course has significantly grown. However, the course fees, which applied in Europe, have hardly been affordable to most African participants. Additionally, the local context of African societies, businesses, and challenges, had to be addressed to achieve the desired impact of the training. Therefore, the KM Academy has established knowledge.city as a network of local African (and European and Asian) companies, who deliver local services—including local training—at local prices and considering African context. The combination of the global and local training finally created a significant impact and allows inclusion and adjustments (Table 5.2).

TABLE 5.2

Elements of Inclusion Applied to the Certification Course of the KM Academy

Criteria of Inclusion	Elements of Inclusion in the Certification Course
Diverse course content	The Curriculum reflects the KM standards and general components of KM. However, in the preparation of the courses, the participants are already requested to share their specific background and questions to allow lecturers to adjust their content. Basic course contents are general enough to allow lecturers to adjust to specific contexts of participants.
Inclusive teaching methods	Impulses from theory and practice always conclude in discussions, groupworks and co-creative components. Participants create their specific understanding and apply the learned in their context. Equal participation and contribution of all participants is given priority. More advanced and experienced participants are encouraged to share their background and experiences and support the peers.
Diverse faculty, guest speakers and industry experts	The KM Academy facilitated a wider spectrum of lecturers, including professional trainers/consultants, as well as scientists, and practitioners from both public and private sector, at least one large and one small organization. Gender balance is given priority.

(Continued)

TABLE 5.2 (Continued)

Criteria of Inclusion	Elements of Inclusion in the Certification Course
Bias and stereotypes	The KM Certification Course has a high focus on the facilitation of Communities of Practice/Knowledge Partnerships and the related aspects of diversity. This gives opportunity to address knowledge inclusion and exclusion and to train participants in facilitating communities/partnership with equal opportunities of participation and contribution.
Cultural/Intercultural competence	Due to the international participation in the KM Certification Courses, the intercultural competence is not only addressed, but applied. Participants learn about different cultures and communicate, learn, share, co-create with participants from other continents. Due to the high linkages to sustainable development, global perspectives as well as local contexts are considered equally relevant.
Inclusive language and communication	The global online course is provided in English language and allows participants from a large international community to join. However, there are still a huge number of countries, which do not speak English commonly, like for instance in Western Africa or Latin America. The use of terms and expressions is made as practical and understandable as possible to any participant. Academic background is no precondition for participation, while all contents are on a very solid scientific basis.
Accessibility	The online courses have a high accessibility. Classroom trainings have strong limitations from a time and financial perspective.
Power dynamics and inclusive leadership	Focused on knowledge, the ways of balancing power, eloquence, status, or other components that could hinder equal participation in knowledge processes, are addressed explicitly in the modules on Communities of Practice and Knowledge Partnerships. This is also an explicit component of the leadership training module, which should favor the development of knowledge independent of age, gender, eloquence, etc.
Research on inclusiveness	The KM Academy, as a partner of K4DP's School of Knowledge Sciences, is highly engaged in developing a research program on knowledge inclusion. Action research is applied by the trainers/consultants integrated into their practical work with various customers.
Inclusive assessment	The assessment is a highly contextualized process, as the ability to apply the key principles in real context is paramount. It is therefore unavoidable that the assessors understand and reflect the individual background and context of the participant. Whereas the subjects of assessment are generic, the assessment of the implementation is fully tailored.

5.7 SUMMARY AND CONCLUSION

The idea of social inclusion is one that is in mainstream literature and is at the forefront of many organizations (e.g., World Bank, United Nations) as evidenced by the sources referenced in this chapter. Knowledge inclusion, however, is a newer concept and one that is not widely discussed. Yet, the role of inclusiveness in knowledge sharing and KM, in general, is vital to the support of social inclusion and in sharing our understanding of ourselves and each other, particularly across our social and cultural experiences.

The purpose of this chapter is to bring together the concepts of social inclusion and knowledge inclusion/exclusion to better develop the interaction of these concepts as well as identify literature on these topics and how they go together. Perhaps more unique to this chapter is the furtherance of how we can implement knowledge inclusion and social inclusion in KM education. The presentation of two case studies in educational programs in KM offer examples and insights into how knowledge inclusion is embedded in these programs. While there are good examples of the particular curricular criteria for assessing knowledge inclusion in these programs, there is clearly room for more growth and strengthening. KM is about people and inclusion to facilitate knowledge sharing and improved organizational performance. Knowledge inclusion can be helpful to strengthen this focus throughout the curriculum.

5.8 SUGGESTIONS FOR FUTURE RESEARCH

There is a limited amount of research on knowledge inclusion and much of its relation to social inclusion and social impact is inferred from definitions and descriptions. One suggestion for future research is to develop principles for knowledge inclusion that would help guide the development of knowledge inclusion in KM education. A further suggestion for future research would be to find more case studies and consider more cross comparison to develop best practices in KM education in the area of knowledge inclusion. It should also be further explored how dedicated educational modules on knowledge inclusion would fit into other educational programs as knowledge inclusion is a matter of any societal domain and thereby any educational program.

REFERENCES

Al-Hawamdeh, S. (2003). *Knowledge management: Cultivating knowledge professionals.* Oxford: Chandos Publishing. https://www.google.com/books/edition/Knowledge_Management/HfOiAgAAQBAJ?hl=en&gbpv=1

Armstrong M. A. (2011). Small world: Crafting an inclusive classroom (no matter what you teach). *Thought & Action, Fall,* 51–61.

Barney, J. B. (1991). Firm resources and sustained competitive advantage. *Journal of Management, 17,* 99–120.

Bishop J. L., Verleger M. A. (2013). The flipped classroom: A survey of the research. *120th American Society for Engineering Education Annual Conference and Exposition,* 30, 1–18.

Bodla, A. A., Tang, N., Jiang, W., & Tian, L. (2018). Diversity and creativity in cross-national teams: The role of team knowledge sharing and inclusive climate. *Journal of Management & Organization, 24*(5), 711–729.

Bourke, J., Titus, A., & Espedido, A. (2020). The key to inclusive leadership. *Harvard Business Review, 6,* H05GLB.

Branch S., Stein L., Huynh H., Lazzara J. (2018, October). *Assessing the value of diversity statements in course syllabi: Annual Conference on Teaching (ACT).* Talk presented at the Society for the Teaching of Psychology ACT, Phoenix, AZ.

Caniglia, G., Luederitz, C., von Wirth, T., Fazey, I., Martín-López, B., Hondrila, K., ... & Lang, D. J. (2021). A pluralistic and integrated approach to action-oriented knowledge for sustainability. *Nature Sustainability, 4*(2), 93–100.

Cumming-Potvin, W. (2013). "New basics" and literacies: Deepening reflexivity in qualitative research. *Qualitative Research Journal, 214*(2), 214–230. https://doi.org/10.1108/QRJ-04-2013-0024

Dei G. J. S. (2006). Introduction: Mapping the terrain—Towards a new politics of resistance. In Dei G. J. S., Kempf A. (Eds.). *Anti-colonialism and education: The politics of resistance* (pp. 1–25). Sense Publishers.

Dinwoodie, D., Pasmore, W., Quinn, L., & Rabin, R. (2015). *Navigating change: A leader's role. Center for Creative Leadership. White Paper,* 1.

Falicov, C. J. (2014). Psychotherapy and supervision as cultural encounters: The multidimensional ecological comparative approach framework. In C. A. Falender & E. P. Shafranske (Eds.). *Multiculturalism and diversity in clinical supervision: A competency-based approach* (pp. 29–58). American Psychological Association.

Fombad, M. (2018). Knowledge management for poverty eradication: a South African perspective. *Journal of Information, Communication and Ethics in Society, 16*(2), 193–213.

Freire, P. (1996). Pedagogy of the oppressed (revised). *New York: Continuum, 356,* 357–358.

Fuentes, M. A., Zelaya, D. G., & Madsen, J. W. (2021). Rethinking the course syllabus: Considerations for promoting equity, diversity, and inclusion. *Teaching of Psychology, 48*(1), 69–79.

Gidley, J., Hampson, G., Wheeler, L., & Bereded-Samuel, E. (2010). Social inclusion: Context, theory and practice. *The Australasian Journal of University Community Engagement, 5*(1), 6–36.

Ginsberg, M. B., & Wlodkowski, R. J. (2009, November). Professional learning to promote motivation and academic performance among diverse adults. In *CAEL Forum and News* (pp. 23–32).

Greenwald, A. G., & Banaji, M. R. (1995). Implicit social cognition: attitudes, self-esteem, and stereotypes. *Psychological Review, 102*(1), 4.

Johnson R. T., Johnson D. W. (2008). Active learning: Cooperation in the classroom. *The Annual Report of Educational Psychology in Japan*, 47, 29–30.

Kissová, L. and I. Rapošová (2017). *Social Inclusion: Perspectives, Practices and Challenges within the Visegrad Region*. Faculty of Social Studies, Masaryk University. Soc607.

Lam, L., Nguyen, P., Le, N., & Tran, K. (2021). The relation among organizational culture, knowledge management, and innovation capability: Its implication for open innovation. *Journal of Open Innovation: Technology, Market, and Complexity*, 7(1), 66.

Miminoshvili, M. and M. Cerne (2022). "Workplace inclusion–exclusion and knowledge hiding behaviour of minority members." *Knowledge Management Research & Practice* 20(3): 422–435.

Muddiman, D. (2000). Theories of social exclusion and the public library. In *Open to all?: The public library and social exclusion* (1–15). London: The Council for Museums, Archives and Libraries.

Overall, P. M. (2009). Cultural competence: A conceptual framework for library and information science professionals. *The Library Quarterly*, 79(2), 175–204.

Qureshi, I., Sutter, C., & Bhatt, B. (2018). The transformative power of knowledge sharing in settings of poverty and social inequality. *Organization Studies*, 39(11), 1575–1599.

Stein S. &, de Oliveira Andreotti, V. (2016). Decolonization and higher education. In Peters M. (Ed.), *Encyclopedia of educational philosophy and theory*. Springer Science+Business Media.

Sutz, J., & Tomasini, C. (2013, July). Knowledge, innovation, social inclusion and their elusive articulation: when isolated policies are not enough. In *International Workshop on "New Models of Innovation for Development,"* University of Manchester.

Suveren, Y. (2022). Unconscious Bias: Definition and Significance. *Psikiyatride Guncel Yaklasimlar*, 14(3), 414–426.

Thorndike, E. L. (1920). A constant error in psychological ratings. *Journal of Applied Psychology*, 4(1), 25–29.

Tiwari, S. P. (2022). Knowledge management and emerging technologies: An overview of the underpinning concepts. *International Journal of Innovative Technologies inEconomy* 1(37), 1–3.

Tsiplakides, I. (2018). Social Inclusion and Equity in Modern Information and Knowledge Societies. *Journal of Sociology and Anthropology*, 2(1), 9–13.

Vaccaro A. (2019). Developing a culturally competent and inclusive curriculum: A comprehensive framework for teaching multicultural psychology. In Mena J. A., Quina K. (Eds.), *Integrating multiculturalism and intersectionality into the psychology curriculum: Strategies for instructors* (pp. 23–35). American Psychological Association.

United Nations. (2015). Transforming our world: the 2030 Agenda for Sustainable Development. https://documents.un.org/doc/un.oc/gen/n15/291/89/pdf/n1529189.pdf?token=yikRwItBlLD09VD5P3&fe=true

United Nations. (2016). Chapter 1; Social inclusion. In United Nations (UN), Report on the world social situation. https://www.un.org/esa/socdev/rwss/2016/chapter1.pdf

UNESCO (2005): UNESCO World Report. Towards Knowledge Societies. Paris UNESCO, 2005, p. 159.

U.S. Department of Education, Office of Educational Technology. (2022). *Advancing digital equity for all: Community-based recommendations for developing effective digital equity plans to close the digital divide and enable technology-empowered learning.* https://tech.ed.gov/files/2022/09/DEER-Resource-Guide_FINAL.pdf

The World Bank. (n.d.). *Social inclusion.* Retrieved July 30, 2023, from https://www.worldbank.org/en/topic/social-inclusion#:~:text=Social%20inclusion%20is%20the%20process,the%20basis%20of%20their%20identity

6

Addressing Epistemic Injustice in Scholarly Communication at Individual and Collective Levels

Angel Y. Ford
University at Albany, State University of New York, Albany, NY, USA

Daniel Gelaw Alemneh
University of North Texas, Denton, TX, USA

6.1 INTRODUCTION

Epistemic injustice affects many individuals and groups of people around the globe. Epistemic injustice occurs when an individual or group of people experience negative effects regarding their ability to know and communicate what they know and experience (Fricker, 2007). In this chapter, the focus is on epistemic injustice impacting scholars and researchers when they try to engage in scholarly communication within their disciplines; particularly scholars and researchers that find themselves in low- and middle-income countries (LMICs). In academic work and specifically in scholarly communication, injustices related to knowing and communicating have far reaching implications for individuals and beyond (Canagarajah, 2002; Demeter, 2020; Ford & Alemneh, 2022a).

Ongoing research around epistemic injustice in scholarly communication examines both possible causal factors of the injustices, as well as the negative effects created by the injustices. The focus of this chapter is not about either causes or effects, but rather about efforts, both individual and collective, to reduce the injustices. Zheng (2019) discussed analyzing the structures and systems and taking action to decrease social injustices

DOI: 10.1201/9781003407966-6

when they are identified. Vasilyeva and Ayala-López (2019) suggested we use structural thinking, examining the way past and current structures have led to the present situation and what can be done to relieve the negative impacts.

In addition to considering ways to reduce injustices, it is important to consider that scientific publishing paradigms are shifting (Tang et al., 2021). Examples of that shift include efforts to move to Open Access (OA) and Open Science (OS), and although this is affecting publishers, this has by no means taken them out of the picture. Publishing houses still have a great deal of influence over how publications are disseminated and how the associated costs are covered. A full discussion on OA and OS is outside of the scope of this chapter, however, requires mentioning as both impact the discussion at hand. Individuals and groups that have any influence could consider ways to promote OA and OS and stand against unfair systems. Policy makers could consider engaging the publishing house stakeholders in discussions about efforts to reduce inequities as well.

To start our discussion in this chapter, we will discuss the broad categories of epistemic injustice and move into a deeper examination of the two main types, distributive and discriminatory. We will then explore ways both individual actors and collective groups can work to address these injustices. After we have explored ways to work against the injustices, we will examine evidence that shows this would be good for science and society. Finally, we will discuss implications as well as future research efforts that could advance this justice work even further.

6.2 BROAD CATEGORIES OF EPISTEMIC INJUSTICE

Many terms float around when referring to epistemic injustices or issues of knowing and sharing knowledge. Patin et al. (2020) uses the term epistemicide to express what happens when a people group is silenced, or their knowledge is completely extinguished or disregarded. This causes what they call a third harm or, "future, intergenerational harm stemming from past injustices" (Patin et al., 2020, p. 2). Nkoudou (2020) uses the term epistemic alienation to explain, "(D)istortion of one's native way of communicating about one's reality, causing cognitive distortion" (p. 32). Bernal and Villalpando (2023) discuss "an apartheid of knowledge" when referring to keeping the races within academia separated. Dotson (2012) refers to epistemic injustices as "epistemic exclusion" or "an infringement on the epistemic agency of knowers that reduces her or his ability to participate in a given epistemic community" (p. 24).

We could also discuss several other terms used to describe injustice in relation to individuals and groups of people as knowers and disseminators of knowledge. However, rather than include an extensive list, which benefits from nuanced ways of examining the issue, we will focus on broad types and efforts to reduce or eradicate them. For this purpose, it is more important to recognize that injustices are occurring, than to be concerned with the names. In fact, Kidd et al. (2017) suggest we do not attempt to come up with an exhaustive list, lest we then stop trying to identify new types of epistemic injustice. The two main types we will examine will be *distributive* and *discriminatory* epistemic injustices. We discuss these two categories to help clarify ways to address each, however, keep in mind that ultimately, we are suggesting ways to reduce *epistemic exclusion* and include scholars in conversations where many are currently being discounted.

The injustices we are examining occur at the individual levels for students, early career scholars, minorities in certain fields, and a particular focus for this chapter is on the effects experienced by scholars based on their countries of residence. The effects on individuals include increased challenges when attempting to publish in top-tiered journals or when submitting proposals to present at conferences. In turn, when individual scholars are affected, negative effects ripple into disciplines, institutions, and even at times national development. We will not go into a more complete list of the effects here as the focus of this chapter is on ways to address the inequities.

6.3 DISTRIBUTIVE EPISTEMIC INJUSTICE

One of the main categories of epistemic injustice is *distributive*. Fricker (2013), considered a pioneer in identifying and describing epistemic injustice, defined *distributive* epistemic injustice as the "(U)nfair distribution of epistemic goods such as education or information" (p. 1318). *Distributive* epistemic injustice in scholarly communication occurs when the distribution of research outputs or the access or methods to obtain knowledge are uneven. Consider the differences in access provided by academic libraries.

At elite research universities in high-income countries such as the United States, Canada, or many European countries, resources are mostly plentiful, and yet at academic libraries in LMICs the opposite is true. Due to academic library access and through other means, scholars in affluent countries can access research outputs with greater ease than their counterparts in poorer countries.

These inequities occur for a variety of reasons, with the most apparent being funding. Funding affects the ability to subscribe to scholarly journals either through individual journal subscriptions or through subscription bundles from larger publishing houses (Roehrig et al., 2018). However, funding also affects access to training in information sciences and ICT infrastructure. In addition to funding differences, disparities appear due to social capital. Scholars in higher income countries, even if they lack access to particular journals through their own academic library affiliations, often have social capital in the form of colleagues or associates that can help them gain access through extended affiliations. Less fortunate scholars may not have the ability to reach out to others for such assistance, as many of their colleagues and associates are in similar situations.

When scholars do not have ready access to research outputs, it causes barriers in the work they can do and can delay or stall their individual professional advancements as well as the growth and advancements they could bring to their institutions, and their disciplines. This can cause them to be unable to help their students advance as well. This inability to advance starts a cycle that contributes to *discriminatory* injustices, which will be the focus of the next section.

6.4 DISCRIMINATORY EPISTEMIC INJUSTICE

Whereas *distributive* epistemic injustice affects scholars through challenges to accessing necessary research outputs, *discriminatory* epistemic injustice in scholarly communication affects the ability to actively engage in conversations either verbally or through publications, both key avenues of genuine engagement. *Discriminatory* epistemic injustice is often broken down into three or more types. The main three are often labeled as testimonial, hermeneutical, and contributory and will be the focus of this section. Even though these three types do not cover all injustices experienced, they encompass a vast majority.

Fricker (2007) defined testimonial epistemic injustice as that occurring "when prejudice causes a hearer to give a deflated level of credibility to a speaker's word" (p. 1). This can be applied to readers and writers as well. When scholars are deemed not credible for some type of prejudice, this causes obstacles for engagement. If this happens before their research is even considered, scholarship could be suffering from the lack of their contributions.

Hermeneutical epistemic injustice is related to understanding and communicating about one's lived experiences. Fricker (2007) defines it as, "(W)hen a gap in collective interpretive resources puts someone at an unfair disadvantage when it comes to making sense of their social experiences" (p. 1). Hermeneutical epistemic injustice is related to social standing and social situations and affects scholars who live and work in contexts different from those widely embraced as Western or Westernized. It may also occur when scholars use methodologies different from those widely accepted. This type of injustice could also be experienced when scholars work on novel findings or findings that might not appear beneficial to the wider audience or those in a Western context.

Sometimes the bias on the part of publication management (reviewers and editors) is due to not possessing the correct hermeneutical heuristics to examine the findings being posited and rather than seeking them out, they simply reject the outputs as not fitting into the norm. These rejections can also occur when the outputs do not appear to be applicable within a Western lens but are rather seen as applicable for a regional or less than dominant group. Dotson (2012) posits that this type of injustice, whereas it is hermeneutical in nature, can also be willful. Contributory or willful hermeneutical epistemic injustice as described by Dotson (2012) is a situational or willful ignorance occurring when hearers or readers could make the effort to understand the communication of the speakers or authors but choose not to. This could be occurring because there would be additional effort necessary to use a foreign heuristic.

Epistemic injustices occur when scholarly outputs are either accepted or rejected based on an individual or group's identity, social standing, or unfamiliar perspective or heuristic as opposed to the quality of their work (Demeter, 2020). *Discriminatory* injustice occurs when proposals or manuscripts are rejected due to bias. These proposals could be for academic or professional conferences, they could be proposals for funding, or they could be manuscripts for peer-review publication. Whatever the type of proposal, their rejections have negative effects on the authors and possibly the disciplines. Now that we have examined different types of injustice and how these injustices occur in scholarly communication, we will begin to explore actions that can be taken to lessen or eliminate their occurrences.

6.5 ADDRESSING EPISTEMIC INJUSTICE IN GLOBAL SCHOLARLY COMMUNICATION

General efforts to reduce bias will be a great way to start, however, we want to reflect for a moment on how long and how much concerted effort eradicating injustice can take. Working toward justice can bring about weariness, however, that does not mean it should not be attempted. Even though we are not confident that we will completely eradicate epistemic injustice in scholarly communication, we intend to put forth great effort in addressing and reducing incidences. Dotson (2012) stated, "One can advocate for better, more responsible epistemic conduct capable of *reducing* epistemic oppression, without also harboring unrealistic expectations for superior epistemic conduct and abilities necessary for *eliminating* epistemic oppression entirely" (p. 25).

With a positive mindset we will begin to examine efforts that can be made at both individual and collective levels to decrease both *distributive* and *discriminatory* epistemic injustice in scholarly communication. Since *distributive* and *discriminatory* injustices impact scholarly communication in different ways, although with some overlap, we will begin with efforts to address *distributive* and then move on to those that would address *discriminatory*.

6.6 ADDRESSING DISTRIBUTIVE EPISTEMIC INJUSTICE

One of the biggest efforts to increase equity in the distribution of scholarly outputs and therefore decrease inequities experienced by scholars around the globe is OA, (Arunachalam, 2017; Ford & Alemneh, 2022b). The OA movement has continually evolved over the last two decades, focusing on the enhancement of scientific communication through limiting restrictions on access and therefore consumption. With the changing landscape of academic publishing and the growing interdisciplinary field of studies,

OA facilitates amalgamations of a diverse set of methods, originating from different disciplines. Although the global efforts to increase OA have made a positive impact on access and research, just over a quarter of such peer-reviewed research is available through OA. This still means many academics find themselves unable to access the peer-reviewed publications they need to complete their work.

The shift to emergency remote teaching and work due to the global COVID-19 pandemic caused national and disciplinary mandates to share research outputs and open educational resources (OER). Since then, the need for such open resources has been highlighted (Ford & Alemneh, 2021) and the OA and OS movements continue to expand. In August of 2022, the President of the United States gave an executive order that all federally funded research be made open (Nelson, 2022). This means that any federally funded projects need to publish with OA publishers even if costs are incurred.

In addition to global OA and OS efforts, both individual and collective efforts can be made to reduce or eliminate *distributive* epistemic injustices in scholarly communication. Individuals can work to make their research outputs open globally through publishing in OA peer-reviewed journals or publishing with OA book publishers. When not infringing on any copyright laws, individuals can also make their publications available through other means such as their institutional repositories or other networks. Individuals can also be open to sharing work with scholars who request copies from them either via email or at conferences. Sometimes it may be a pre-print that is made available; however, this is still helpful if that is the only means to share research findings that will help other scholars advance.

Collectively, efforts can also be made to promote OA by institutional or organizational mandates, and through the use of repositories, and also through disciplines. We must also mention the importance of transparent, open, and timely access to data and information through all avenues of OS. In the post-pandemic academia, institutions worldwide continue to adjust to the new normal, be it remote teaching and learning or telecommuting. More importantly, we continue to witness increased levels of research outputs generated in a short period of time and shared globally as well. Any effort institutions or organizations can make to encourage open scholarly communication may help to reduce *distributive* epistemic injustices.

6.7 ADDRESSING DISCRIMINATORY EPISTEMIC INJUSTICE

We recognize that OA, OS, and OER have been critical in the context of equity and the democratization of knowledge and a great start toward justice in scholarly communication, however, much remains to be done to ensure scholars from LMICs have a fair chance of publication and dissemination of their research outputs (Roh et al., 2020). In order to have a fair chance, *discriminatory* epistemic injustice in scholarly communication, must be identified and disrupted. First, we will explore efforts individuals can make and then move on to collective efforts that can be made to address *discriminatory* epistemic injustice.

Several of the ideas discussed for individuals could easily cross over into collective levels when leadership in institutions of higher education or in organizations encourage and promote these actions by their faculty and students. One of the first steps for individual scholars is to understand *discriminatory* epistemic injustice. What does it mean to either embrace or exclude scholars who are different from you? Do individual scholars recognize inclusion of scholars as a moral issue or issue of justice? Or is the issue more professional in nature where embracing scholars with different backgrounds would expand science? It is challenging for individuals to change behavior unless they feel an internal motivation to do so. Of course, policies can be implemented that mandate change, and although that may be necessary at times, if individuals have an intrinsic reason for change, they are more likely to put forth sustained effort toward that change. Therefore, leadership that can help individuals see the bigger picture and the relevance of embracing diverse scholars as beneficial to all will help their faculty and students tap into reasons for change that may sustain their efforts.

Another step individuals can take is active reflection on positionality and where scholars fit in reference to power within research communities, power both professionally and geopolitically. If a researcher happens to be in a high-income country and working at a top-rated university, the influence may be greater than a researcher in a high-income country that happens to be at a teaching university, where research is not the focus. This is not to say that the second individual does not have a part to play; this simply means that the influence level may be reduced. Through self-reflection, individual scholars can determine how they interact with other scholars in their disciplines and if those interactions are affected by biases, explicit or implicit. Do we hold stereotypes about scholars from LMICs that may be contributing to testimonial or hermeneutical epistemic injustices? Deeper still, if we hold stereotypes, what are they? Are they in reference to intelligence, ability, communication skills, or other perceived deficits? Another question for scholars' self-reflection could be about the willingness to interact and possibly even collaborate with scholars who are very different, culturally, experientially, or ideologically. What is the willingness level to engage? Are there power dynamics that need to be considered in regard to any of these differences? If so, how can efforts be made to change the power dynamics? Do scholars from core countries remain neutral about embracing marginalized scholars to protect themselves? If so, how can what Dotson (2012) calls contributory injustice or willful injustice be prevented?

Another area individual scholars can consider is who they cite in their literature reviews or use as authors of readings in their curriculum. Are any scholars being cited or referred to actually positioned outside of the main culture? This demonstrates which scholars are valued and promoted. Scholars should be cognizant of the published literature they use as instructors and as writers and researchers. How we interact with scholars through our networks and the communities we are involved in demonstrates the value we place on other scholars.

When it comes to involvement in actual publication, are scholars aware of the influence they have when performing peer-reviews? Do individual scholars hold credibility deficits for individuals or groups of people before getting to know their thoughts and views? (Dotson, 2012). Sometimes reviewers are the gatekeepers to whether a person's proposal, presentation, or manuscript is moved forward or eliminated from further review or advancement, meaning individuals in these positions should be cognizant of their biases.

Are scholars able to examine the value of a proposal or study when language differences might affect the readability? Are methodologies or ways of conducting research that fall outside of the norm still considered for what they may contribute to a wider body of knowledge or are they rejected without further consideration? Specifically examining hermeneutical issues, are the articulations of scholars when they position themselves in their research trusted, or are their different lenses rejected because the reviewer(s) would need to put forth effort to see from this different perspective? As stated earlier, many of the individual level factors are easily taken on at the collective levels as well, however, it is important to look at factors that are specifically addressed at the collective levels.

At the collective levels, a number of things can be done to address *discriminatory* epistemic injustice in scholarly communication including, the development of policies and procedures that promote global equity; training scholars, peer-reviewers, and others involved in knowledge management about avoiding biases; embracing global scholars as peer-reviewers and as parts of the editorial boards for academic journals; developing and promoting funding sources for scholars with limited access to financial resources; adjusting current academic networks and communities for equity; and developing new collaborative communities. All of these efforts help to break down the barriers experienced by scholars from LMICs as well as promote better science in the affected disciplines.

Developing policies and procedures as well as training at institutions and in organizations that deal with global knowledge management could promote fair and equitable consideration for scholars from marginalized groups. These efforts could include initiatives that expose unconscious biases, not to be punitive, but rather to shed light on areas that remain hidden even from those perpetuating the wrongs. This could have both direct and indirect effects that promote equity. In addition, editorial boards could embrace marginalized scholars as peer-reviewers and as board level leadership allow their voices to influence management, giving fair and equitable consideration to what they bring to the table, and increasing cultural and ideological diversity in scholarship. Currently, evidence shows that peer-reviewers and editorial boards are not inclusive of scholars from LMICs (Liu et al., 2023).

The next consideration could be to develop funding mechanisms that specifically support the research of scholars from marginalized groups as well as topics relevant to their contexts. Demeter (2020) discusses how grant funding is more difficult to obtain for marginalized scholars due to methodology decisions as well as topic choices. In addition, work could be done to create more equitable academic networks and communities that connect scholars from marginalized groups with each other and with scholars from dominant groups. More consideration could be afforded scholars who would like to present research topics that might not readily appear globally valuable but may nonetheless have applicability by having the voices of the scholars engaged in the conversation (Demeter, 2020). Efforts could also be made to honor marginalized scholars with appropriately earned awards.

Efforts at both the individual and collective levels are critically important to reduce the injustices felt by scholars in LMICs; however, in addition to the efforts discussed previously there are things that can be considered and carried out at both levels. These include the general and overall way we work with scholars globally and how we handle science. Both individuals and leadership could encourage the move toward OS (Thibault et al., 2023), which could help to increase equity. Then we could ask ourselves and our organizations some challenging questions. Are the invitations we put out to scholars from LMICs, either as individuals or as organizations, to "join the scholarly conversations" actually valid or are they just words we use for appearances? Should we also ask to "join their conversations?" and therefore validate what marginalized scholars are already doing, rather than expecting them to join in what we are doing? Do we acknowledge that those that have been excluded from conversations in their disciplines have a lot to offer that will benefit everyone? Are we willing to become advocates and engage gatekeepers to challenge the status quo?

6.8 WHY ADDRESSING THESE INJUSTICES IS BENEFICIAL

In addition to the negative effects injustices have on individuals, the effects on institutions, and society alert us to the fact that eliminating them will be beneficial not only to affected individuals, but also to the wider collective. Dotson (2012) states, "A compromise to epistemic agency, when unwarranted, damages not only individual knowers but also the state of social knowledge and shared epistemic resources" (p. 24). Reducing injustices in knowledge diversity and production is good for science and it's good for society. The world witnessed this while we all lived through the COVID-19 pandemic when science around prevention and cure was shared widely, and solutions were quickly reached and disseminated to the public to reduce the spread of the virus. This real-world example of OS through the widespread sharing of all aspects of research, was not only good for science, it was good for society. The pandemic related restrictions were lifted when science provided the confidence that aspects of life could return to pre pandemic conditions.

Addressing epistemic injustice in scholarly communication benefits science through diversifying perspectives and allowing and even encouraging more rapid growth. This growth enhances disciplines. The movement toward OS is being embraced as a movement that is good for science. Addressing these injustices goes hand in hand with the principles of OS in that scholars who have struggled to engage in scholarly communication will be more readily able to do so when their work is embraced as opposed to rejected due to biases. Reducing injustice benefits society through a more transparent system of research, a more rapid form of dissemination, and more quickly transforming research into practical change.

Embracing diversified research outputs as acceptable could be crucial for the advancement of science because when scholars are closed out of scientific discourse their unique knowledge is not being combined synergistically with their peers, leading to a lack of diversity in perspectives, hindering progress and innovation. When a diversity of voices and perspectives is embraced, it encourages more robust and innovative scientific discoveries. Furthermore, addressing epistemic injustice can help to promote scientific literacy and public engagement with science. By making scientific research and communication more accessible and inclusive, we encourage more people to engage, promoting scientific literacy and thinking critically about findings.

Teams of individuals when working together to solve problems may bring beneficial cognitive diversity (Page, 2019) and ideological diversity (McBrayer, 2024). "Groups offer epistemic advantages over individuals" (McBrayer, 2024, p. 1). Longino (1990) highlighted the need to view science as social knowledge, a view that has been embraced in some spheres and has not been in others. Longino challenged the idea that science is value free and posited that science is more of a social process. She also argued that context is a critical consideration with science. By promoting fairness and equity in scientific research and communication, we can ensure that scientific knowledge is produced and disseminated in a way that benefits everyone.

6.9 IMPLICATIONS

Access to knowledge refers not just to mere ability to retrieve and use but also the right to participate in the creation, distribution, and acquisition of raw information, secondary analyses of data, and knowledge-embedded tools and services (National Institute of Chemistry, 2023). Willinsky (2006) focused on aspects of the social epistemology of scholarship and noted the need for a democratization of knowledge and the role OA might play to help achieve this. Similarly, many OA advocates (Alemneh, 2022; Nobes & Harris, 2019, among others) highlighted the desired objective of the OA movement in terms of reducing historical disparities in access and promoting equitable access. However, Knöchelmann (2021) approached the accessibility issue from the consumption of knowledge side and coined the term "The Democratisation Myth" to dismiss that notion and argue that OA cannot solve an accessibility problem even in Global North scholarly communication.

In a different vein, Gök and Karaulova (2024) investigate the internal heterogeneity of international research collaborations. Although their critical discourse did not emphasize the value of openness, the impact of the presence of OA supportive policies and infrastructure can be considered as relevant phenomena to build the link and further disambiguate the effects of shared heritage to promote international collaboration and partnerships in different countries and territories. Exposing and understanding the injustices experienced by scholars from LMICs and the negative effects these experiences have not only on the scholars but also on science should be considered by policy makers, higher educational leadership, and scholarly output management teams. Many of the efforts to discuss ways to address the injustices could be reiterated here. In general, anyone or any organization that has any leverage to encourage diversity in scholarly communication should consider the implications that doing so could deliver positive impacts to science.

Just as mandates have been made to increase scholars publishing in OA and engaging in OA, initiatives could be instituted that would ensure equity in scholarly communication as far as inclusion in the peer-review process and scholarly output management. The phenomenon could be addressed from a social justice lens as well as from the perspective that diverse science is good science. The promotion of OS and global inclusion of scholars could be leveraged to promote equity in scholarly communication.

6.10 FUTURE RESEARCH

Evidence already shows that injustices are occurring both at individual and systemic levels; however, much remains to be understood. Future research should include both the factors contributing to the injustices as well as the effects the injustices have on individuals, institutions, disciplines, and society in general. As discussed above, when access to knowledge is limited, scholars cannot engage openly within their disciplines. As a result, they are less likely to be invited to collaborate and engage with dominant scholars, causing a negative spiral effect on their professional lives. Ford and Alemneh (2024) suggest several areas of future research as well as the establishment of a new critical lens to define the phenomenon experienced by scholars from LMICs. This new critical lens would provide a framework for future work examining the effects on diverse geopolitical locations as well as the effects on specific fields or disciplines.

Studies could be initiated to better understand from the point of view of scholars from LMICs what injustices they actually feel they experience. Those injustices could include whether they feel they are not believed or deemed credible (testimonial), whether they do not feel they are able to articulate their knowledge or experiences (hermeneutical), or whether they feel the hearer or reader is not trying to understand their message (willful or contributory) (Dotson, 2012). Scholars from outside of LMIC contexts can think they understand, but until they have empirical evidence from the affected scholars themselves, injustices may be misunderstood and even perpetuated. Before work can be done to reduce these injustices, a better understanding of the experiences of the scholars would ground reduction efforts in better solutions. In other words, we need to understand which epistemic injustice the scholars feel they are experiencing in order to help reduce those injustices.

As stated earlier in the chapter, studies could be done that examine relationships and predictability between the obstacles faced and individual effects of frustration and motivation. Other personal effects that should be considered could be feelings of isolation and reduced self-confidence in one's ability to perform the research aspect of their position. Evidence shows a need to address the infrastructure issues and even the culture of research in some LMICs (Fussy, 2019; Nakijoba & Awobamise 2022); however, some of the issues may be closer tied to the frustrations that scholars feel when they attempt to engage in scholarly conversations than cultural issues. Research could be done to examine these different factors. As far as we are knowledgeable in this area, no research has been done showing causation between frustration and lack of motivation. Some of these factors may be found to be direct effects and some may be found to be mediating effects. Empirical research is needed to determine the effects, so that they can be addressed.

An infinite number of research studies could be done on how involving scholars with diverse backgrounds could enhance science in a variety of disciplines. How diversity affects natural sciences such as biology or chemistry may be very different from how diversity affects social science research such as psychology or education. Evidence shows that scholars involved in international projects produce more research outputs

(Heng et al., 2020); however, empirical data collection and analysis on the benefits of equitable international partnerships on advancing science would go a long way in advancing this equity work. Understanding the effects on specific disciplines could be very beneficial for those specific fields of study and initiatives could be implemented to advance science through encouraging fair and equitable cross-national partnerships.

6.11 CONCLUSION

In conclusion, epistemic justice in scholarly communication is an interesting study of a widespread issue that is not currently adequately addressed or understood. Yet enough is known that efforts can be made to address and reduce identified injustices. Even efforts based on the elementary level understanding of the present is better than maintaining the status quo that is perpetuating and possibly even exacerbating the phenomenon.

Individuals and collective groups involved in consuming and producing research outputs have an influence on how the future unfolds. Being aware of that influence through who is presenting or publishing, through whose work is promoted through readings and citations, is a big part of exposing the injustices. Whereas efforts should be made to embrace diverse scholars through research output use and consumption, efforts also need to include who is allowed to engage in scholarly communication and scholarly communication management.

Emphasizing the value of openness, we hope that this chapter highlights ways for approaching this rarely discussed topic from a perspective of both individual and collective levels. We also hope that our approaches and findings spark more critical discourse around this intriguing research topic so that it can be analyzed and understood across different disciplines, stakeholders, and of course, geopolitical positions.

REFERENCES

Alemneh, D. (Ed.) (2022), *The Handbook of Research on the Global View of Open Access and Scholarly Communications*. IGI Global.
Arunachalam, S. (2017). Social justice in scholarly publishing: Open access is the only way. *The American Journal of Bioethics, 17*(10), 15–17. https://doi.org/10.1080/15265161.2017.1366194

Bernal, D. D., & Villalpando, O. (2023). An apartheid of knowledge in academia: The struggle over the "legitimate" knowledge of faculty of color. In *Foundations of Critical Race Theory in Education* (pp. 77–92). Routledge.

Canagarajah, A. S. (2002). *A Geopolitics of Academic Writing.* University of Pittsburgh Press.

Demeter, M. (2020). *Academic Knowledge Production and the Global South: Questioning Inequality and Under-representation.* London: Palgrave Macmillan.

Dotson, K. (2012). A cautionary tale: On limiting epistemic oppression. *Frontiers: A Journal of Women Studies, 33*(1), 24–47. https://doi.org/10.5250/fronjwomestud.33.1.0024

Ford, A., & Alemneh, D. (2022a). Scholars experiencing epistemic injustice due to management of scholarly outputs. *Proceedings of the Association for Information Science and Technology, 59*(1), 67–75. https://doi.org/10.1002/pra2.605

Ford, A. Y. & Alemneh, D. G. (2021). Equitable educational planning with open educational resources: Tooling up for the post-pandemic era. *Educational Planning. Educational Planning, 28*(3), 21–30.

Ford, A. Y. & Alemneh, D. G. (2022b). The role of open access in equitable research curriculum and research outputs. In D.G. Alemneh (Ed.), *Global View of Open Access and Scholarly Communications* (pp. 126–147). IGI Global. https://doi.org/10.4018/978-1-7998-9805-4

Ford, A. Y. & Alemneh, D. G. (2024). Inclusive global scholarly communication: Toward a just and healthier information ecosystem. *Journal of the Association for Information Science and Technology, 76*(10), 1058–1069.

Fricker, M. (2007). *Epistemic Injustice: Power and the Ethics of Knowing.* Oxford University Press.

Fricker, M. (2013). Epistemic justice as a condition of political freedom? *Synthese, 190*(7), 1317–1332.

Fussy, D. S. (2019). The hurdles to fostering research in Tanzanian universities. *Higher Education, 77*(2), 283–299. http://doi.org/10.1007/s10734-018-0276-8

Gök, A., & Karaulova, M. (2024). How "international" is international research collaboration? *Journal of the Association for Information Science and Technology, 75*(2), 97–114. https://doi.org/10.1002/asi.24842

Heng, K., Hamid, M., & Khan, A. (2020). Factors influencing academics' research engagement and productivity: A developing countries perspective. *Issues in Educational Research, 30*(3), 965–987.

Kidd, I. J., Medina, J., & Pohlhaus, G. (2017). Introduction to the Routledge handbook of epistemic injustice. In *The Routledge Handbook of Epistemic Injustice* (pp. 1–9). Routledge.

Knöchelmann, M. (2021). The democratization myth: Open access and the solidification of epistemic injustices. *Science & Technology Studies, 34*(2), 65–89. https://doi.org/10.23987/sts.94964

Liu, F., Rahwan, T., & AlShebli, B. (2023). Non-White scientists appear on fewer editorial boards, spend more time under review, and receive fewer citations. *Proceedings of the National Academy of Sciences, 120*(13), e2215324120. https://doi.org/10.1073/pnas.2215324120

Longino, H. E. (1990). *Science as Social Knowledge: Values and Objectivity in Scientific Inquiry.* Princeton University Press.

McBrayer, J. P. (2024). the epistemic benefits of ideological diversity. *Acta Analytica,* 1–16. https://doi.org/10.1007/s12136-023-00582-z

Nakijoba, R., & Awobamise, A. (2022). Building educational research capacity: Challenges and opportunities from the perspectives of faculty staff of selected private universities in Uganda. *The Uganda Higher Education Review, 10*(1), 19–34. https://doi.org/10.58653/nche.v10i1.02

National Institute of Chemistry (2023). Co-Creating the Future. *Bulletin of NIC,* published on Jan 26, 2023. https://issuu.com/nataajagerradin/docs/nic

Nelson, A., (2022). *Memorandum for the Heads of Executive Departments and Agencies: Ensuring Free, Immediate, and Equitable Access to Federally Funded Research.* Executive Office of the President.

Nkoudou, T. H. M. (2020). Epistemic alienation in African scholarly communications: Open access as a Pharmakon. In M. P. Eve & J. Gray (Eds.), *Reassembling Scholarly Communications: Histories, Infrastructures, and Global Politics of Open Access.* (pp. 25–40). MIT Press.

Nobes, A., & Harris, S. (2019). Open Access in low-and middle-income countries: Attitudes and experiences of researchers. *Emerald Open Research, 1,* 17. https://doi.org/10.35241/emeraldopenres.13325.1

Page, S. E. (2019). *The Diversity Bonus: How Great Teams Pay Off in the Knowledge Economy.* Princeton University Press.

Patin, B., Sebastian, M., Yeon, J., & Bertolini, D. (2020). Toward epistemic justice: An approach for conceptualizing epistemicide in the information professions. *Proceedings of the Association for Information Science and Technology, 57*(1), e242. https://doi.org/10.1002/pra2.242

Roehrig, A. D., Soper, D., Cox, B. E., & Colvin, G. P. (2018). Changing the default to support open access to education research. *Educational Researcher, 47*(7), 465–473. https://doi.org/10.3102/0013189X18782974

Roh, C., Inefuku, H. W., & Drabinski, E. (2020). Scholarly communications and social justice. In M. P. Eve & J. Gray (Eds.), *Reassembling Scholarly Communications: Histories, Infrastructures, and Global Politics of Open Access.* (pp. 41–52).

Tang, R., Mehra, B., Du, J. T., & Zhao, Y. (2021). Framing a discussion on paradigm shift(s) in the field of information. *Journal of the Association for Information Science and Technology, 72*(2), 253–258. https://doi.org/10.1002/asi.24404

Thibault, R. T., Amaral, O. B., Argolo, F., Bandrowski, A. E., Davidson, A. R., & Drude, N. I. (2023). Open Science 2.0: Towards a truly collaborative research ecosystem. *PLoS Biology, 21*(10), e3002362. https://doi.org/10.1371/journal.pbio.3002362

Vasilyeva, N., & Ayala-López, S. (2019). Structural thinking and epistemic injustice. In B. R. Sherman & S. Goguen (Eds.), *Overcoming Epistemic Injustice: Social and Psychological Perspectives,* (pp. 63–85). Rowman & Littlefield International.

Willinsky, J. (2006). *The Access Principle: The Case for Open Access to Research and Scholarship,* MIT Press.

Zheng, R. (2019). What kind of responsibility do we have for fighting injustice? A moral-theoretic perspective on the social connections model. *Critical Horizons, 20*(2), 109–126.

7

Perspectives on Diversity in Knowledge Management Research

Irene Kitimbo
Conference Board of Canada, Ottawa, Ontario, Canada

Cynthia Kumah
Independent Researcher and Consultant, Montreal, Quebec, Canada

7.1 INTRODUCTION

Diversity commonly refers to including people who hold different identities, perspectives, and training (Hattery et al., 2022). In addition, the Editors Association of Canada (About Editors Canada, 2024) defines diversity "as increasing the presence of people of diverse identities in the editorial process." For our purposes, we extend the editorial process to include all aspects involved in the research production process such as reviewing manuscripts, journal acceptance guidelines, research funders, and avenues for accessing research.

Diversity has emerged as a foundational pillar for fostering creativity and driving innovation across various sectors. In the world of business, scholars have extensively investigated the relationship between diversity and organizational performance, noting that while correlation exists, causality is not always evident (Hunt et al., 2015). Pioneering companies like IBM recognized the strategic importance of diversity in nurturing talent pipelines and fostering sustainable success long before it became a mainstream concept (Thomas, 2016).

Making the case for why diverse teams are smarter and why increasing team diversity is a good business decision, Rock and Grant (2016) found that diverse teams are more likely to reexamine facts and remain

DOI: 10.1201/9781003407966-7

objective, encourage greater scrutiny of each member's actions, and keep their joint cognitive resources vigilant. In addition, diverse teams are more likely to outperform homogeneous ones in decision making because they process information more carefully. Furthermore, individuals who do not look, talk, or think like us can allow us to dodge the costly pitfalls of conformity which discourages innovating thinking.

In academia, the benefits of diversity extend beyond scholarly output to encompass broader societal outcomes. Studies have consistently shown that diversity within educational settings significantly enhances civic mindedness among students, fostering a culture of inclusivity and social responsibility (Cole and Zhou, 2014).

A notable study by Freeman and Huang (2014) revealed compelling insights into the impact of diversity on research outcomes. Their research demonstrated that scholarly work produced by researchers from diverse ethnic backgrounds tends to have a more significant influence on the research literature compared to contributions from non-diverse backgrounds. This underscores the enriching effect of diverse perspectives on academic discourse and knowledge creation.

7.2 KNOWLEDGE CREATION AS RESEARCH

Research can be viewed as a journey of exploration or the generation of fresh insights. Organizational knowledge creation, as defined by Nonaka and von Krogh (2009), involves the act of harnessing knowledge produced by individuals, amplifying it within social contexts, and selectively integrating it with existing organizational knowledge.

Various theories in the extant literature have been proposed to explain knowledge creation, with Nonaka and Takeuchi's SECI knowledge spiral being particularly prominent. This theoretical framework elucidates knowledge creation as a dynamic process wherein the interplay between tacit and explicit knowledge facilitates the generation of new insights, fostering their dissemination across individual, team, and organizational levels (Nonaka, 1994; Nonaka and Takeuchi, 1995). The process of transitioning knowledge from one form to another, thereby enriching the organizational knowledge base and enhancing its utilization, is conceptualized as the knowledge spiral (Nonaka, 1994). This spiral encompasses four fundamental conversions:

1. Tacit-to-tacit knowledge transformation, often occurring through mentor-apprentice relationships, where skills are passed down from master to apprentice.
2. Explicit-to-explicit knowledge transformation, typically through formal learning mechanisms focusing on factual knowledge.
3. Tacit-to-explicit knowledge transformation, wherein tacit knowledge is articulated, such as when a skilled practitioner explains their actions, rendering tacit knowledge explicit.
4. Explicit-to-tacit knowledge transformation, as newly acquired explicit knowledge is internalized, enriching, and refining one's tacit knowledge.

These knowledge transformations are commonly referred to as socialization, combination, externalization, and internalization modes, respectively (Nonaka and Nishiguchi, 2001). In the context of scientific knowledge creation, novel research is similarly fostered through externalizing new ideas, socializing and engaging stakeholders in discourse, combining and amalgamating fresh insights with established paradigms to enhance outcomes, and internalizing resultant advancements to propel the field forward.

Rather than engaging in debates over the nuances of various knowledge creation theories, this chapter concentrates on the outcomes or outputs of the knowledge creation process. Research output in knowledge management manifests through academic articles, journals, monographs, conferences, and other industry publications. Bibliometric analyses (Farooq, 2024; Gaviria-Marin et al., 2019; Schiuma et al., 2023) have facilitated researchers in comprehending the intellectual landscape of the domain, identifying emerging trends, assessing journal performance, discerning collaborative patterns, and evaluating scientific productivity. For our purposes, we focus on the five top-ranked journals in knowledge management research.

7.3 METHODOLOGY

In this chapter, our exploration into diversity within knowledge management research takes shape through a multidimensional lens. To achieve a comprehensive understanding, we embarked on a thorough analysis across various facets of diversity. This included examining the geographical distribution of authors, exploring collaboration patterns between different regions, scrutinizing authors' departmental affiliations, quantifying the occurrence of the term "diversity" in publication titles, and editorial composition of the journals of interest among other things.

Our methodology was anchored in the examination of data sourced from the top five journals in the field, as indicated by the 2021 knowledge management journal rankings (Serenko and Bontis, 2022). These include the Journal of Knowledge Management, the Journal of Intellectual Capital, Knowledge Management Research and Practice, VINE Journal of Information and Knowledge Management Systems, and the Learning Organization. By adhering to this rigorous approach, our aim was to unveil insights into how diversity manifests and is addressed within the context of knowledge management research.

7.3.1 Data Search Process

We conducted a search within the Scopus database, using "knowledge management" as our primary search term. To refine our focus, we narrowed down the search results to the top five journals of the 2021 rankings. Furthermore, we limited the publication date range from 2013 to January 2024. We chose this time frame because most diversity, equity, and inclusion initiatives in organizations began about 10 years ago.

Following this initial search, we retrieved a dataset comprising over two thousand publications. Subsequently, we exported this dataset to Excel for further analysis. Prior to conducting our analysis, we cleaned the dataset to eliminate any entries with empty or incomplete information, ensuring the integrity and accuracy of our findings.

7.3.2 Qualitative Document Analysis

Central to our methodological framework was the adoption of a qualitative document analysis approach. This methodology facilitated an in-depth exploration of the multifaceted dimensions of diversity evident within scholarly publications. Through meticulous examination, we aimed to uncover recurring themes, patterns, and discourses pertaining to diversity, while also capturing nuanced insights and perspectives embedded within the literature.

Our analysis traversed a diverse array of elements within publications sourced from the top journals in the field. This qualitative lens enabled us to transcend mere quantitative metrics, delving into the nuanced conceptualizations and operationalizations of diversity prevalent within scholarly discourse.

Through our qualitative document analysis, we sought to contribute to a more profound and holistic understanding of diversity within the field of knowledge management. By shedding light on these intricate dynamics, our endeavor aimed to inform future research, practice, and policy interventions geared toward fostering inclusivity, equity, and social justice within the realm of knowledge management.

7.4 FINDINGS AND DISCUSSION

In this section, we delve into the multifaceted approaches through which diversity can be harnessed and accentuated within knowledge management research, thereby fostering a culture of sustained creativity and innovation within the discipline. We explore various dimensions and strategies for leveraging diversity, recognizing its pivotal role in enriching perspectives, catalyzing novel ideas, and driving forward the frontiers of knowledge management. Through an in-depth examination, we illuminate how embracing diversity across various facets—be it cultural backgrounds, disciplinary expertise, cognitive styles, or demographic characteristics—can serve as a catalyst for transformative advancements in the field. Furthermore, we underscore the importance of inclusive practices and equitable representation in research endeavors, advocating for the amplification of diverse voices and experiences to nurture a vibrant ecosystem conducive to continuous innovation and breakthroughs in knowledge management theory and practice.

7.4.1 Geographical Locations

When examining the diversity of geographical locations among authors contributing to these journals, we observed a commendable global representation, with contributors hailing from every continent. This diversity signifies a broad spectrum of perspectives and insights being brought to the forefront of scholarly discourse, enriching the collective knowledge pool. However, upon closer analysis, disparities in publication density across continents become apparent. Western Europe and North America emerge as focal points, hosting a substantial proportion of authors and publications. This concentration may reflect historical trends in academic leadership, infrastructure, and funding within these regions. Additionally, Australia and various Asian countries demonstrate significant participation, contributing to the global tapestry of knowledge dissemination.

Despite these notable contributions, a concerning imbalance arises when considering the representation of African institutions. Among the over 1800 publications scrutinized, a mere fraction—less than 50—originated from authors affiliated with institutions in Africa. This stark underrepresentation raises important questions about access to resources, research infrastructure, and systemic barriers faced by scholars in the region. Addressing this disparity is imperative for fostering a more inclusive and equitable scholarly landscape. Efforts to amplify the voices of African researchers, facilitate collaboration, and enhance research capacity are essential for harnessing the full potential of global knowledge exchange. By bridging these gaps, we can cultivate a more diverse, representative, and impactful scholarly community that reflects the richness of global perspectives.

7.4.2 Collaboration Patterns

When examining collaboration patterns across different geographical locations within the field, our analysis revealed robust collaboration networks primarily among researchers from Europe, the United States, China, Canada, and Australia. These collaborations underscore the global nature of knowledge management research and the cross-pollination of ideas across diverse cultural and geographic boundaries.

However, a notable observation emerged regarding the limited extent of collaboration involving African researchers. Despite the vast potential for fruitful collaborations and the wealth of knowledge within African academic institutions, there appears to be a gap in the level of engagement with researchers from the African continent. This finding highlights an opportunity for fostering greater inclusivity and diversity within collaborative research endeavors in the field of knowledge management.

Furthermore, our analysis unveiled instances where the same cross-country collaborations yielded multiple publications spanning various topics. This observation suggests that these collaborative partnerships are characterized by sustained engagement and mutual interest, leading to ongoing scholarly output across different domains within knowledge management.

Overall, while collaboration among certain regions is thriving, there is a clear need to promote and facilitate more extensive engagement with researchers from underrepresented regions such as Africa. By fostering inclusive collaboration across diverse geographical locations, the field of knowledge management can benefit from a broader spectrum of perspectives, expertise, and insights, ultimately advancing the collective understanding and application of knowledge management principles on a global scale.

7.4.3 The Term "Diversity" in the Title

The presence of the term "diversity" in only eight (8) publication titles within our dataset raises thought-provoking considerations about the extent to which diversity is actively addressed within knowledge management research. These titles include:

- The impact of gender diversity on corporate social responsibility knowledge: empirical analysis in European context
- Improving school performance and student academic orientation: the role of safety-oriented knowledge management and diversity
- TMT entrepreneurial passion diversity and firm innovation performance: the mediating role of knowledge creation
- Cognitive diversity, creativity, and team effectiveness: the mediations of inclusion and knowledge sharing
- Co-creation in coworking-spaces: boundary conditions of diversity
- Knowledge diversity and firm performance: an ecological view
- Challenges to the learning organization in the context of generational diversity and social networks
- Team psychological safety and team learning: a cultural perspective

This finding suggests a potential disparity between efforts to promote diversity in other academic disciplines and the level of attention it receives within the domain of knowledge management. In many fields, there has been a concerted push to enhance diversity across various dimensions, including but not limited to gender, race, ethnicity, and socioeconomic background. However, the relatively limited use of the term "diversity" in publication titles within knowledge management may indicate a gap in prioritization or awareness regarding diversity-related issues.

It is essential to recognize that diversity encompasses more than just demographic characteristics. In the context of knowledge management, fostering diversity can encompass a wide array of considerations, including diverse perspectives, methodologies, and interdisciplinary collaborations.

Thus, the apparent underrepresentation of diversity-focused publications in our dataset prompts reflection on whether the field is adequately addressing the multifaceted aspects of diversity.

This observation underscores the importance of actively integrating diversity considerations into knowledge management research agendas. Embracing diversity not only enriches the breadth and depth of scholarly inquiry but also promotes inclusivity, innovation, and social equity. By fostering a culture of diversity and inclusion within the field, knowledge management researchers can contribute to more robust, contextually relevant, and impactful scholarship that addresses the complex challenges of our interconnected world.

7.4.4 Language

The inclusion of diverse languages in knowledge creation and dissemination is crucial for fostering a truly global exchange of ideas. However, a notable bias exists within the top journals, which predominantly privilege publications in the English language. This bias poses a significant challenge for authors whose first language is not English, compelling them to generate and present knowledge in a language divergent from their native tongue. This linguistic shift can potentially impede the depth and complexity of their writing, as well as hinder the articulation of intricate thoughts and ideas. This challenge is particularly pronounced in cases where the language of publication lacks direct equivalents for concepts or expressions present in the author's native language, thereby limiting their ability to convey nuanced meanings effectively. In addition, not everyone has the resources to pay for translation services or access to professional translators; many depend on assistance from friends. Furthermore, journals may reject submissions based on language quality or require language improvement before approving them for publication. This places an additional burden on non-English speaking researchers.

Addressing this linguistic disparity is essential for promoting inclusivity and enhancing the richness of scholarly discourse. Embracing multilingualism in academic publishing not only acknowledges the diverse linguistic backgrounds of researchers but also facilitates a more comprehensive understanding of complex phenomena across different cultural contexts. By recognizing and accommodating the linguistic diversity inherent in knowledge creation, we can cultivate a more equitable and robust scholarly landscape that transcends linguistic barriers.

7.4.5 Open Access

Exploring diversity in access options is pivotal in ensuring equitable dissemination of research findings. There has been growing discourse advocating for the democratization of research publications, emphasizing the importance of making scholarly knowledge accessible to all interested individuals. In this regard, we scrutinized the accessibility of publications within the subject area under investigation. Our analysis encompassed nearly 1800 publications spanning from 2013 to January 2024, sourced from the top five journals in the field. Surprisingly, only a fraction of these publications—approximately 360—were accessible online free of charge. This finding underscores the prevalence of access barriers that hinder widespread dissemination of scholarly work, potentially limiting the reach and impact of valuable research findings.

The disparity in access options highlights the need for concerted efforts to enhance inclusivity in scholarly communication. In his 2020 editorial on social justice in the information context, Raju (2020) argues that it is important to create space for voices from the Global South, recognize multiple ways of knowing in the face of dominant cultures and intellectual traditions, and represent the less advantaged in a spirit of transformative activism. Embracing open access initiatives can foster greater accessibility to knowledge, empowering researchers, practitioners, and the general public alike to engage with cutting-edge research findings. By championing open access principles, we can foster a more equitable and transparent scholarly ecosystem that promotes collaboration, innovation, and societal progress.

7.4.6 Departments of Affiliation

In our exploration of authors' departments of affiliation, a notable trend emerges with a significant proportion of authors being affiliated with business schools. This observation shows the central role of business education in knowledge management research and highlights the interdisciplinary nature of the field. However, our analysis also reveals a diverse landscape of affiliations across a multitude of academic domains.

Beyond business schools, we observed a considerable presence of authors affiliated with departments and schools of economics, engineering, computer science, information science, humanities, social sciences, education, law, and medicine. This diversity of affiliations reflects the interdisciplinary nature of knowledge management, drawing expertise and insights from a wide array of academic disciplines.

The involvement of researchers from such varied backgrounds enriches the discourse within knowledge management, bringing unique perspectives and methodologies to the table. It underscores the interdisciplinary collaboration and cross-pollination of ideas that characterize the field, fostering innovation and advancing our collective understanding of knowledge management principles and practices.

The diverse range of perspectives brought forth by authors from various disciplines within knowledge management underscores the field's capacity to tackle intricate challenges and seize emerging opportunities within our ever-evolving information landscape. Embracing this multidisciplinary approach not only broadens the scope and depth of research endeavors but also fosters invaluable connections between theoretical insights and practical applications across a myriad of knowledge domains.

We can harness insights from disciplines such as economics, engineering, computer science, information science, humanities, social sciences, law, medicine, and beyond; knowledge management researchers are equipped to confront complex issues with versatility and innovation.

Furthermore, this collaborative ethos nurtures a rich tapestry of interdisciplinary dialogue, cultivating a fertile ground for the cross-pollination of ideas and the co-creation of knowledge. Such symbiosis not only propels the advancement of knowledge management as a field but also facilitates the translation of research findings into actionable strategies and impactful practices that resonate across diverse sectors and industries.

7.4.7 Editorial Composition

The composition of editorial boards and teams serves as a pivotal component in both facilitating and regulating research production within the realm of knowledge management. Beyond establishing editorial guidelines, determining authors' publishing fees, negotiating copyright agreements, and ensuring journal accessibility and audience reach, these editorial bodies play a crucial role in shaping the direction and scope of research in the field.

In our analysis of the top five journals in knowledge management research, we conducted a comprehensive review of the listed addresses of editorial team members by country. Our findings revealed a notable skew toward Western countries, with more than three-quarters of the editorial team hailing from these regions. Delving deeper into the data, it became apparent that the United States boasted the highest concentration of contributing editors. Moreover, when examining regions, Western Europe emerged as the primary domicile for a significant portion of editors involved in knowledge management research. While there were pockets of representation from Asia, and the occasional presence from South America, notably Brazil, the inclusion of editors from Africa was limited to just one journal, The Learning Organization. This observation echoes Witt's (2019) finding from a review of bias in the peer review process, that submissions from Africa and the Asia Pacific region are rejected at rates above the average while those from North America, Europe, and Latin America surpass the average. He further argued that there is a clear need to work toward review processes, organizational structures, and professional development programs that can help make research and publishing more accessible to all colleagues in the library science field.

When comparing the geographic distribution of editorial teams with the locations of contributing authors, a clear trend emerges, indicating a disproportionate emphasis on productivity emanating from Western Europe and North America. However, it is imperative to acknowledge the contextual nature of knowledge. The models, frameworks, and mental paradigms championed by Western academia may not necessarily address the multifaceted knowledge-related challenges prevalent in the global South. Simultaneously, the flow of knowledge in a northward direction is often impeded by gatekeepers operating within dissemination avenues, such as editorial policies and ranking scales that predominantly align with Western standards.

This disparity underscores the necessity for a more inclusive and diverse representation within editorial bodies, allowing for a broader spectrum of perspectives and experiences to inform the discourse surrounding knowledge management research. By fostering greater collaboration and exchange between scholars from diverse geographical backgrounds, there exists the potential to enrich the field with novel insights and approaches that resonate more profoundly with the intricacies of global knowledge landscapes.

7.5 CONCLUSION: CHALLENGES AND OPPORTUNITIES

As explained, our purpose is to encourage discussion and further exploration of what constitutes diversity in research and how we can together make the research enterprise more inclusive. The foregoing discussion is based on the findings gleaned by analyzing data from the five top-ranked journals in knowledge management research as reported by Serenko and Bontis (2022). The seven attributes chosen to review diversity in knowledge management research could be applied to any field of study. In this context they serve as proxies through which to conceptualize the framework of knowledge production.

There are several challenges that come with working in diverse teams. Teams may be diverse along disciplinary lines, across countries, languages, cultures, conceptual frameworks, and many more aspects. In a study of diversity in academic research teams, Siemens and Buur (2012) examined the need to accommodate multiple differences when collaborating with team members across different institutions, and countries. They highlighted problems in scheduling meetings across different time zones, issues with communication, and frustration when expressing conflict in different languages. Other scholars cited hurdles in defining appropriate team behavior across different cultures and some others noted disparities in access to information, technology, and/or research tools due to differences in infrastructure.

Cognizant of the complexity involved in working across countries and cultures, our call for broader inclusion of research teams from non-Western countries is not naive. We aim to find solutions in spite of the challenges recorded in the literature. In the pursuit of diversity within research, efforts have predominantly aimed at extending invitations to individuals from various backgrounds, spanning gender, race, nationality, and disciplinary affiliations. However, it is crucial to recognize that diversity does not automatically translate into true inclusion within research teams. Our analysis of the institutional affiliations of contributing authors to the top five journals in knowledge management underscores this disparity, revealing a landscape rich in diversity of source countries but lacking significant inclusion of authors from the global South.

Inclusion, as articulated by Hattery et al. (2022), transcends mere representation; it entails a process that ensures every member of a research team not only occupies space but is also welcomed, valued, and empowered to contribute meaningfully on par with their peers. The solitary presence of editorial team members from Africa within The Learning Organization, among the top-ranked journals in knowledge management research, serves as a poignant reminder of the work that remains to be done.

As leaders in the field of knowledge management, we are called upon to scrutinize the very structures that shape the intellectual landscape of our discipline. It is incumbent upon us to champion initiatives that foster genuine diversity and inclusion, encompassing a multitude of perspectives, knowledge producers, and contextual understandings. By dismantling barriers and embracing a more inclusive approach to knowledge creation, we can unlock the full potential of our collective wisdom, ushering in a new era of innovation and understanding that transcends geographical boundaries and cultural divides. Together, let us commit to building a future where every voice is not only heard but also celebrated in the rich tapestry of knowledge creation.

Education and training may help to mitigate the impact of differences when conducting and publishing research with team members from different countries and across academic disciplines. This is not to say that there are zero contributing authors to knowledge management journals from the global south. Rather, the argument here is to increase participation. While the education system(s) may differ in different countries, it would be beneficial to broaden the framework of learning to include cultural exchanges, recognition of local expertise, and commonly accepted certification. There is a chance to explore the development of professional norms around the knowledge management field that could be customized for regional preferences. For example, the accounting field has global and regional standards that are recognized and respected across the world. This doesn't hold true for knowledge management. Implementing standards, particularly regional ones, would address local needs, enhance participation, and reduce barriers to publishing for researchers from non-Western regions.

Another area where education can help is in raising awareness about citation diversity and training authors to address this bias. Citation diversity has a significant impact on the way research is written, presented, and perceived. The question of how a scholar's identity impacts citations is important because biases related to social identity can impact equity, diversity, and inclusion in scientific research and have a lasting effect on an individual's career development. Ray et al. (2022) suggest that "citation diversity can be understood as an indicator of the diversity of perspectives that inform one's thinking and writing and an understanding of (and appreciation for) the value diversity brings to research." It is intended to counter the bias that is found in how scholarly work is published, used, and cited. Consider a name-agnostic citation such as: "Other authors [x] have studied...." In such cases, it would be more inclusive to use the author's (un-common) name explicitly when citing their work. For example, "S. R. Ranganathan (1931) studied...." Identifying biases and injustices is an important first step in creating solutions. We must keep working toward more diverse and inclusive practices across all fields of research.

One of the limitations of our study is that we selected only the top five journals in knowledge management research and limited our research to the SCOPUS database. As such, more research is needed to better understand the topic of diversity in knowledge management research. While Serenko and Bontis (2009, 2013a, 2017, 2022) have been consistent in updating the global ranking of knowledge management and intellectual capital academic journals every five years, there are other researchers writing about journal ranking that we have not considered. The debate on what is the most suitable method to rank journals is not new. Serenko and Bontis (2013b) recognize two major ranking approaches (expert surveys and journal citation impact measures) and discuss advantages and disadvantages of each, using a triangulation of both. Given that we are highlighting under representation of certain world regions from Western journals to begin with, the solutions may begin with greater inclusion. We would suggest an initiative to review the common system of journal rankings, acknowledging that current sources are not truly representative of global diversity of thoughts and perspectives in knowledge management. We would encourage regional and/or linguistic rankings such as top knowledge management journals in South Asia, top knowledge management journals in Africa, top Knowledge management in the Spanish language, etc. This would help to democratize what is perceived as an approved/ranked list of the establishment. The criteria for ranking would be determined by stakeholders in the regions and would therefore be more accessible for researchers and audiences in those regions.

Since our focus is on the research production framework, access to knowledge management research is a critical issue. Many of the top journals in the field are only accessible via subscription and kept behind the firewall of publishing houses. Although limited in diversity, this research is important for reference, contributing to framing of issues and providing a scaffold upon which customized, context-specific, nuanced research is developed. However, access is a consistent issue for both research producers and consumers from the developing world. Most research are not accessible outside the West. Different open access initiatives have made attempts to make research available, but we have a long way to go. Emerald Publishing is responsible for four of the top five journals in knowledge management and they have two pathways to open access (green and golden). In addition,

Knowledge Management Research and Practice has an open select pathway to open access publishing. Despite these provisions, our data analysis showed that only a small fraction of articles was freely accessible online. There is a need to engage with stakeholders, review where and why the need is not met, and create more pathways to open access.

Diversity and inclusion statements are considered a transparent, public way of demonstrating an organization or institution's efforts to improve diversity and inclusion practices. In the case of academic journals, the diversity statement would include goals to work toward and a plan of action to keep evolving and making changes and adaptations needed to address any issues. These statements help to communicate a welcoming and inclusive space for everyone thereby increasing engagement, submissions, and usage from all areas of the research community.

Diversity statements are increasingly common on journal homepages and are used by editors and journal owners alike to raise awareness and to signal a clear position and intent to improve diversity outcomes for the entire research community. We examined the journal websites and corresponding publishing houses for diversity statements. Emerald Publishing, which distributes the Journal of Knowledge Management, the Journal for Intellectual Capital, The Learning Organization and VINE Journal of Knowledge Management Practices has made their stake in including diverse voices very clear. Some of Emerald's diversity and inclusion initiatives include the global survey on gender equality across its journals, giving more visibility to content that discusses issues of diversity and inclusion, and efforts to align with the United Nations Sustainable Development Goals.

As the foregoing discussion has shown, there are many opportunities for leaders in knowledge management research to explore practical solutions to system-wide challenges that will impact how the field is shaped going forward. More research is needed to understand the finer nuances of diversity in research teams and how to evolve research infrastructure into more inclusion and sustainable practices to advance knowledge. The 2022 global inclusivity report from Emerald Publishing and the Power of Diverse Voices campaign is a wonderful example of how the publishing industry can participate in increasing diversity and inclusion in research. Not surprisingly, survey results from academics in low- and middle-income regions, specifically Asia, Latin America, Middle East, and Africa recoded the highest scores for benefits to inclusion. The work that needs to be done will involve partnering with different stakeholders across the research production spectrum. Whereas publishing houses may have a biggest say in research dissemination, there is enough work for the institutions that train researchers, the research funders, and the researchers themselves.

7.6 RECOMMENDATION

In our study, we examined seven non-scholarly attributes to assess diversity, or its absence, within knowledge management research. These attributes include:

- Geographic location of authors
- Collaboration patterns
- Frequency of the term "diversity" in document titles
- Language
- Accessibility of journals
- Departmental affiliation of contributing authors
- Editorial composition of each journal

While these elements are fundamental to academic publication, they are not unique to our dataset. We contend that they are foundational to almost any scholarly work. The discourse on diversity and inclusion, both in society and within academic research, has made significant strides, evidenced by recent outputs and diversity policies of prominent publishing houses such as Emerald Publishing, Wiley, and Springer. Inspired by The Royal Society of Chemistry's (2024) set of requirements suggested to improve EDI in academic journals, Dewidar et al. (2022) proposed six approaches to improve EDI in academic publishing, including:

- Adopting a journal diversity statement with clear, actionable steps to achieve it
- Promoting the use of inclusive and bias-free language
- Appointing a journal's equity, diversity and inclusion director or lead
- Establishing a mentoring approach
- Monitoring adherence to equity, diversity, and inclusion principles
- Publishing reports on equity, diversity, and inclusion

To advance this discourse, we propose the above seven attributes as building blocks for a preliminary diversity and inclusion (D&I) scholarly publishing checklist. Drawing from findings in the *Emerald Publishing report* (2002), which highlighted issues such as language barriers, homogeneity within editorial boards, and journal accessibility, we advocate for a comprehensive approach to inclusivity.

Additionally, we suggest incorporating the following three elements, identified in the literature, into the checklist (and welcome others to further develop and refine the checklist):

- Indigeneity: including indigenous thoughts and perspectives, challenging exclusionary practices, as well as embracing indigenous research methods (Eaton, 2022).
- Citation diversity: a declaration from authors regarding the balance of sources consulted and cited in their work (Ray et al., 2022).
- Gender: addressing gender bias in academic research (e.g., Witterman et al., 2019) demonstrated that when controlling for age and domain of research, a gender bias exists in peer review processes that judge the caliber of the investigator: there was a 4% lower success rate for women grant applicants.

By integrating these elements into a comprehensive checklist, we aim to foster greater diversity and inclusivity within scholarly publishing practices, thereby enriching the academic landscape.

REFERENCES

About editors Canada. Editors Canada. (2024, July 30). https://editors.ca/about/ Accessed Februaary 26, 2024. https://www.editors.ca/about-editors.canada

Cole, D., & Zhou, J. (2014). Do diversity experiences help college students become more civically minded? Applying Banks' multicultural education framework. *Innovative Higher Education, 39*, 109–121.

Dewidar, O., Elmestekawy, N., & Welch, V. (2022). Improving equity, diversity, and inclusion in academia. *Research Integrity and Peer Review, 7*, 4.

Eaton, S. E. (2022). New priorities for academic integrity: equity, diversity, inclusion, decolonization and Indigenization. *International Journal for Educational Integrity, 18*(10). https://doi.org/10.1007/s40979-022-00105-0

Emerald Publishing Report. (2002). Agents of change for an inclusive world. *Global Inclusivity Report 2022*. The Power of Diverse Voices.

Farooq, R. (2024). A review of knowledge management research in the past three decades: a bibliometric analysis. *VINE Journal of Information and Knowledge Management Systems, 54*(2), 339–378.

Freeman, R. B., & Huang, W. (2014). Collaboration: Strength in diversity. *Nature, 513*(7518), 305–305.

Gaviria-Marin, M., Merigó, J. M., & Baier-Fuentes, H. (2019). Knowledge management: A global examination based on bibliometric analysis. *Technological Forecasting and SocialChange, 140,* 194–220.

Hattery et al. (2022). Diversity, equity, and inclusion in research teams: The Good, The Bad, and The Ugly. *Race and Justice, 12*(3), 505–530.

Hunt, V., Layton, D., & Prince, S. (2015). *Diversity matters.* McKinsey & Company, *1*(1), 15–29.

Nonaka, I. (1994). A dynamic theory of organizational knowledge creation. *Organization Science, 5,* 14–37.

Nonaka, I., & Nishiguchi, T. (2001). *Knowledge Emergence: Social, Technical, and Evolutionary Dimensions of Knowledge Creation.* Oxford, UK: Oxford University Press.

Nonaka, I., & Takeuchi, K. (1995). *The Knowledge Creating Company.* New York, NY: Oxford University Press.

Nonaka, I., & Von Krogh, G. (2009). Perspective—Tacit knowledge and knowledge conversion: Controversy and advancement in organizational knowledge creation theory. *Organization science, 20*(3), 635–652.

Raju, J. (2020). Diversity, inclusion, and social justice in the information context: Global South perspectives: Editorial. *The International Journal of Information, Diversity, & Inclusion, 4*(3/4), 1–4.

Ranganathan, S. R. (1931). *The Five Laws of Library Science.* Madras Library Association.

Ray, K. S., Zurn, P., Dworkin, J. D., Bassett, D. S., & Resnik, D. B. (2022). Citation bias, diversity, and ethics. *Accountability in Research, 31*(2), 158–172.

Rock, D., & Grant, H. (2016). Why diverse teams are smarter: Diversity and inclusion. *Harvard Business Review,* Nov 4, 2016.

Royal Society of Chemistry. 2024. Our work to improve inclusion, diversity, accessibility and culture in the Chemical Sciences. Accessed February 26, 2024. https://www.rsc.org/policy-evidence-campaigns/inclusion-diversity/

Schiuma, G., Kumar, S., Sureka, R., & Joshi, R. (2023). Research constituents and authorship patterns in the knowledge management research and practice: A bibliometric analysis. *Knowledge Management Research & Practice, 21*(1), 129–145.

Serenko, A., & Bontis, N. (2009). A citation-based ranking of the business ethics scholarly journals. *International Journal of Business Governance and Ethics, 4*(4), 390–399.

Serenko, A., & Bontis, N. (2013a). Global ranking of knowledge management and intellectual capital academic journals: 2013 update. *Journal of Knowledge Management, 17*(2), 307–326.

Serenko, A., & Bontis, N. (2013b). The intellectual core and impact of the knowledge management academic discipline. *Journal of Knowledge Management, 17*(1), 137–155.

Serenko, A., & Bontis, N. (2017). Global ranking of knowledge management and intellectual capita academic journals: 2017 update. *Journal of Knowledge Management, 21*(3), 675–692.

Serenko, A., & Bontis, N. (2022). Global ranking of knowledge management and intellectual capital academic journals: a 2021 update. *Journal of Knowledge Management, 26*(1), 126–145.

Siemens, L., & Buur, E. (2012). A trip around the world: Accommodating geographical, linguistic, and cultural diversity in academic research teams. *Literary and Linguistic Computing, 28*(2), 331–343.

Thomas, D. A. (2016). Diversity as strategy. In *Readings and Cases in International Human Resource Management* (pp. 105–118). Routledge.

Witt, S. W. (2019). Can journals overcome bias and make the peer review process more inclusive? *IFLA Journal, 45*(4), 275–276.

Witterman, H. O., Hendricks, M., Straus, S., & Tannenbaum, C. (2019). Are gender gaps due to evaluations of the applicant or the science? A natural experiment at a national funding agency. *Lancet, 393*(10171), 531–540

8

The Role of Artificial Intelligence in Inclusive Knowledge Management

Yang Lin
Penn State University, University Park, PA, United States

Kimiz Dalkir
McGill University, Montreal, Quebec, Canada

8.1 INTRODUCTION

The role of artificial intelligence (AI) in knowledge management (KM) continues to grow and evolve. Tsui et al. (2000) consider KM to be:

> a discipline that encompasses processes and techniques for the creation, collection, indexing, organisation, distribution, access to and evaluation of institutional knowledge for improvement of performance, and more generally, for the exploitation of intellectual capital, including reuse opportunities.
>
> *(Tsui et al., 2000, p. 235)*

The authors note the predominant application of AI to KM lies in enhanced searching for content online. However, they emphasize that there are many other ways in which AI can add value to knowledge processing activities such as data mining and big data for knowledge discovery, automated organization of knowledge, and synthesizing different existing knowledge to generate new knowledge.

AI-driven KM has rapidly become the linchpin of organizational success, and its significance only continues to burgeon. The wealth of data generated daily content with the exponential growth of digital content,

DOI: 10.1201/9781003407966-8

necessitates intelligent systems that can not only organize and retrieve information but also distill meaningful insights from the vast expanse of knowledge. AI, with its formidable capacity for data analysis, natural language processing, and machine learning, stands as the vanguard of this knowledge revolution.

Yet, amid the transformative power of AI, a crucial imperative emerges—inclusive AI-driven KM. This imperative resonates with the understanding that the benefits of AI should not be limited to a select few but should extend inclusively to diverse communities and individuals. Accessibility and diversity must form the bedrock upon which AI-driven KM systems are built. In an increasingly interconnected world, where knowledge is the currency of progress, ensuring equitable access and representation within the digital knowledge ecosystem is not just a choice; it's an ethical obligation.

Inclusivity in AI refers to the ethical and social responsibility of ensuring that AI technologies are developed, deployed, and utilized in a way that considers the diverse needs, perspectives, and experiences of all individuals and groups. AI systems should not discriminate against or disadvantage any particular demographic, culture, ethnicity, gender, or other characteristic.

> For AI to be truly inclusive, changes are required at all three levels—the algorithm, the data, and the end-users. Existing ethical frameworks address mainly individual, human responsibility, not distributed responsibility.
>
> *(Avellan et al., 2020, p. 142)*

This means AI needs to be developed by diverse teams, that the data used to train AI is representative and not biased and that AI applications are accessible by all users regardless of their socioeconomic status or any disability.

Efforts are being made to address these issues and promote inclusivity in AI. Researchers, policymakers, and organizations are working on developing techniques to mitigate bias in AI, improving transparency, diversifying development teams, involving stakeholders in the design process, and implementing guidelines and regulations that prioritize inclusivity. We explore the ways in which AI can be harnessed not only to enhance efficiency but also to foster inclusivity, ensuring that the wealth of knowledge and information benefits all, irrespective of background, ability, or circumstance. As we traverse this terrain, it becomes evident that the path to a brighter, more inclusive future lies in harnessing the boundless capabilities of AI in KM, guided by principles of accessibility and diversity.

This chapter focuses on the connection between AI and KM, how and why AI can lack inclusivity and makes use of a case study to discuss how AI for KM can better integrate DEI in both conceptual and practical projects. The specific ChatGPT AI application is used to illustrate how inclusive AI can enhance knowledge processing activities.

8.2 LACK OF INCLUSIVITY IN AI SYSTEMS

As noted in the introduction, there are three general reasons why AI systems may not be inclusive: the makeup of the teams of people involved in the design and development processes, the nature of the training datasets, and the accessibility of the final system.

If the teams responsible for designing and developing AI systems may lack diversity themselves, this can lead to the oversight of important considerations and perspectives. A lack of diverse voices can result in systems that do not adequately address the needs of different groups and may suffer from over-representing the perspectives, biases, and values of the development team members. Similarly, if AI systems are tested and validated only with a limited group of users, the technology might not be effective or inclusive for a broader audience. Biased feedback from users can further reinforce existing biases in AI systems. If a system's output is biased due to initial training data, user feedback based on those biased outputs can lead to a feedback loop that strengthens the bias.

AI algorithms, though potent, are not immune to the biases inherent in their training data. Bias in training data refers to the presence of systematic and non-random errors that reflect underlying social, cultural, or historical inequalities. If the training data used to develop an AI system is biased or unrepresentative, the system can inherit and perpetuate those biases. For instance, if historical data reflects existing societal biases, the AI system may learn and replicate those biases in its outputs. When these biases seep into AI-driven KM systems, they risk perpetuating stereotypes, discrimination, and unequal representation. Bias can emerge in various forms, from gender and racial biases to socioeconomic and cultural biases. Recognizing and mitigating these biases is a moral and ethical imperative, as AI systems wield significant influence over what knowledge is accessed and by whom. Some well-known examples include the US AI system used to assess the likelihood of people repeating a crime, which was unfairly skewed toward minority groups and the Amazon recruitment algorithm that had a strong gender bias and rejected qualified female job applicants. "Having diverse teams in the technology design can eliminate such discrimination, unethical use, and unfair practices" (Kinnula et al., 2021, p. 2).

Training data can be biased in various ways, which can lead to biased or unfair outcomes when training machine learning models or AI systems. Biases can be introduced during the data collection, preprocessing, and labeling phases.

The way data is collected can introduce a number of different biases. If the data collection process is not carefully designed to be representative and unbiased, the resulting dataset may not accurately reflect the true distribution of the real world. When the data used for training is not a random or representative sample of the target population, it can introduce *sampling bias*. Biased sampling can lead to incorrect generalizations and predictions. If certain groups or classes are underrepresented in the training data, the AI system might not learn to recognize or understand those groups effectively. This can result in the system performing poorly or making inaccurate predictions for those underrepresented groups (*underrepresentation bias*). Biased training data can also contain stereotypes about particular groups, which the AI system might learn and perpetuate in its outputs. For example, if a dataset contains biased descriptions or labels for certain ethnicities, genders, or professions, the AI might generate content that reinforces those stereotypes, resulting in *stereotype bias*. If historical data reflects past societal biases, these *historical biases* can be learned and amplified by AI systems. For example, if a hiring dataset is biased toward a particular gender for certain job roles due to historical hiring practices, an AI model trained on that data might continue to favor that gender. Finally, *context bias* can result if, for example, social media data might reflect biases present on those platforms, which can be learned by AI systems.

Decisions made during the data preprocessing phase, such as filtering or normalization, can inadvertently introduce bias. For example, if certain data points are excluded during preprocessing, it might disproportionately affect specific groups (preprocessing bias). In addition, the process of labeling data (assigning categories or attributes to data points) can introduce bias if the labeling is influenced by subjective judgments or preconceived notions. *Labeling bias* can lead to inaccurate model predictions.

For example, data that have been labeled by humans for training a model may be subjective, even among experts. Different models may need to be developed for different genders, cultures, etc., as it is rarely possible to generalize models to an entire human population based on limited training data. Fairness is about treating people equally through developing models that encapsulate moral standards in the decision-making process. Explainability is required, so all stakeholders, including people impacted by the decisions of automated systems, can understand how a decision is made and the user knows why a system has made a decision.

(Crockett et al., 2021, pp. 779–780)

In order to address these biases in training data, is a critical challenge in AI development, researchers and practitioners employ techniques such as:

- *Data Augmentation*: Creating additional training examples by applying transformations to existing data, which can help mitigate bias by making the model more robust to variations.
- *Balancing Data*: Ensuring that each class or group is represented proportionally in the training data.
- *Collecting Diverse Data*: Actively seeking out data from different sources to capture a broader range of perspectives and experiences.
- *Bias Mitigation Algorithms*: Developing algorithms that aim to reduce bias during training and prediction phases.
- *Fairness Evaluation*: Measuring and assessing the fairness of AI models to identify and mitigate biased outcomes.

While these approaches can help mitigate bias, it's important to recognize that complete elimination of bias remains a very challenging task, and ongoing research and efforts are needed to create more inclusive and equitable AI systems.

8.2.1 Bias in AI Algorithms

Biases can also arise from the underlying assumptions embedded in the algorithms. These include the design of an algorithm, including the choice of model architecture and parameters. For instance, if an algorithm inherently favors certain groups or types of data, it can lead to biased outcomes. The process of selecting and engineering features (input variables) for an algorithm can introduce bias if certain features are given more weight or importance based on subjective judgments or preconceived notions. Algorithms developed in one cultural or geographic context may not generalize well to other contexts, leading to biased outcomes. Algorithms often make assumptions about the relationships between variables or the distribution of data. These assumptions can be biased if they do not accurately represent the real-world context. As discussed earlier, biased feedback from users interacting with algorithmic outputs can reinforce existing biases, leading to biased results over time. Finally, algorithms can have unintended consequences that disproportionately affect certain groups. For example, an algorithm used in hiring may inadvertently disadvantage certain demographics if the features it considers are biased.

A number of approaches can be used to address these biases. In addition to trying to ensure that the training data is diverse, representative, and free from bias to the extent possible, *bias audits* can be conducted to identify and mitigate bias in algorithms, both before deployment and as part of ongoing monitoring. *Regular evaluation* can be used to continuously assess the performance of algorithms to detect and correct biased behavior. *Fairness metrics* can be developed and used to quantify and evaluate bias in algorithmic outcomes and steps can be taken to try to make algorithms more transparent and understandable to users, allowing users to be able to identify and address potential biases. It's important to recognize that while algorithms themselves are not inherently biased, the biases that emerge are often reflections of human biases present in data and decision-making processes. Efforts to make algorithms more inclusive and unbiased require careful consideration, ongoing vigilance, and interdisciplinary collaboration.

8.2.2 Bias in Feedback Loops

Biases can also occur from biased feedback from users. A feedback loop occurs when the output of an AI system influences user behavior or decisions, and those user interactions are then used as new data to further train or refine the system. Feedback loop biases may be due to an *initial bias propagation* which occurs if the AI system is trained on biased data or has biased algorithms, its initial outputs can already be biased.

When users interact with these outputs, they may unintentionally reinforce those biases by selecting or promoting certain options over others, leading the AI to further emphasize those biased outputs. User interactions with the AI system's outputs, such as clicking on recommendations or providing feedback, generate new data. If certain groups of users are more likely to interact with the system, their preferences and behaviors can become overrepresented, causing the AI to adapt more to their preferences and potentially marginalizing other groups. Feedback loops can amplify the views or preferences of a minority group, especially if they are more engaged or vocal. This can result in the AI system catering to the interests of the minority at the expense of the broader population.

Confirmation bias can occur if the AI system's initial outputs align with users' existing beliefs or preferences; they may be more likely to engage positively with those outputs. This can reinforce users' existing views and limit exposure to diverse perspectives. AI systems may also prioritize recommendations that they think users are more likely to engage with, based on past interactions. This can lead to a lack of diversity in recommendations, reducing exposure to new or different information. This can lead to a vicious cycle where the AI system's outputs become more and more aligned with certain biases, making it increasingly difficult for the system to provide diverse and unbiased recommendations. Finally, as the AI system relies on user interactions for feedback, certain groups of users may provide more feedback than others, leading to an imbalance in the feedback data. This can skew the AI's perception of user preferences.

To mitigate bias introduced through feedback loops, AI developers and researchers can try to actively seek feedback and input from a diverse set of users to ensure that the AI system considers a wide range of perspectives and preferences. When collecting feedback data, they should ensure that it represents a balanced sampling of the entire user population and not just certain groups. They can continuously assess the performance and potential biases of the AI system, identifying patterns that could indicate skewed feedback loops. They can also implement algorithms and techniques that reduce bias during the feedback loop, such as re-ranking recommendations to ensure diversity. Overall, careful design, ongoing monitoring, and thoughtful intervention are essential to prevent bias from being amplified and reinforced through feedback loops in AI systems.

8.2.3 Accessible AI

AI bias extends beyond data sampling and algorithmic errors; it touches on issues of discrimination and fairness. Biased AI can result in unequal access to knowledge, discrimination against certain groups, and the perpetuation of historical prejudices. The consequences are profound, impacting individuals, communities, and society at large. The ethical implications of allowing such biases to persist in KM systems are undeniable. In the absence of clear regulations and guidelines, developers might not have a framework to follow for ensuring inclusivity in their AI systems. Developers may also be in heterogeneous teams, perhaps from different organizations but also from different countries where guidelines may differ greatly. As a result, there are no inclusivity or accessibility "standards" for AI systems. This results in a chaotic landscape where some applications are very inclusive due to organizational DEI requirements (for example, the World Bank has an accessibility policy that requires on-screen readers and other assistive technologies for their website content[1] in compliance with their Web Content Accessibility Guidelines[2]). On the other hand, other organizations do not have any policies and any applications, including AI-based applications, can be developed without much thought given to accommodating all users. In the absence of clear regulations and guidelines, developers might not have a framework to follow for ensuring inclusivity in their AI systems. Thus, they might not anticipate all the ways in which an AI system could be used, leading to unintended consequences that disproportionately affect certain groups.

There are a number of barriers to accessibility in AI systems. This is partly due to the lack of representation of users with disabilities when designing and developing AI systems, as discussed. If AI systems are tested and validated only with a limited group of users, the technology might not be effective or inclusive for a broader audience. In addition, developers might not anticipate all the ways in which an AI system could be used, leading to unintended consequences that disproportionately affect certain groups. A number of studies have tackled the issue of how to remove these barriers. For example, Park et al. (2021) conducted semi-structured interviews and online surveys to gather data from people with disabilities. They note that while some existing AI systems such as Microsoft Seeing AI and Google Lookout use sound to describe online images to visually impaired users and others such as DragonDictate transcribe speech into text to accommodate users with physical or speech disabilities (e.g., dyslexia), these too have limitations. For example, computer vision has limited accuracy in describing images if these images were taken by blind users rather than sighted users and speech transcription doesn't work as well with diverse communication skills such as those of deaf users. Assistive technologies aimed at increasing accessibility to a broader range of diverse users may in fact make things worse!

> In many ways, AI has augmented existing inequalities inherent in societal structures that are sexist and patriarchal but also racist and colonial.
>
> *(Roche et al., 2021, p. 644)*

Roche et al. (2021) go on to note that we have already seen evidence of gender bias in AI systems. There is a clear risk that the digital divide will be further increased if AI technologies do not accommodate the needs of marginalized and underrepresented user groups such as ethnic, racial, disabled, senior, and LGBTQ users. Women and those in lower socioeconomic categories remain very underrepresented globally.

> These findings could be considered evidence of a worrying absence of significant voices in the AI ethics debate, specifically those often most marginalised by the technology, namely women and the Global South. If the debate is being shaped disproportionately by higher-income countries and a largely male-dominated industry, are gender diversity, global fairness and cultural pluralism being neglected?
>
> *(p. 650)*

Given the dominance and imbalance, geographically, linguistically, and demographically, a much more inclusive framework is needed for AI systems. Ethical and inclusive AI needs to include representation of the diversity of all users. It is no longer enough to assume that everyone lives in North America and speaks English. This way of thinking is clearly outdated and results in AI systems that implicitly require all users to try to adapt. Many cannot or choose not to which results in a catastrophic loss of significant voices in design, development, and use of AI systems. The AI community needs to address the power imbalance with an international discourse on the ethics of AI. Any exclusion of significant voices means much of the globe (and half the world's population) could be forced to use and adapt to technologies developed without their participation.

> Additionally, there is a lack of representation of data from diverse users, this includes people with special needs and marginalized communities (e.g. inclusion). Representation of minorities and special groups is crucial for AI to be inclusive. Lastly, the application or service being designed should cater

to diverse users' needs, regardless of disability by designing an application that ensures it is accessible by a larger group of users or by targeting the application towards a specific group of users (e.g. accessibility).

(Kinnula et al., 2021, p. 2)

A further challenge is discussed by Morris (2020) who cautions that user disabilities can be detected by AI based on their online interaction patterns which can then make it easier to discriminate. The author discusses research on X (formerly Twitter) where AI inferred whether people were blind based on their profiles and activity patterns. Other AI systems can detect whether someone has Parkinson by analyzing their mouse movements while they search online.

The potential for peoples' disability status to be implicitly revealed through their computing actions means that algorithms could treat users differentially based on inferred disability status, such as the possibility for health insurers to deny coverage or employment advertisements to be targeted to avoid display to people with disabilities. Developing ethical and legal frameworks regarding the application of AI to inferring disability status is a crucial issue.

(p. 36)

Crockett et al. (2021) looked at 77 AI systems and ranked Microsoft's Responsible innovation: A Best Practices Toolkit [111] as the highest while noting it still had limitations when it comes to implementing these best practices in actual organizations. The authors concluded that there is currently no single approach that can help overcome all the accessibility barriers and note the need for "case studies, clear compelling stories of benefits, and step-by-step instruction manuals on how to use and embed toolkits into operations (and how much time/cash it will cost. Crockett et al., 2021, pp. 786–787). Finally, Avellan et al. (2020) discuss another good way forward toward more inclusive AI:

Several organizations and universities across the world have created a foundation called AI and Inclusion that aims to be inclusive to a diverse group of users, including "urban and rural poor communities, women, youth, LGBTQ individuals, ethnic and racial groups, people with disabilities—and particularly those at the intersection of these identities."

(p. 2)

Other good practices include targeting AI systems toward specific types of accessibility such as Microsoft's AI for Accessibility,[3] which provides grants to development teams.

In summary, AI can help increase accessibility but at the same time, it can also be used to make it worse! Our recommendation is to ensure that ethical considerations are used to create best practices and guidelines for inclusive AI.

8.3 HOW CAN INCLUSIVE AI HELP MAKE KM MORE INCLUSIVE?

While the shortcomings of AI and inclusive AI are continuing challenges, AI can provide a number of valuable methods to help make KM more inclusive throughout the knowledge processing cycle.

8.3.1 Knowledge Capture and Creation Phase

In knowledge capture and creation processes, also referred to as knowledge elicitation, capture, or even discovery, knowledge is obtained from knowledge workers by interviewing and observing them. However, knowledge can also be created "automatically" through the use of AI. Some examples include data mining to detect novel patterns, automated text summarization and abstraction, automated knowledge organization, and automated translations.

In our digital age, the sheer volume of information available can be overwhelming. The challenge is not just accessing knowledge but also discovering it amid the vast sea of data. AI can play a valuable role in search and knowledge discovery through techniques such as data augmentation and semantical validation. AI-powered search engines have redefined the way we find information. Gone are the days of sifting through endless search results. AI algorithms, backed by machine learning and natural language processing, now understand context, semantics, and user intent. This understanding enables search engines to deliver more relevant results, reducing search time and increasing the accuracy of knowledge discovery.

The essence of AI-powered knowledge discovery lies in personalization. Search results and content recommendations are no longer generic; they are finely tuned to cater to individual preferences and needs. AI systems consider a user's historical search patterns, the content they've engaged with, and even their demographic information to craft a unique knowledge exploration experience. This personal touch enhances engagement and ensures that every user's quest for knowledge is met with content that resonates.

AI's power extends beyond personalization; it adapts to evolving interests. As users explore new topics or shift their focus, recommendation systems dynamically adjust their suggestions. This adaptability encourages continuous learning and serendipitous discoveries. Knowledge seekers are guided toward uncharted territories, broadening their horizons with each interaction.

We cannot stress enough AI's advantages of processing and making sense of vast amounts of data that would be extremely overwhelming and difficult for humans to handle—just imagine the potential errors and inconsistency that could happen. AI can efficiently analyze large datasets (even in real time); identify patterns, trends, and anomalies; and extract valuable insights. This capacity not only accelerates the knowledge discovery process but also ensures that critical information is not overlooked due to data volume, significantly improving discovery efficiency and effectiveness.

Some illustrative use cases include training a generative AI tool, such as ChatGPT, on past case results to help the legal team better predict and plan for next best course of action given anticipated outcomes based on past decisions. Another is training generative AI tools on historical dataset (rules, decisions, and arbitration results) on trade and tax compliance cases to predict likely outcome or decision to help compliance and tax departments to predict outcomes or impact of a potential violation on business.

AI-powered summarization algorithms can analyze lengthy documents and generate concise summaries, capturing key points, insights, and takeaways. This makes it easier for individuals to quickly grasp the main ideas from documents, helping users determine whether a document is relevant to their needs. Some examples would be to extract key information from detailed technical documentation and synthesize field reports in a specific format to enable engineers and on-field resources to quickly digest complex information and extract salient parts from contracts and legal documentation on lands and rights. These algorithms could also be used to summarize large columns of drone footage, generate key clauses and main takeaways from legal contracts to increase productivity of the legal team through quickly synthesizing key information and generate actionable items out of customer feedback. Finally, AI-based summarization could automate the creation and publishing of knowledge content to optimize and increase accessibility. Synthesize and summarize issues and resolutions from data available in various forum threads to add to the KM corpus to minimize future resolution timelines and improve customer experience.

AI can also help analyze knowledge contributions and usage over time to identify critical knowledge gaps and areas where organizations need to focus their knowledge retention efforts. Knowing which knowledge gaps exist can then trigger knowledge creation and capture activities in the organization. Use cases include parsing government case files for actionable details which are then sorted and prioritized for maximum impact, analyzing electronic health records (EHRs) to identify patterns and predict outcomes to help healthcare professionals make more informed decisions about patient care and treatment and reviewing supplier shipment for accuracy. Other examples include:

1. Onboarding assistant to support new employees with a personal AI assistant.
2. Synthesize fragmented HR policy information spread across multiple talent portals, onboarding packages, employee handbooks, and emails to answer questions and free HR FTE hours spent replying to general questions.
3. Build a multimodal "supply-chain" insights module that can detect trends and be queried with natural language to automatically detect risks and problems from a knowledge base consisting of video feeds, images, and text data from the end-to-end production chain.
4. Make various government or banking regulations easy to find and understand.
5. Chatbot to allow frontline or online support banking employees to query information (product and service catalog, rules and legal notes, account feeds, account opening policy, etc.) for customers in real time using natural language processing.
6. Synthesize publicly available information in real time on macroeconomic trends, financial market, sector outlook via a Gen AI market dashboard which creates summaries for portfolio managers to better guide decision making in investment management.
7. Visual support chatbot to help citizens navigate government services through interactive answers and also redirect citizens to appropriate course of actions, websites, and resources.

8. Generate text in patient health portals to consult patients on general health questions about symptoms, medications, treatments, nutrition and wellness, diseases, medical test procedures, appointments and provider availability, insurance and billing, self-care, and mental health.
9. Generate insights from social media posts to Identify adverse events and inform future launch and quality efforts.
10. Generate draft reports from quality events (complaints, deviation), alongside creation of communication materials to external and internal stakeholders.
11. Better understand customer distribution experience by analyzing high volume of data across case management, order management, call recordings, and surveys.

AI-driven language models have emerged as invaluable writing and editing companions. Generative AI systems, such as ChatGPT, are examples. These models, trained on a vast corpus of text, assist writers by suggesting improvements in text grammar and tone. They analyze context and provide constructive feedback, facilitating the crafting of polished and engaging content. Additionally, they offer language enrichment suggestions, ensuring that content resonates with a wider audience. This capability is extremely important to people who have domain knowledge that is worth sharing but worry about their own communication skills. Gen AI can help increase efficiency in content creation by automating repetitive tasks such as brainstorming topics, writing outlines, writing a first draft, repurposing content for different channels, doing research and editing content for grammar, readability, and conciseness.[4] It can also help create hyper-targeted content by generating personalized content based on user data.[5]

AI-driven language models excel in translation tasks. They can translate content between languages with remarkable fluency and accuracy. For content creators in multilingual environments, these models simplify the process of creating content that reaches a global audience. The fluidity of AI-driven translations ensures that the essence and nuances of the original content are preserved, transcending linguistic boundaries.

In addition, AI can help generate new and creative ideas for your content by analyzing your audience's interests and suggesting relevant topics for you to write about.[6] AI can help automate repetitive tasks such as brainstorming topics, writing outlines, writing a first draft, repurposing content for different channels, doing research and editing content for grammar, readability, and conciseness. AI can generate personalized content based on user data, which can help create hyper-targeted content.[7] AI can also learn from existing artifacts to generate new, realistic artifacts that reflect the characteristics of the training data but don't repeat it. It can produce a variety of novel visual content such as images, video, music, speech, text, software code, and product designs. Finally, AI can help optimize and improve marketing copy, add creative and customer messaging by analyzing data patterns and user feedback[8]. Some examples include:

1. Create training content can improve efficiency by assisting content development, driving personalization, enhancing delivery methods, and creating more engaging learning experiences for employees.
2. Generate and update HR portal content, including employee handbooks, policies, event postings, etc.
3. Review incidents to identify opportunities for improvement, and update procedures, documentation, and training materials accordingly.
4. Compose new material design and substances with desired characteristics by exploring a wide array of material structures and properties to meet certain specified criteria
5. Generate customer-facing insights and personalized sales recommendations.
6. Generate personalized property recommendations based on a buyer's search history and preferences.
7. Generate investor communication letters and articles to keep investors up-to-date and develop a strong investor relationship.
8. Collate various government reports across different topics or within the same subject area to create entirely new reports based on the information from the underlying structured and unstructured reports.
9. Create summaries and documentation to reduce development costs.

Generative AI is a powerful tool that can help create content in various forms, including visual and written content. It can learn from existing artifacts to generate new, realistic artifacts that reflect the characteristics of the training data but don't repeat it. It can produce a variety of novel content, such as images, video, music, speech, text, software code, and product designs. However, it's essential to understand the complexities of generative AI tools before using them. For instance, it's crucial to know the copyright rules for AI-generated content and ensure that you are not violating any terms. Additionally, generative AI should be used as the first step in the content creation process rather than the final step.

8.3.2 Knowledge Sharing and Preserving

In the knowledge sharing and preserving phase AI algorithms can also assess the quality and reliability of contributed knowledge by analyzing factors like source credibility, fact-checking, and sentiment analysis. AI can automatically extract metadata from documents, including titles, authors, publication dates, and keywords. This metadata enhances document findability. AI can also categorize documents and content based on their topics, themes, and subject matter. This simplifies the organization and retrieval of knowledge assets. AI-powered entity recognition tools can identify and extract names, organizations, dates, and other entities from documents, which can be leveraged to further facilitate document indexing and search as well as building knowledge graphs.

In the realm of collaborative content creation, AI emerges as a unifying force. Real-time translation and transcription services, fueled by AI, bridge language barriers, fostering inclusivity in global collaborations. Teams dispersed across the globe can seamlessly communicate and contribute, transcending linguistic differences. Content becomes accessible to a diverse audience, irrespective of their native languages, thereby amplifying the reach and impact of collaborative efforts. Speech recognition technologies transform spoken words into text or vice versa, ensuring that the contributions of individuals with diverse abilities are integrated effortlessly. Screen readers powered by AI enable visually impaired individuals to engage in collaborative writing, thereby creating a more inclusive environment where everyone's voice is heard. Some examples include:

1. Convert audio recordings of speech into searchable text details and create summary of the conversation with key points (e.g., ChatGPT offers to summarize your Zoom meetings with a popup that appears at the end of the meeting).
2. Cater to unique strengths and weaknesses of students at higher education institutions to adapt course content to their needs to enable students to better address their areas of weakness thus resulting in better academic performance; help to generate content which best suits a student's profile, academic performance, interests, etc.

3. Provide community moderators advanced tools to rapidly summarize opinions in community discussions and provide automated Q&A across multiple channels, and manage in game voice chat, and use tailored language to nudge players and save community manager workloads. Gen AI could also be used to generate user-specific content or disseminate user-relevant posts, queries and tasks to include more peripheral members of a community of a virtual community of practice to participate and collaborate.

8.3.3 Knowledge Preservation, Use and Reuse

In the modern world, the acquisition and dissemination of knowledge have transcended the boundaries of print media and physical libraries. The digital age has ushered in an era where information is not only abundant but also rapidly accessible. However, for a significant portion of the global population, barriers to accessing this digital knowledge persist. This includes individuals who face challenges in reading, comprehending, or interacting with digital content.

Natural Language Processing (NLP) and speech recognition technologies have revolutionized the way individuals interact with digital content. NLP algorithms enable text comprehension, making it possible for AI systems to convert written content into spoken languages or other accessible formats for individuals with diverse needs and backgrounds. AI-driven Text-To-Speech (TTS) systems convert written text into spoken words with remarkable accuracy. From e-books to news articles, digital content becomes accessible through the spoken word, empowering individuals with visual impairments or learning disabilities to access written content. Speech recognition technologies allow users to engage with digital platforms using their voices, bridging the gap for those who may have limited or no use of traditional input devices.

In addition, AI-powered translation tools have transcended language barriers, opening a world of knowledge to multilingual audiences. These tools, bolstered by machine learning, have made it possible to translate vast bodies of work efficiently. Whether it's a scientific paper, a historical manuscript, or a literary masterpiece, AI-driven translation enables knowledge to transcend linguistic boundaries, making it accessible to individuals around the globe. Some examples include:

1. Help validate information from different sources to determine its accuracy and authenticity.
2. Translate from one language to another for proper grammar, spelling, and cultural context for websites to increase accessibility of information.
3. Generate captions and subtitles in various languages for multimedia content such as video and audio.
4. Real-time sales or customer service support (e.g., actively monitoring phone calls and offering solutions or next steps).
5. Automate content localization process to reduce time in translation and improve accuracy and consistency.

In conclusion, AI technologies, such as NLP, speech recognition, and content conversion tools, are at the forefront of revolutionizing knowledge accessibility. AI can help us access a much greater volume of knowledge content, while at the same time help us access much more diverse and inclusive knowledge content. Knowledge can be contributed by and accessed by all users, content can be in the language of their choice and it can even be more multimedia content. These advancements not only enhance the lives of individuals with diverse backgrounds but also usher in an era of inclusivity where knowledge knows no bounds. Researchers, educators, and content creators can reach a more diverse and global audience, fostering a culture of knowledge exchange that transcends borders and abilities.

8.4 SUMMARY AND RECOMMENDATIONS FOR INCLUSIVE AI IN KM

There is a clear and urgent need for strategies on the ethical application of AI in KM and this includes the need for more research on this (from the academic side) and also for proven practices from organizations (from the practitioner side). These strategies must include diversity in data, transparent algorithms, and ongoing mitigation and monitoring. One strategy to combat bias is to ensure diversity in the training data. A more comprehensive representation of voices and perspectives helps AI systems to learn without undue influence from a narrow demographic. Diverse datasets lead to more inclusive KM systems that cater to a broader audience. Transparency is another critical aspect of ethical AI. Organizations should strive to make their AI algorithms transparent, understandable, and interpretable. This allows users to comprehend how decisions are made and detect biases when they arise. Transparency also aids in accountability and responsible AI deployment. Ethical AI requires continuous monitoring and mitigation of biases. Organizations should implement robust mechanisms for bias detection, evaluation, and correction. Regular audits of AI systems can help identify and rectify bias-related issues before they escalate. These key components are critical success factors for AI applications in KM. The ultimate end goal would be to work toward an ISO standard for inclusive AI and, ideally to incorporate inclusivity requirements in the existing KM ISO standard (ISO 30401-2018).[9]

KM practitioners always have to (sometimes painfully) find a balance between theory and practice. They want to deliver quality products and services (researching best practices is often not the challenging part), but are forever confined with the famous scope-cost-time triangle. On top of that, there are factors such as upper leadership support, organizational culture, and strategic priorities which by no means favor what they are trying to achieve. Thus, even if building an inclusive and diverse AI-powered KM solution is absolutely the right thing to do, the real question is: will they be able to do it?

One of the few areas of consensus in the KM world is that there is no one fit for all approach for organizations who want to adopt KM. This likely becomes more obvious when AI, particularly inclusive AI, is part of the equation. We just talked about a few key factors earlier which can cause AI to be biased during KM implementation.

First, practitioners don't often have a lot of choices when deciding what data to use to train AI. Ideally, data for training inclusive AI should be diverse and representative of target users. For example, when building a conventional search for a global consulting firm, user demographics such as geography, business, and industry must be counted in. But, what about gender, age, socio-cultural contexts? Many organizations have set strict privacy policies against using sensitive personal information. Even if such personal information is anonymized and aggregated so that no individuals can be identified, the process of dealing with internal legal teams often tends to be long, complex, and out of control. In practice, time is often the single most challenging resource that product teams don't have. In the end, they must compromise and go with whatever data available, with serious concerns around data diversity and representativeness.

Besides training data, product teams tasked to develop and test AI are often biased. There are not many companies which can afford the luxury of a large, experienced, diverse data science team, so that they are able to factor in inclusiveness during project resource planning—they often get whoever is available and already feel lucky if the "good ones" are part of the project. There's research indicating the issue of lack of female developers and data scientists (e.g., de Hond et al., 2022, Young et al., 2023; D'ignazio & Klein, 2023). Many even decided to move or outsource their entire development and tech support units in one country or two to save cost, and people working there may not understand the business and users much.

In addition, when it comes to prioritization, important decisions or tradeoffs are often made by a few senior product leads (sometimes only one person) who are under significant pressure to deliver on time and within budgets, and ultimately account for the overall product success. Thus, the concept of Minimal Viable Product (MVP) is often adopted, which is unlikely in line with the idea of inclusiveness and diversity. As a result, inclusiveness is often ignored or fortunately becomes a nice to have item shoved into backlogs for future releases. And don't get me started on how backlog items are *supposed* to be treated vs. how they are *actually* treated.

There is therefore a strong parallel between best practices to increase inclusivity in both KM and in AI. These are summarized in the next section.

8.5 CONCLUSIONS AND NEXT STEPS

In the ever-evolving landscape of AI-driven KM, ethics stand as the compass guiding responsible innovation. The journey toward ethical AI is marked by the unwavering commitment to combat bias, foster diversity, inclusion, and ensure equitable knowledge access. By acknowledging the ethical imperatives, implementing strategies for fairness, and drawing inspiration from organizations leading the way, we pave the path to an inclusive and equitable future in KM. One way to address this is to develop ethical guidelines that may form the basis for inclusive AI-enabled KM.

Both KM and AI are in themselves complex areas and given the earlier discussion that there cannot be a one-size-fits-all approach to either area, the framework guidelines can only provide high-level guidelines. There needs to be additional work done to customize the DEI approach to each organization, and even to each organizational microculture. The broad areas where guidelines are needed for AI-enabled inclusive KM are:

1. Governance
   a. Need for international, national legislation, and organizational policies,
   b. Human oversight of AI,
   c. Participation with broadest possible representation.
2. Ethics
   a. Prioritize human privacy and dignity.
3. Standards
   a. Identify and mitigate biases through better "sampling" and data triangulation,
      i. ensure diversity in AI and KM development teams,
      ii. develop and use fairness metrics to assess AI algorithms and KM processes,
      iii. find more representative set of users to provide feedback.
   b. Assure algorithmic transparency (referred to as the visibility and understanding of how algorithms arrive at suggestions and decisions).
   c. Accessibility (ensure accommodation for any physical disabilities and accommodate linguistic diversity
   d. Emphasize human-centric AI solution design and development to address different groups of users' needs and preferences.
   e. Define inclusiveness metrics.
   f. Implement algorithms to regularly self-examine for inclusiveness, including a regular feedback loop to seeking and processing inclusiveness-oriented feedback.

8.5.1 Preparing for the Future: AI and Inclusive Knowledge Management

As we stand on the precipice of an era defined by exponential technological growth, the role of Artificial Intelligence (AI) in KM is poised to undergo profound transformations. With emerging technologies like Gen AI on the horizon, the possibilities are boundless. In this concluding section, we embark on a journey into the future, speculating on the evolving role of AI in KM, envisioning advancements that promote inclusivity, and advocating for a future where AI is harnessed as a force for good, guided by ethical and inclusive principles.

At least at present, AI is being created, trained, and used by humans, and thus its limitations and biases ultimately come from humans, and can be explained using Simon's bounded rationality theory. Like humans who have access to only a limited subset of all relevant and accurate information in any given situations and are subject to their own cognitive complexity and contextual constraints, AI also suffers from similar restrictions, perhaps in a lesser scale, and its rationality is inevitably bounded. Data and algorithms used to create and optimize AI and the various points of interactions AI deal with people are potential sources of biases that may affect its reliability, accuracy, and ultimately inclusiveness, which can have serious consequences for individuals, organizations, and the entire society, especially in domains such as legal justice, employment, education, and healthcare.

The emergence of AI models like GenAI, characterized by unprecedented creativity and human-like capabilities, foretells a future where KM transcends traditional boundaries. Gen AI can be envisioned as a virtual collaborator, capable of generating content, summarizing knowledge, and aiding in creative endeavors. It could potentially revolutionize content creation, making it more accessible and inclusive for a global audience.

The future of AI-driven KM may be one of personalized knowledge experiences. AI algorithms will understand individual preferences, learning styles, and needs, curating knowledge that aligns with diverse user profiles. This customization ensures that knowledge is not just accessible but also engaging and relevant to each individual.

Future AI systems will likely be more proficient in processing and understanding multimodal data, such as text, images, audio, and video. This will enable more inclusive knowledge representation, accommodating diverse forms of content and interaction. It will break down barriers for individuals with different abilities, making knowledge more accessible through various sensory channels.

Advancements in AI-driven language models may lead to real-time language translation capabilities that seamlessly break down language barriers in knowledge sharing. Users from diverse linguistic backgrounds will be able to communicate and collaborate effortlessly, fostering global inclusivity.

As AI evolves, it is imperative that we uphold ethical standards in its development and deployment. Organizations and individuals must commit to identifying and mitigating biases, ensuring fairness, and prioritizing inclusivity. Ethical AI should be the cornerstone of our KM practices, promoting equitable access to knowledge.

The future of AI-driven KM is collaborative. Organizations, communities, and AI developers should work in concert to create AI systems that reflect the values of inclusivity and diversity. Collaboration fosters innovation, and by combining our collective wisdom with AI's capabilities, we can pave the way for a more inclusive knowledge ecosystem.

In closing, as we gaze into the future of AI in KM, let us do so with anticipation and responsibility. The transformative potential of AI, when harnessed ethically and inclusively, knows no bounds. It is a tool that has the power to bridge divides, transcend barriers, and democratize knowledge on a global scale. As we prepare for this future, let us commit to embracing AI while upholding the highest standards of inclusivity and ethics, ensuring that knowledge truly becomes a beacon of enlightenment for all.

The journey continues, and the future beckons—a future where AI and inclusive KM combine to unlock the limitless potential of human understanding and collaboration.

NOTES

1 https://www.worldbank.org/en/who-we-are/site-accessibility
2 https://www.w3.org/WAI/standards-guidelines/wcag/
3 https://www.microsoft.com/en-us/ai/ai-for-accessibility-grants
4 What is generative AI and what are its applications? | Google Cloud. https://cloud.google.com/use-cases/generative-ai
5 Content Productivity: Harness Generative AI to Create Content - Databox. https://databox.com/using-generative-ai-for-content-creation
6 Applications of AI for Content Creation - Buffer. https://buffer.com/resources/ai-content-creation/
7 Crafting Effective AI Prompts For Improved Content Generation: A https://build5nines.com/crafting-effective-ai-prompts-for-improved-content-generation-a-chatgpt-guide/
8 Top 5 Ways AI Can Enhance Your Content-Creation Process - Entrepreneur. https://www.entrepreneur.com/science-technology/top-5-ways-ai-can-enhance-your-content-creation-process/413954
9 https://www.iso.org/obp/ui/#iso:std:iso:30401:ed-1:v1:en

REFERENCES

Avellan, T., Sharma, S., & Turunen, M. (2020, January). AI for all: defining the what, why, and how of inclusive AI. In *Proceedings of the 23rd International Conference on Academic Mindtrek* (pp. 142–144).

Crockett, K. A., Gerber, L., Latham, A., & Colyer, E. (2021). Building trustworthy AI solutions: A case for practical solutions for small businesses. In *IEEE Transactions on Artificial Intelligence*. pp. 778–798.

de Hond, A. A., van Buchem, M. M., & Hernandez-Boussard, T. (2022). Picture a data scientist: a call to action for increasing diversity, equity, and inclusion in the age of AI. *Journal of the American Medical Informatics Association, 29*(12), 2178–2181.

D'ignazio, C., & Klein, L. F. (2023). *Data feminism*. MIT press.

Kinnula, M., Iivari, N., Sharma, S., Eden, G., Turunen, M., Achuthan, K., ... & Tulaskar, R. (2021, June). Researchers' toolbox for the future: Understanding and designing accessible and inclusive artificial intelligence (AIAI). In *Proceedings of the 24th International Academic Mindtrek Conference* (pp. 1–4).

Morris, M. R. (2020). AI and accessibility. *Communications of the ACM, 63*(6), 35–37.

Park, J. S., Bragg, D., Kamar, E., & Morris, M. R. (2021, March). Designing an online infrastructure for collecting AI data from people with disabilities. In *Proceedings of the 2021 ACM Conference on Fairness, Accountability, and Transparency* (pp. 52–63).

Roche, C., Lewis, D., & Wall, P. J. (2021). Artificial intelligence ethics: an inclusive global discourse? *arXiv preprint arXiv:2108.09959* and in, *Proceedings of the 1st Virtual Conference on Implications of Information and Digital Technologies for Development,* May 26-28, 2021. 643–658.

Tsui, E., Garner, B. J., & Staab, S. (2000). The role of artificial intelligence in knowledge management. *Knowledge based systems, 13*(5), 235–239.

Young, E., Wajcman, J., & Sprejer, L. (2023). Mind the gender gap: Inequalities in the emergent professions of artificial intelligence (AI) and data science. *New Technology, Work and Employment, 38*(3), 391–414.

9

A Toolkit for Inclusive Knowledge Management

Susan McIntyre
KM Consultant, Ottawa, Ontario, Canada

9.1 INTRODUCTION

During the Second World War, an Austrian émigrée living in California was deeply concerned about the loss of life, particularly of children, due to the lack of countermeasures against torpedoes that made allied submarines and ships sitting ducks against the German Navy. She enlisted an eclectically talented composer to work with her on a frequency-spectrum hopping solution that could protect the fleet from attack. When the inventors received the patent for the novel approach, the US Navy would not engage with them and stayed with their old, less effective methods. The technological solution was sound and went on to have an impact on events in the Cuban missile crisis, other electronic warfare countermeasures and the modern use of Wi-Fi, Bluetooth and GPS technology (Rhodes, 2011).

Why then was the joint work of Hedy Lamarr (Hedy Kiesler Markey) and George Anthell rejected at the time. It was not because the invention was not ready for prime time, i.e., an idea that had no current application. What were the biases that prevented this life-saving idea from being adopted? Was it because of their careers as actress and musician that got in the way perceived as not serious enough? Was it that neither were formally trained in the topic and were "citizen scientists" of their generation? Or perhaps it was their ethnicities or even more likely, that Hedy was a woman? Whatever the cause, the inclusion of these inventors and their ideas did not happen.

DOI: 10.1201/9781003407966-9

This small illustration, even when indicative of the culture of the times, demonstrates a real cost when exclusion versus inclusion in knowledge sharing occurs. In this case, there was likely loss of life, but in the less dramatic workplace, a Knowledge Management (KM) program that does not check itself for inclusiveness will lose out as well. This chapter looks at how the practitioner can ensure that the organization's KM program has checks and balances in its toolkit that protect it from being too introverted and to be inclusive of voices and knowledge that matter to the KM objectives, in short to be Inclusive KM.

9.2 BACKGROUND AND ASSUMPTIONS

Knowledge Management, no matter the definition, is concerned with the management of knowledge flows for effective or improved productivity or innovation. As a matter of principle, KM theorists and practitioners tend to assume that because "we do not know what we do not know," the more diversity, equity and inclusion, (DEI) the better. KM philosophy also leans toward a holistic approach that has often assumed, erroneously, that all knowledge is important. The result has been drowning in good intentions with questionable value in results.

The notion of diversity as an underlying premise of KM, specifically when it comes into play in innovation, turns out to not be as obvious as might have been assumed. In fact, it appears from meta-reviews of the literature (Mannix & Neale 2005, Horwitz & Horwitz, 2007) that groups with "surface-level" diversity with such visible differences as gender, age and race are not more creative and generally suffer from conflict, lack of cohesion and/or lower performance. On the other hand, groups with deep-level diversity such as in skills, information, expertise and educational credentials tend to be stronger in creativity and improved problem solving.

That is not to say that surface-level diverse groups are to be avoided. Rather, there are advantages and issues that simply must be identified and managed. There are indications that divergent thinking is necessary for creative ideas, but it is convergent thinking that brings these ideas into actionable innovations (Chamorro-Premuzic, 2017). The role of leadership in bringing cohesion to these groups for actionable results will become apparent.

The current trends for organizations to seek out and grow surface-level diversity is therefore not necessarily tied to KM or innovation drivers. Fundamentally, DEI is a societal movement to address years of bias and inequity in hiring practices. Whether the efforts are overt or not, the workplace is becoming more diverse. Immigration, migration, multidisciplinary, demographic, and generational change are driving diversity in the workplace. The issue is not so much that KM drives the need for diversity programs, but that diversity will drive the KM approach. What seems to be most important for diversity to effectively contribute to creativity is being able to develop the leadership skillsets that will build the cohesiveness to optimize deep level cognitive and skilled diversity. This in turn will contribute to a better knowledge sharing culture.

The DEI concepts of equality and equity are also basic premises in the world of KM and perhaps lead to one of the greatest challenges that KM advocates encounter. The push to change from "knowledge is power" to "knowledge shared is knowledge squared" (or some other catch phrase) is rooted in this assumption that if only everyone had access to the entire corporate corpus, KM would have achieved its goals. There is an awareness that all employees or stakeholders must have equal access to corporate or community knowledge and information management systems and that equity plays a role in cases where access is limited. For example, although everyone in an organization may have access to the in-house knowledge bases, equity of access may be compromised for those with visual limitations. Similarly, remote or northern workers could have limited or even debilitating access because of time zones or bandwidth. Design of such systems must always consider these conditions.

At its nub, KM is about inclusion. Whereas diversity is an "imposed" condition and equity is a design consideration, inclusion is a KM driver. Scott Page (2008) dispels the notion of the solitary genius hitting upon the big ideas in favor of a diversity of skills and intellect collectively reaching this goal. He describes how it is group diversity of thought that gets the upper hand in innovation over groups of like-minded experts. Managing inclusion is how KM practitioners identify the breadth of capture, the components required for creation, who can access, receive and share knowledge, and the extent to which it can be assimilated and applied. A KM system without a focus on inclusion will fail because it will not be comprehensive; nor will it leverage all opportunities, some of which we "don't know that we know."

There are four premises in the following discussion. Firstly, diversity is a good thing, both at the surface level where the workforce should reflect the breadth of society, and at the attribute deep-level of skills and experience, which provide innovation thought and action. The result should be a point where both are balanced within the same samples. Secondly, strong leadership from all levels must be present to bring cohesion to diverse working groups; leaders should demonstrate and foster the skill sets necessary for diverse working groups to understand and respect one another that they might optimize individual attributes. Thirdly, KM systems should be designed with equality and equity in mind. This is not to treat any individuals specially but to ensure that knowledge is accessible to the entire workforce so they might contribute to the highest level possible. Finally, diversity is going to happen in the workplace, whether a DEI initiative exists or not; demographics indicate the future. What KM must do is ensure that the conditions are right for inclusivity and build them into an effective KM program.

9.3 THE KNOWLEDGE MANAGEMENT CYCLE

Integrating these principles into KM requires a quick review of the KM cycle. To manage knowledge is to manage its process flows. KM is a holistic approach that considers knowledge within a life cycle from creation through analysis and organization to use and application. The Integrated KM Cycle in Figure 9.1 (Dalkir, 2017) illustrates this clearly.

9.3.1 Knowledge Capture and/or Creation

The KM cycle begins with the creation of new source material or the capture of existing knowledge. This could mean employing any number of processes, involving the creation of tacit knowledge or the creation of explicit knowledge through capture and codification (in written, visual, numerical, theoretical, oral, or other forms). Some examples would be:

- codifying tacit or implicit knowledge into useable, transferable forms
- providing conditions for investigation, experimentation, or study of subject matter
- facilitating conversations, communities of practice, or knowledge sharing events
- scheduling scrums for rapid problem-solving
- interviewing or recording experts

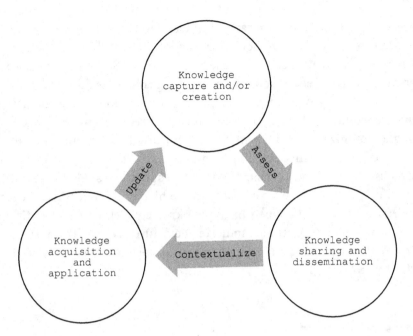

FIGURE 9.1
Integrated KM Cycle. (After Dalkir, 2017).

- providing technological tools for exchange and development of ideas
- embedding neophytes into groups of experts, apprenticeships, or mentorships.

9.3.2 Assess

Not all knowledge captured or created will have the same level of value and the feeds going into this hopper must be sorted and assessed. How to do this is non-trivial, but the most important thing to remember is that not all knowledge has to be codified, nor that all knowledge has longevity. Principles of information and archival management can be very helpful here as those disciplines are adept at determining long-term value of codified knowledge and methods of structuring retention. Does the information have sufficient context to be meaningful to a current or future reader? If not, is the effort to provide that context worth the investment of time? Will the knowledge be useful beyond the immediate tasks? Should it be destroyed after initial use? Is there a process to "publish" new knowledge in meaningful ways? Imagine if Hedy Lamarr had not filed for a patent, how would that lost knowledge have impacted future technology developments?

9.3.3 Knowledge Sharing and Dissemination

This aspect of the life cycle is what we tend to think about when we talk about KM. It is how to "get people to share" and how to get access to the knowledge needed to do our jobs well. These are the processes that tend toward technological solutions. Let's face it, knowledge workers are expecting knowledge to literally be at their fingertips and will continue to expect even more as large effective search engines and artificial intelligence evolve better and more robust products. The issues here are two-fold: a) feeding the machine with quality explicit knowledge for retrievability, and b) recognizing that most knowledge is tacit and requires human contact for transmission. A third consideration is whether new retrieval systems will overcome the current requirement to structure knowledge for accurate retrievability.

9.3.4 Contextualization

The process of contextualization is perhaps the most labor intensive and underfunded aspect of the KM cycle. Nonaka and Takeuchi (1995) call this process "combination" in their KM spiral model. This involves an explicit-to-explicit knowledge conversion that provides additional value. For example, think about bibliographic databases or manual card catalogs, which draw together a corpus of related literature and provide taxonomies for effective retrieval. Think about a textbook, which has been compiled from the subject area to give students a comprehensive understanding of the field without having to find every reference. In the workplace, think about annual reports or training manuals that save employees hours of figuring "it" out themselves.

9.3.5 Knowledge Acquisition and Application

Now the knowledge story turns to usage. Capture and dissemination are only as useful as the uptake. The organization must have the processes in place to allow employees and stakeholders to assimilate and apply that which is available to them. Are the employees encouraged to check for lessons learned or consult with experts before starting new projects? Are they required to build multidisciplinary teams or to check the organization's knowledge bases for background on similar projects? Does the organization provide training based on the best knowledge they have for increased results? This is how the organization ensures that knowledge is acquired and applied.

9.3.6 Update

The last process step in the cycle is keeping both the knowledge and processes up-to-date and relevant. This could involve creating new systems or content and better access, but there are two very important processes that must be present. The first is the need to monitor the goals of the system and ensure that KM is working toward that end. This requires a built-in monitoring of the business plan and a maturity model check on the system. The second tool is Lessons Learned, which is frankly the most effective means of organizational learning and process improvement. By inserting lessons learning into the cycle at all levels, the KM system will evolve and adapt to the benefit of the organization (McIntyre, 2015).

9.4 APPROACH

This toolkit for Inclusive KM has been developed as a guide for KM practitioners to use in designing KM systems that are inclusive of knowledge voices and sources. It should assist, as well, to ensure that all components of the knowledge cycle are designed to be inclusive in a manner that works toward the goals of the organization and its KM program. The toolkit is not prescriptive; it is only a starting point. It is not possible for it to be comprehensive because, like any process or guide, it must be tested and reformed based on analysis and lessons learned. The practitioner reading this will see gaps immediately that can be filled in and adapted according to the specific requirements of individual KM systems.

The approach taken is based on years of practitioner experience and knowledge, but it takes guidance from experts in DEI fields. It begins with a KM Framework, first describing the main elements and then how to manage each step of building a framework to be inclusive. A case study demonstrates how Inclusive KM can happen. Finally, the approach includes the tried-and-true method of a checklist as a guide. It is constructed to be used as a means of monitoring progress in inclusive KM.

9.4.1 A KM Framework

The ISO Standard on KM requirements (International Standards Organization, 2018) provides any practitioner with all the components for a KM system. It is a succinct introduction to KM, but every organization must adapt its own approach based on its own organizational goals and structure. Table 9.1 illustrates the steps in a process to develop a KM system within an organization, a meta-organization or a community. A brief description of each step follows.

9.4.2 Understanding the Organizational Mission, Vision and Outcomes

KM, while laudable, does not exist for any other reason than to bring value to the organization it serves. It is critical when embarking on the development of a KM system and at regular intervals to ensure an understanding of the raison d'être of the organization and to align KM objectives accordingly. This is why KM looks so different in each instance: it is unique to the culture, the goals and aspirations of its own organization.

At this initial stage, it will be necessary to look at any second-tier policies that might impact KM objectives as well. The organizational DEI policy should be considered to determine applicable requirements. It is not

TABLE 9.1

Eight Steps to Build a KM Framework

Knowledge Management Framework
1. Understanding the Organizational Mission, Vision and Outcomes
2. Identifying the Problem
3. Articulating the Solution: KM Vision and Strategy
4. Choosing to be Leaders
5. Creating the Culture
6. Fleshing out the Framework
7. Building Processes, Technology, Tools
8. Measuring and Realigning

the role of the KM strategy developer to compensate for any lack of said policies but there should be awareness of the impacts on the KM approach.

9.4.3 Identifying the Problem

One of the greatest lessons of planning a KM system is not to take too large a bite. So many organizational challenges are related to knowledge flow that there is a tendency to want to address all of the issues identified. Take the time to identify the problem through interviews, surveys or documents, but stay focused on the main issues. We recall a time when the initial problem was thought to be knowledge retention because of high staff turnover. The solution grew to creating a web-based system when it was possible a simple hand-over process might have sufficed.

9.4.4 Articulating the Solution: KM Vision and Strategy

A KM vision and strategy are high-level documents by their very nature. Unfortunately, they are often initiated at lower levels of the hierarchy with little input, other than a rubber stamp from the top management. It is imperative that senior management is engaged at all stages and that the KM Strategy speaks for them and demonstrates that value will be forthcoming. The Strategy must articulate how it will meet their goals, more so than lofty ideals. Senior management must see the vision as their own, and it is up to the lower management to provide that and demonstrate it for them.

9.5 CHOOSING TO BE LEADERS

Stephen Covey (2020) has said that "leadership is a choice," not a position. This bit of wisdom comes to play in most workplace environments, but here we recognize that it is a critical success factor for both KM and DEI. Covey's guidance is that the aspiring leader must strive to understand those they lead and to understand differences in individuals. By doing this, the leader can foster collaboration and minimize conflict. The linkage between conscious leadership and change initiatives, such as KM or DEI programs, will require training and top management expectations. To be clear, anyone can be a leader, and everyone should aim to be a leader. Leadership is a value.

9.6 CREATING THE CULTURE

To be sure, it is not enough to cross fingers, toes and eyes and shout the mantra, "Change the culture!" Too often we hear that we must change from a knowledge hoarding culture to a knowledge sharing culture. How to do this may not always be simple, but it is always related to <u>trust.</u> Knowledge holders must trust that knowledge users will do the right thing with their knowledge, that they understand it, will give them credit for its creation and protect it from unauthorized usage. Although protections can be built into systems, e.g., security clearances, the only sure way to build trust is through personal interaction. Fortunately, KM has its ways.

There has been a lot said about incentives for participation in change and KM initiatives. These ideas can range from monetary to status rewards. Fundamentally, it comes down to whether there is an inherent reward in the activity for the individual. Participation often depends on whether the activity produces the outcomes that meet the goals of the individual or their organization. When there is a clear intent on the part of the activity or organization in which the employee wants to participate and it is an objective that coincides with their own, there will be "buy-in." Other rewards will be superfluous.

9.7 FLESHING OUT THE FRAMEWORK

The KM Framework is a critical piece of documentation that will serve as doctrine, albeit subject to review and change. One of the greatest knowledge weaknesses in systems is the lack of supporting documentation that is reviewed and updated cyclically. A framework document provides the foundation of vision, goals, assumptions and high-level policy that will direct procedures and roadmaps. It will become a reference point for the organization to understand the whys and hows of the KM program and prevent mission drift. The framework is the document that gets the blessing of senior management and sets in motion the KM initiatives in the organization.

9.7.1 Building Processes, Technology and Tools

Now it is time to design the kind of activities that will support the objectives of the KM Vision and Framework and do the work of KM; this is where the *KM cycle* is inserted and managed. For DEI principles, it is the most critical area where unconscious bias can enter design. It is also the highest resource management and there will be pressure to cut corners that will impact long-term results. It is critical to manage the creation of processes, technology and tools as projects that have built-in checks on alignment with goals and values.

9.7.2 Measuring and Realigning

In many ways, this final step of the KM Framework is the most crucial. It is the step where value of KM systems is measured and used to justify investment and continued support. It is a challenging step and requires methods to measure intangibles. Measures must be considered before the activities are launched, although serendipity can play a role in providing other unexpected benefits. This measurement information is important for organizational learning and to adjust the KM systems to be more effective. The framework should provide a management cycle in which the KM system is evaluated and updated regularly. However, this cannot be an annual or bi-annual event. In fact, lessons learned should be an integral part of any activity or stage of the cycle. By embedding learning in management of the KM cycle, it will become more robust.

9.8 PLANNING FOR INCLUSION

We will consider each stage of the KM Framework planning process through an inclusion lens. The practitioner who is committed to the principles of DEI must ensure that they are acting in consort with their objectives. A structured approach will ensure consistency and the ability to report and measure progress. There is no certain way to assure that the perfectly inclusive KM system is created; but by providing some rigor, the practitioner can demonstrate due diligence.

9.8.1 Understanding the Organizational Mission, Vision and Outcomes

At this first step, the practitioner must consider high-level objectives, identifying critical issues to manage, mitigate or leverage. Looking through the DEI lens:

- Determine what the workforce looks like and will soon look like, quantifying and understanding the impact of diversity. Diversity can be a result of intentional recruiting policies; it can be a result of changing demographic factors, or even the nature of the work or location. Start thinking about some of the high-level objectives and considerations of KM to engage or serve the workforce.
- Identify the main stakeholders and their diversity profile. These could be customers, sector partners, citizens, business or any number of categories. Will any of these be served or partners in knowledge products or processes?
- Establish the mission, goals and outcomes of the organization and how knowledge flows are embedded or could improve the organizational outcomes. Investigate policy, economic or other drivers internal to the organization.
- Determine what the current external environmental drivers are that will influence the business case for KM and for services. These could be political, environmental, social, demographic or others.
- Identify the challenges particularly as they relate to inclusion. These could be related to diversity and social cohesion, a result of subcultures within the organization, or exclusion of underrepresented groups. Look for the outliers.
- Consider the second level organizational policies that direct business activities in the organization. These could include DEI or other sociocultural policies or could be more operational such as Information Management or digitization directives.

9.8.2 Identifying the Problem

The question to answer is: what problems prevent the organization from achieving its goals? The follow-up question is: can the better management of knowledge assist with the problem? That may seem self-serving but in fact, it is almost impossible to get past the first question and answer without seeing that there is an element of KM in either the problem or the solution. A documentation review will be part of this process to understand the organization and its challenges.

Interviewing a cross-section of 20–30 key stakeholders will undoubtedly get to the root of the issues in any organization. Unless there is a desire to collect large datasets, a relatively small sample of informants will be able to help identify the key issues and possibly even some of the solutions, if not the details of how those solutions could be implemented.

In choosing these informants, ensure that the sample includes voices that might otherwise not be heard, but be careful to consider spurious input that might not be representative. It is a fine balance to include unique input but not be led into unhelpful dead-ends. A simple interview approach could include questions such as these:

1. What are your biggest challenges in accomplishing your organizational objectives?
2. What would you need to meet these challenges?
3. What knowledge and information issues or gaps are barriers to accomplishing your goals?
4. What are some of the sources that you rely on for knowledge? For information? (People, Systems, Tools, Expertise)
5. What advice would you give someone new to the organization to accelerate their time to competency in your area, i.e., how could they become effective in the shortest possible time?
6. Who has the greatest challenge getting the knowledge or information they need to accomplish their tasks?
7. When you think of KM, what best practices exist in the organization or elsewhere that you would recommend? Why?
8. Who are the go-to people in the organization, i.e., the ones you depend on for their knowledge and expertise?

9.8.3 Articulating the Solution: KM Vision and Strategy

The data and analysis produced by the first two phases will allow the practitioner to draft the KM Vision and Strategy for the organization. The document does not have to be large and may in fact benefit from a sharp, direct approach. It will include environmental and policy context and drivers. It will identify the key issues for productivity with an analysis of each issue. It will then make the case for a KM system approach, which may be new, revised or dovetailed into existing programs.

How this KM approach will address DEI issues is necessary to the degree that it could be an example of how these goals are embedded in KM processes, rather than being another thing to "do." Getting the decision-makers to review and endorse the strategy at this point is critical. The tendency is to wait until there is a whole package to present for approval. The difference here is that senior leaders must have time to digest the concepts and if the KM Strategy presents itself as a solution for a holistic set of change initiatives, such as DEI, it will be better received.

9.8.4 Choosing to Be Leaders

The other key reason to gain senior leadership endorsement is because leadership is so fundamental to DEI success in the workplace. Given that surface differences can lead to conflict and hinder productivity, these situations cannot be left unmanaged. (Hovell, 2022) proposes that intentional and managed conversation will provide the mechanism to bring cohesion to diverse groups. He also points out that DEI training is notable for its success in helping participants *actually* change their view of these issues, helping them to see different perspectives. Aspiring leaders in the KM and DEI space share traits of humility, empathy and listening with an open mind (Brown, 2019).

In our work in meta-organizational KM, it was found that the most effective leaders were boundary spanners who were comfortable with multiple disciplines collaborating (MacGillivray, 2006). They were also comfortable with sharing leadership with subordinates, recognizing that leadership could come from any level or nature of expertise. While it goes without saying that certain people are "natural" leaders, (Covey, 2020), (Hovell, 2022) and others are clear that anyone can choose to study, attain and use the skills of leadership. If KM practitioners want to have the most significant impact on building the culture of successful DEI and KM, this is the training and awareness area with the most potential impact.

9.8.5 Creating the Culture

Culture change occurs constantly but not easily by planning. The introduction of technology is the most definitive driver as those of us who have experienced the introduction of the cellphone into our midst can attest. With large-scale demographic changes happening, culture change will happen without our intervention. However, for organizations to be productive and innovative, they must manage that change in a positive, rather than conflictive, manner.

Trust and respect are the two most significant values to nurture optimal collaboration. In an increasingly diverse workplace, this must take place at two levels. First, there must be facilitation of mutual understanding, inclusive conversation and leadership with employees of surface-level diversity. The objective is to be able to respect and empathize with individuals' experiences and perspectives to the extent possible. This does not occur when left to chance but must be handled with tact and kindness. Diversity and leadership training can assist the process.

The second aspect is inclusion of attribute-level employees. This will occur through intentional interpersonal communication, facilitation and, yes, face-to-face interaction. The trend to a virtual workplace may be comfortable for many, but there is a danger in excluding others and preventing the building of trust among diverse team members. Research indicates that cognitive trust is more likely in face-to-face situations, followed by video display and last by voice only (Baker, 2018). In the post-COVID world, the reluctance to return to in-person work and even the reluctance to show one's face on a video meeting could have serious repercussions for the level of trust and collaboration in the workplace required for innovation and productivity.

In fact, our experience has demonstrated that it is shared experience that builds trust and respect between members of different working cultures necessary to achieve mutual objectives (McIntyre, 2009). It is through the tacit exchange of knowledge, referred to as *Socialization* by (Nonaka & Takeuchi, 1995) that trust is built, and teams succeed. When attempting to influence culture change conducive to Inclusive KM, consider the impact of being present physically or to compensate in ways so that team members can build trust. When employees feel trust and are trusted, they have a sense of belonging and that is both a strong incentive and reward.

9.8.6 Fleshing out the KM Framework

Once the background research is done, the KM Framework can almost write itself. At this point, it should be clear what the organization needs from KM to achieve its aims. In general, a KM Framework follows these main sections, but can be adapted to each organization.

- The KM Mission
- The Drivers
- Knowledge Management Value Proposition
- Governance, Roles and Responsibilities
- Results-Based Logic Model
- Measurement.

The Mission section is the "what" of the Framework and will take its lead from that of the organization and any sub-objectives. The Drivers are the background "whys" of the need for KM and will come from policy and environmental factors as well as from interviews or other research done.

The KM Value Proposition is also a "why"; it is the justification for employing KM as a solution to the challenges of the organization. Some research on savings and productivity from employing new processes or technologies will likely be required for a business case. Turning to the "how," every management scheme needs governance, spelling out resources, responsibilities and accountabilities. Roles and management structures should also be sketched out, if not in detail.

Finally, a Results-Based Logic Model, or some structured equivalent of outcomes, outputs, activities and measures should be created to give credibility to the Framework. At this point, the practitioner is looking for approval and resources and will require this level of rigor. The actual project management or planning details will start to be fleshed out after senior approval. Table 9.2 illustrates the contents of a logic model with examples. Note that the model is the basis for the last part of the Framework, the measurement regime.

9.8.7 Building Processes, Technology and Tools

Now begins the hard part: putting flesh on the bones of the Framework. Making the link between objectives and activities is critical to the success of KM and even more so with Inclusive KM. An implementation plan begins with determining what processes, technologies or tools can produce the outputs that impact the desired outcomes. Too often organizations or managers begin with a technology that seems as if it is the latest great solution, only for the implementers to discover it is incompatible with resource allocation, culture or objectives. Often beginning with a scaled-down pilot project can provide the affordable and measurable test to determine what will work or prove its worth in the workplace.

A project management approach, albeit generally not as rigorous as big technology or construction projects, will be a good lead to follow. Here are some of the steps to keep in mind when building an implementation plan with processes, technology and tools.

1. Establish a governance and resourcing structure as outlined in the Framework and operationalize its business flow.
2. Re-examine and state KM objectives and ensure that they are aligned with the organizational goals and drivers.
3. Identify activities, tasks and outputs for each outcome and identified objectives. Create a management plan for resources, timetables and

TABLE 9.2

Results-Based Logic Model with Examples

Results-Based Logic Model

Organization Outcomes					Knowledge Management Activities and Outcomes		
Ultimate Outcomes	Strategic Outcomes	Operational Outcomes	Outputs	Intermediate Outcomes	Immediate Outcomes	Outputs	Activities
The very highest level impacts on the society or industry	Overall long-term objectives to gain advantage	Measurable through activities and results	Products or services, generally tangible	The impact that KM will have on organizational outputs within 2–3 years	Impact that KM will have within 1–2 years	Measurable results of the activities moving toward achieving the outcomes	Planned actions that will create outputs and impact eventual outcomes
e.g., the World is a better place because of us	e.g., we make the best products in our sector	e.g., we lead in innovative practices and ideas	e.g., product suite, reliability, sales, and market share	e.g., cohesive and diverse teams are creating innovative products	e.g., Indicators of Inclusive KM leadership; Indicators of knowledge sharing in communities	e.g., x number of new leaders trained in Inclusive KM; new communities of practice on platform	e.g., develop leadership course for Inclusive KM; KM Content Management Platform

milestones. Assign human resources. Employ a risk management plan.

4. Develop both engagement and communication plans for stakeholders. It is particularly important to keep senior decision-makers constantly in the know. Remember that it takes more than simply informing them; they must participate to make KM their own. Engage natural allies, whether that is in DEI, Change Management, Information, Data or Technology Management, or other areas.

5. Determine what awareness and training is required for the end-users, both internal and external to the organization. Focus on increasing awareness with the critical mass and not necessarily with the reluctant adopters. They can be the focus after some success.

6. Establish a learning environment and cycle. Exploring lessons learned and adapting processes, technology or tools at every stage will create an inclusive learning environment and produce better results.

7. Develop Return on Investment (ROI) measures for KM and effectiveness measures for the activities. Ensure an annual cycle of review and updating processes and documentation.

8. It is one thing to have a diverse workforce, but if there is a problem of retention, then it is for nought. KM should consider how its plans can contribute to a feeling of belonging and worth in the workplace.

9.8.8 Measuring and Realigning

Of all stages of KM planning and implementation, the measurement is most likely to fall to the side because it is difficult to perform. Often the results appear intangible and linking them to outcomes seems futile. At the very least, it is possible to quantifiably measure usage and uptake over time. Qualitative measures are a bit more challenging as they tend to rely on opinion. Satisfaction levels are valuable and can help make a case for future support for KM initiatives.

There are many types of measurement structures that have been used in KM. We have found that the Results-Based Management Framework provides a usable structure for measurement (Dalkir & McIntyre, 2011). One mechanism is to search for KM anecdotes and then quantify the resulting data from that. For example, we recall a time when a scientist located a document that had not been available to him due to lack of a KM approach. He estimated that had cost him the equivalent of two years of research.

That information can easily be quantified, and the opposite is true. Scientists have told us that through knowledge shared in Communities of Practice, they have been able to save months of work. There is a cost savings but without a measurement regime, the knowledge of that value would be lost.

9.9 A CASE STUDY

Now the Framework is in place, and we know what we want to accomplish and why. We wonder if KM really can do its part for inclusion. The good news is yes! This case study tells of a time when corporate cultures had to work together to achieve mutual aims. While in this case, surface diversity was more about uniforms than ethnicity or gender, it demonstrates the same basic issues.

In the post-9-11 timeframe, in the early 2000s, there was a realization across governments and industries that many heads were better than one. Perhaps it was because of suspected intelligence failures from not sharing information or an economic push to enhance resources or the tendency to draw together in the face of a shared threat or even coinciding with a more cooperative time in history. The result, in Canada at least, was to initiate "whole-of-government" collaborations. These, by their very nature, were KM initiatives by other names.

In one case, the objective was to protect citizens from "weapons of mass destruction," an alarming term for chemical, biological, radiological, nuclear and explosive threats. Because of jurisdictional differences and the breadth of the topics, there was a need to include subject matter experts from science, policy, policing and military agencies. Each sector had its own culture and ethos, which did not always mix well. Even within sectors, there were differences and rivalries. The challenge was not on managing diversity in the DEI sense, but on diversity in worldviews, loyalties, expertise, perspectives and even biases.

The cultures and personalities from each sector created artificial barriers to cooperation. Police and military organizations are both considered "closed" cultures where they have somewhat rigid and rule-based operations. Yet, the two are very different. In a police-led event, the first on-scene is in charge until relieved. In a military situation, there is a clear hierarchy of roles and depending on the event, some level of officer will be in charge. Scientists and policy makers come from "open" organizations where they are accustomed to making individual decisions based on expertise. It is no surprise that scientists tend to be introverted and dedicated to the integrity of their knowledge. Policy folks are concerned with maintaining the government's course. All-in-all, these differences can create conflicts.

The objective for the managing organization's KM approach was to provide opportunities for these diverse individuals to develop an understanding of the strengths and motivations of their new colleagues and to develop the trust that would allow them to achieve the stated and mutual objectives. The approach was to build relationships through communities of practice, tabletop, and field exercises (experiential learning), joint projects and eventually operations. In other words, face-to-face interaction and sharing experience in real time was the way that individuals began to tacitly understand how they could trust the others when faced with a live situation.

It was observed that over time, those groups with leaders who were comfortable with boundary spanning and diversity were able to bring groups together cohesively. They shared leadership and inspired their communities of practice toward their objectives collectively. A second factor for group cohesion was the benefit from shared experience in exercising incident response. An observation can illustrate how this looked in one community. On the first day of the first exercise, away from home, the group went to the bar for a drink after a long day. The individuals sat in self-selected groups from their own organization. The next time they exercised it was impossible to see who belonged to which organization as they all mixed in together.

Over the years, the cohesion grew, and the veterans introduced new members and could mentor them in the meta-culture. On a small scale this worked, but it often proved to be a relationship-dependent situation. In large security events where the same groups were involved, the planning, exercising and co-location could create workable teams, but these relationships could not be transferred to inter-agency trust as a standard operating procedure. This factor illustrates how important it is to constantly provide opportunities for co-workers to have shared experience to create an Inclusive KM workplace.

One additional lesson can be taken from this case. A KM technology platform was introduced early in the collaboration for the Communities of Practice to share information. It may have been early days in the acceptance of social media–like tools with the culture shift too extreme for the participants. They were reluctant for the most part to add to the system, but they did appreciate having what was there at their disposal. It is clear that trust did and still does play a great role in knowledge sharing, and never more so than in science, policing, and military communities. The lesson for Inclusive KM is to find tools and mechanisms that allow all end-users a way to participate. Some may feel drawn to tools that allow some anonymity while others prefer to share openly (even loudly). Inclusive KM will require a diversity of ways to share knowledge and accommodate individual cultures and personalities.

9.10 A CHECKLIST FOR INCLUSIVE KM

The Government of Canada, in a commitment to gender equity in policy development and programs, has developed an extensive analytical process called Gender-Based Analysis Plus (Government of Canada, 2022). GBA Plus has evolved to include gender diversity and consider intersectionality with factors such as age, class, race, ethnicity, religion and ideology. Our Inclusive KM checklist takes a lead from this analytical approach by asking the relevant questions to ensure inclusivity. A word of caution is necessary: the type of question asked can itself be a cause of bias. We must take the time to evaluate our questions with the simple fishbone approach, asking "why might this question create bias in thinking?" Then ask the "why?" question as many times as it takes to get to the root of the problem. If the answers do not create risk or can be managed appropriately, proceed with the next questions. If issues arise, then risk mitigation is necessary.

The Inclusive KM practitioner is encouraged to use this checklist in Table 9.3 as a guide during planning and lessons learned review. Each step used in building the Framework has questions, which can be modified or expanded, depending on the organization. The middle columns can be used to assess the level of success in achieving the aims or as a means of measuring progress or Inclusive KM program maturity. The final column is there to remind the practitioner of what work must be done to rectify any shortcomings.

TABLE 9.3

Inclusive KM Checklist

Category	Questions	Addressed	In Progress	Struggling	Not Applicable	Remediation Efforts
Organizational Mission, Vision and Objectives	Does the KM Framework align with the organization's objectives?					
	Does the KM framework align with the organization's DEI policies?					
	If there are no DEI policies, are there concepts that should be incorporated into the KM framework to ensure inclusivity?					
	Who are the external and internal stakeholders? What is the demographic composition?					
	Are there gaps in the Organizational Mission, Vision and Objectives that may have an impact on planning?					
Identifying the Problem	Who are the stakeholders who should be interviewed or surveyed?					
	Is there anyone or any group that needs to be included in a different way, i.e., are there language or access differences to consider?					
	Should there be various means of inputting to the survey?					
	What are the demographics of the stakeholders and has the sampling been proportional?					
	Who are the outliers, and do they have unique perspectives that should be considered?					
	What sources should be examined and have all perspectives been covered?					
	Are there groups that are more underserved than others?					

(Continued)

TABLE 9.3 (Continued)

Category	Questions	Addressed	In Progress	Struggling	Not Applicable	Remediation Efforts
Articulating the Solution: KM Strategy and Vision	Does the KM Strategy reflect the objectives and DEI policies of the organization?					
	Does the KM Strategy address the diversity of the stakeholders and how they might be included?					
	Has the senior management seen their concerns for DEI reflected in the KM Strategy in a clear manner?					
	Is inclusive KM an attainable objective rather than a speaking point?					
	Does the vision reflect the broad intent for inclusion?					
Choosing to be Leaders	Is the KM team committed and choosing to be leaders for inclusion?					
	Is it necessary to initiate DEI training for the organization?					
	Is there leadership for KM training that could be initiated?					
	Has the KM team or proposed team taken DEI and leadership training?					
	How can KM be a catalyst for inclusive leadership?					
Creating the Culture	How can KM build the inclusive culture into its structures and activities?					
	Are there processes that can be considered that will facilitate trust?					
	Are there any leaders that can lend their support to this effort?					

Fleshing out the Framework	Are there any embedded biases against any of the stakeholder groups?
	Is retention of diverse employees a goal? Should it be?
	Do any of the drivers relate to biases that can be managed by inclusion activities?
	Does the KM Value Proposition exclude anyone? Does it offer means to include where otherwise excluded?
	Are the governance structure and the KM inclusive and representative?
Building Processes, Technology and Tools	Are we asking the right questions in the design of each activity, process, technology or tool?
	How can KM processes, technology and tools contribute to retention?
	Have we the right teams and stakeholders identified in the design to ensure all perspectives and needs?
• Knowledge Capture and Creation	What are the processes of knowledge capture and creation that could involve the most diversity? Have we thought about different personality types and comfort levels?
• Assess	Do our assessment approaches have inherent biases?
• Knowledge Sharing and Dissemination	Can everyone access knowledge in the forms they require or work best with?
• Contextualization	Do our taxonomies reflect the mental models and cultures of the workforce? Do they have inherent biases? Is the language used appropriate? Is it understandable?

(Continued)

TABLE 9.3 (Continued)

Category	Questions	Addressed	In Progress	Struggling	Not Applicable	Remediation Efforts
• Knowledge Acquisition and Application	Is knowledge translatable into transferrable and usable forms for all?					
• Update	Has the knowledge been updated to account for the identified needs of users? Have the processes, technology and tools been adapted according to discovered needs?					
Measuring and Realigning	Are the right lens being looked through? Are there inherent biases in the measures? Is an audit of inclusivity required?					

9.11 CONCLUSION

Hedy Lamarr's frequency-hopping invention was buried deep in the classified naval establishment and did not surface for years after she had filed the patent. When it did get passed on to researchers in the 1950s, it became a game-changer for military research, and when it was finally declassified and thus able to be used in civilian applications, the patent was then in the public domain. Not only was the invention not used as she had planned, Lamarr was excluded from technical discussions and monetary compensation. Hedy was a victim of non-inclusion and society lost out on her timely gifts and subsequent contributions.

DEI is about increasing our talent pool and ensuring that the very best rise to the top. Whether there will be more surface-level diversity in the upcoming years due to intentional recruitment or because of changing demographics, the challenge of KM remains the same. In its foundational attribute of managing the knowledge flow for enhanced value and innovation, KM must do everything in its power to include all diversity and provide opportunities for participation.

Inclusive KM requires inclusive leadership where respect and understanding for one another's stories occur. It requires managers and employees to choose leadership and be part of the inclusivity solution through training and self-motivation. Inclusive KM requires employees to meet and share experiences, not as in forced team building but in work-related tasks and training. Finally, Inclusive KM requires the intentional building of trust between individuals and with the organization for job satisfaction, incentive and retention. KM can be a significant partner in the creation of an inclusive workplace.

REFERENCES

Baker, A.L. (2018). *Communication and Trust in Virtual and Face-to-Face Teams.* PhD Thesis. DOI: 10.13140/RG.2.2.20907.28963

Brown, J. (2019). *How to be an Inclusive Leader.* Oakland: Berrett-Koehler.

Chamorro-Premuzic, T. (2017). Does Diversity Actually Increase Creativity? *Harvard Business Review,* https://hbr.org/2017/06/does-diversity-actually-increase-creativity accessed 30 Jan 2024.

Covey, S. R. (2020) *The 7 Habits of Highly Effective People: Powerful Lessons in Personal Change.* New York: Simon & Schuster.

Dalkir, K. (2017). *Knowledge Management in Theory and Practice.* 3rd Ed. Cambridge, MA: MIT Press.

Dalkir, K., & McIntyre, S. Measuring Intangible Assets: Assessing the Impact of Knowledge Management in the S&T Fight against Terrorism. In Vallejo-Alonso, B., Rodriguez-Castellanos, A., & Arregui-Ayastuy, G. (Eds.), *Identifying, Measuring, and Valuing Knowledge-Based Intangible Assets: New Perspectives.* 2011: 156–176.

Government of Canada. (2022). *Gender-based analysis plus (GBA Plus).* https://women-gender-equality.canada.ca/en/gender-based-analysis-plus.html accessed 14 February 2024.

Horwitz, S. K., & Horwitz, I. B. (2007). The effects of team diversity on team outcomes: A meta-analytic review of team demography. *Journal of management, 33*(6), 987–1015.

Hovell, J. (2022). Acknowledgement. In *Creating Conversational Leadership: Combining and Expanding Knowledge Management, Organization Development, and Diversity & Inclusion* (pp. V–VI). Berlin, Boston: De Gruyter Saur. https://doi.org/10.1515/9783110731989-202

International Standards Organization. (2018) Knowledge Management Systems: Requirements. ISO 30401:2018.

Mannix, E., & Neale, M. A. (2005). What differences make a difference? The promise and reality of diverse teams in organizations. *Psychological science in the public interest, 6*(2), 31–55.

MacGillivray, A. (2006). Leadership in a Complex, Knowledge Rich Environment. Unpublished report prepared for the Chemical, Biological, Radiological and Nuclear Research and Technology Initiative.

McIntyre, S. (2009). Creating and Sustaining Meta-organizational Memory: a Case Study. In *Building Organizational Memories: Will You Know What You Knew?* Edited by John Girard. Hersey PA: Information Science Reference.

McIntyre, S. G. (2015). Learning Lessons for Organizational Learning, Process Improvement and Innovation. In *Utilizing Evidence-Based Lessons Learned for Enhanced Organizational Innovation and Change.* McIntyre, et al. (eds.) Hershey PA: IGI.

Nonaka, I. & Takeuchi, H. (1995) *The knowledge creating company: How Japanese companies create the dynamics of innovation.* New York: Oxford University Press.

Page, S. (2008). *The difference: How the power of diversity creates better groups, firms, schools, and societies-new edition.* Princeton University Press.

Rhodes, R. (2011). *Hedy's Folly: the life and breakthrough inventions of Ledy Lamarr, the most beautiful woman in the world.* New York: Doubleday.

Index

Pages in *italics* refer to figures and pages in **bold** refer to tables.

Printed in the United States
by Baker & Taylor Publisher Services

Printed in the United States
by Baker & Taylor Publisher Services